GRADUATION:

The Revision of Estimates

Dick London, FSA

ACTEX Publications

Winsted, Connecticut

To Mother
in loving memory

Library of Congress Cataloging-in-Publication Data

London, Dick, 1943–
    Graduation: the revision of estimates.

    Bibliography: p.
    Includes index.
    1. Insurance, Life—Mathematics. 2. Graduation
(Statistics) I. Title.
HG8782.L56 1985   519.5   85-23001

ISBN   0-936031-00-X

CONTENTS

PREFACE

This text is the latest in a series of publications on graduation encouraged by the Society of Actuaries and its predecessor organizations, primarily for the benefit of students preparing for the professional examinations. The first such text was prepared by Robert Henderson and published in 1918, followed by a second edition in 1938. Henderson's work was superseded in 1946 by a monograph which was principally the work of Morton D. Miller. Although Miller's text has been supplemented on the Society's syllabus by study notes for some time, it has remained the principal reference on graduation for actuaries for nearly 40 years.

Interestingly, the subject of graduation has been a popular one for actuarial research and papers. There has been extensive writing on it in the actuarial literature, and various statistical and applied mathematical periodicals. Accordingly, this basic text does not come close to being an exhaustive treatment of the subject. The extensive bibliography in this text, itself far from exhaustive, provides the interested reader with the opportunity for further study. An attempt is made throughout the text to give references for further study on specific topics.

There are several reasons for a new text at this time, and these are reflected throughout the text.

The computer revolution has given us the ability to process large amounts of data, and perform extensive calculations, in a matter of seconds and at very reasonable cost. This permits the use of graduation methods which were impractical, although theoretically valid, in the past. In particular, regression methods for parametric graduations are emphasized. In general, the graduation methods discussed in this text are highly computer oriented, but a knowledge of computer programming languages is not required.

Although fundamentally an actuarial subject, graduation is closely linked to the fields of probability and statistics. This has always been true, but has not always been clearly demonstrated by many of the earlier writers, and consequently not clearly understood by students and practitioners. A fundamental goal of this text is to make clear the nature of the relationship of graduation to statistics.

Similarly graduation has traditionally been thought of as simply data smoothing. This text recognizes the validity of a smoothness objective, but expands that idea to the more general concept of reflecting all elements of prior opinion in a graduation problem. Of the several graduation techniques presented in the text, some will be seen to be mainly (or exclusively) exercises in data smoothing, whereas others will stress a statistical estimation theory, down-playing (or ignoring) the smoothness consideration. These latter methods, mainly the Min-R_0 M-W-A of Chapter 3 and the Bayesian techniques of Chapter 5, frequently tend to produce results that are not appropriate for practical use.

Another feature of this text is a set of exercises at the end of each chapter. In an effort to achieve a smooth presentation of theory in the text itself, many derivations and examples are presented as exercises, with direction given as needed. The reader should be aware that the exercises constitute a very important part of the pedagogy. They are arranged by chapter sections. A good approach is to work the exercises of each section immediately after studying that section. Certain exercises require the use of a computer, or at least a programmable calculator; these are indicated with an asterisk. It can be difficult to obtain numerically accurate answers for such exercises, so the answers given in Appendix A should be viewed as tentative.

Another characteristic of the presentation is that, in each chapter dealing with a particular graduation approach, the theory, assumptions and mathematics of that approach are described, and reinforced through the exercises. Extensive analysis and commentary are deliberately omitted at that time. Critique of the methods is then undertaken in Chapter 9; numerical illustrations are presented in Appendix C.

A general overview of the text is as follows: Chapters 1 and 2 present the general theory of graduation; Chapters 3–5 deal with nonparametric graduation methods; Chapters 6 and 7 deal with parametric methods; Chapter 8 deals with the special problem of two-dimensional graduation; Chapter 9 presents an analysis and summary of the methods. The appendices contain answers to the chapter exercises, the bibliography, and numerical illustrations of the various methods presented in the text.

The text presumes that the reader has a knowledge of calculus, linear algebra, and probability and statistics at the third year university level. It also presumes familiarity with basic life contingency functions, and the mortality curves suggested by Gompertz, Makeham, and Weibull. A basic understanding of finite difference operators is required; since finite differences is not a standard part of an undergraduate mathematics curriculum, a brief description of these operators is presented in Appendix D. Finally, the text presumes some understanding of computerization, but does require familiarity with any particular programming language.

References to the bibliography are indicated in the text in square brackets.

The author gratefully acknowledges the contribution of the Society of Actuaries to the development of this text. A Review Task Force, appointed by the Society's Education Committee, reviewed the drafts of the text, and made many valuable suggestions. Particularly helpful were the contributions of Stuart Klugman and

James Broffit, University of Iowa, Esther Portnoy, University of Illinois, and the legendary Walter B. Lowrie, University of Connecticut, who also served as the Task Force chairman.

The text was published in study note form by the Society for eighteen months, during which time additional corrections and improvements were suggested by various students and academicians.

The numerical illustrations exhibited in Appendix C were produced by Eric Greenhill, then a graduate student at University of Connecticut, and his valuable assistance is gratefully acknowledged.

October, 1985   Dick London, FSA

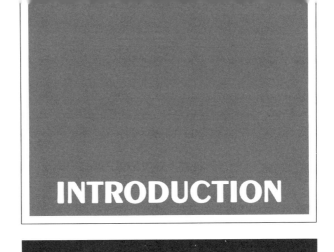

INTRODUCTION

1

1.1
GRADUATION DEFINED

The process of graduation has been defined by many writers on the subject. Andrews and Nesbitt define graduation as

> *"an effort to represent a physical phenomenon by a systematic revision of some observations of that phenomenon"* *([1], page 2).*

This definition suggests that a model-building process is being undertaken; it suggests that we have a set of *observations,* giving us some preliminary information about the model, and that we then *revise* the observations in an attempt to improve our model as a representation of the underlying phenomenon.

Miller describes graduation as

> *"the process of securing, from an irregular series of observed values of a continuous variable, a smooth regular series of values consistent in a general way with the observed series of values"* *([46], page 4).*

Miller, like Andrews and Nesbitt, takes the view that some underlying law (or phenomenon) gave rise to an "irregular" sequence of values, that these should be revised, and that the revised sequence be taken as a representation of the underlying law. But Miller goes beyond the mere instruction to "revise the observations" in two important ways.

First, he suggests that the revised values should not deviate overly much from the original (observed) values. This consideration, referred to as *fit,* is an obviously desirable one in the graduation process, and is further explored in Chapter 2.

More significantly, Miller's description clearly assumes that the underlying law is smooth, regular and continuous. Since the general objective in the graduation process is to revise the observed values so as to produce a "better" representation of the underlying law, Miller's assumption regarding the nature of that underlying law gives a more definite sense of direction to the revision process. The concept of *smoothness* is further explored in Section 1.5.

It should be noted that both of the above definitions identify graduation as the *revision* of the initial, observed data, and not the procurement of that data in the first place. Thus the process of model-building is suggested here to consist of (at least) two steps:

1. Obtain, somehow, the set of observed data.

2. Graduate (i.e., revise) that data to produce a "better" representation of the presumed underlying law, according to criteria which need to be specified.

1.2
AN ACTUARIAL ORIENTATION

As this text is written primarily for actuaries, it will be useful at this point to place the issue of graduation in an actuarial context.

One of the more important tasks for an actuary to perform is the construction of the *survival models* from which insurance values are calculated. These models are generally displayed in tabular form, and are commonly referred to as *mortality tables*. (Those with a less pessimistic bent call them *life tables*.)

Let us assume that the first step of this model-building exercise has been completed. An experience study has been carried out, producing a sequence of age-specific mortality rates (or probabilities) based on the experience of the group under observation, and for this reason is generally referred to as the observed data. (In the next section we point out that "observed" is not the most technically correct term to use for these data.)

The design and procedures of these experience studies are covered in many other texts. For example, Batten [2] treats this subject with an orientation toward insurance company and pension fund data, whereas the text by Elandt-Johnson and Johnson [11] is oriented primarily toward clinical data. In addition, various texts describe such studies in the context of large, general population data, which is a part of the general field of demography.

These observed mortality data constitute an *initial* representation of an assumed underlying law or pattern of mortality. At this point the second phase of our model-building exercise, called graduation, begins. We undertake a systematic revision of the initial data with the aim of producing a "better" representation of the unknown, underlying mortality pattern, than that given by the initial data itself. Note, however, that our revised data is still viewed as a representation of the underlying law. We are not so immodest as to view it as being the true underlying law itself!

At this point it should be noted that there may be a third step in our model-building exercise. Since mortality has been shown to change (generally improve) over time, it may be advisable to reflect any such expected improvement in our model, since the model may well be used to produce economic and demographic values applicable into the future. Although this topic of mortality projection is an important one, it is beyond the issue of graduation, and is not discussed further in this text. Thus, in our actuarial orientation, we view graduation as an attempt to secure our best representation of currently prevailing mortality.

1.3
THE STATISTICAL NATURE OF GRADUATION

The implication of Miller's description quoted in Section 1.1 is that graduation consists of smoothing the observed data while retaining some degree of fit to it; this is technically correct, but does not go far enough. It fails to recognize the statistical nature of the graduation process.

As early as 1887 this was commented on by King, who said

"What is the real object of graduation? Many would reply, 'to get a smooth curve'; but that is not quite correct. The reply should be, 'to get the most probable deaths'." ([36], page 114)

Eighty years later, Kimeldorf and Jones say

"We view graduation not merely as smoothing, but as the more general process of estimating the true rates which actually prevail in the population. . . ." ([35], page 126)

Whittaker stated the nature of graduation quite tersely by saying

"The problem of graduation belongs essentially to the mathematical theory of probability." ([60], page 303)

Finally, lest we leave the reader with the impression that Miller holds an improper view of graduation, we find that he makes this extremely cogent and elegant observation:

"We have only the series of observed probabilities given by our limited observations, from which we must estimate *the unknown true mortality rates. Viewed in this way, the problem of graduation is a mathematical problem in which we are asked to* estimate, *or secure a representation of, the series of true rates of mortality that is assumed to have given rise to the irregular series of observed probabilities."* ([46], page 6, emphasis added)

This quotation from Miller, coupled with that of Kimeldorf and Jones, presents as good a definition of graduation as we are likely to construct. It allows us to place graduation in the context of statistical estimation, in a situation where we wish to estimate a *sequence* of values. By recognizing this statistical basis, we are able to present graduation in terms of familiar concepts such as random variables, means, variances, confidence intervals, and so on.

We recognize that each "observed" value is actually an estimate of the true underlying value prevailing in a population. The estimate has been obtained by applying some *statistical estimation procedure* to the data of a *sample* drawn from the underlying population. Except in the simplest of situations, the estimate is not actually "observed"; it is calculated from experimental data by means of a chosen estimation procedure, such as maximum likelihood or a moment procedure. For this reason, in this text we prefer to use the term *initial estimate* in place of the term "observed value". When we graduate we revise this initial estimate and thereby produce a *revised* estimate (but still an estimate) of the true underlying value. Of course we do this for the entire sequence of estimates.

1.4
THE SPECIAL NATURE OF GRADUATION AS STATISTICAL ESTIMATION

Having obtained our sequence of initial estimates, why do we wish to revise them? Why do we not consider them to be our "best" estimates of the unknown values we wish to estimate? If our estimation procedure was a reasonable, valid one, why change the estimates?

The answer lies in the nature of the data itself. Each initial estimate is an element of a particular kind of sequence in which we suspect there exists a strong relationship among the elements of the sequence. In light of this, not all sequences of numbers are candidates for graduation. Only certain types of data are suitable for graduation, namely those for which "relationships among the elements of the sequence" are believed to exist. Mortality rates by age is an obvious example. In his pioneering work on graduation, Henderson [21] refers to such data as *serial statistics*.

Elphinstone, specifically dealing with mortality rates, also justifies graduation by the hypothesis that there are relations between neighboring rates, and, conversely, if we do not postulate such relations, then it is incorrect to graduate, for the initial estimates are "best". Elphinstone states flatly

> *"The theory of graduation* is *the theory of relations between neighboring rates. . . ." ([12], page 18, emphasis added)*

We can now see why our sequence of initial estimates needs to be revised. In most cases each element in the sequence was obtained independently of each other element, that is, without recognizing the "relation between neighboring rates". When we graduate the initial estimates, these relations are recognized and reflected in these revised estimates.

In general, we are now dealing with knowledge (or perhaps we should say *belief*) that we have about the nature of the sequence under consideration, such knowledge being independent of the information contained in the initial estimates.

That is, we are talking about knowledge (or belief or opinion) held *prior to* procurement of the initial estimates. The sum total of such knowledge we refer to as our *prior opinion*.

This extensive involvement of prior opinion sets graduation apart from other exercises in statistical estimation. In many cases, statistical estimation is based exclusively (or very nearly so) on the observed data itself; in such a case our initial estimates would stand as final. But in graduation, our final estimates are based on the initial (observed data), *as well as* our prior opinion about the sequence under consideration.

All graduation methods, in some manner, reflect this principle of using prior opinion, to greater or lesser extents, and in describing various graduation methods in this text, we will always identify this use of prior opinion as it appears. We will see that prior opinion can be expressed quite informally, or with a considerable degree of formality, as in the Bayesian approach of Chapter 5.

1.5
SMOOTHNESS

Undoubtedly the element of prior opinion most frequently used by actuaries in graduating mortality (or other decrement) rates has been the belief that the true rates form a smooth sequence in some sense. This originally intuitive belief is certainly supported by empirical evidence. In addition, there is an obvious practical justification for the smoothness objective. As Miller states,

> *"The actuary expects to use his tables of mortality for the calculation of premiums, reserve factors, annuities, and so forth. There is nothing to be gained by assuming that mortality varies other than regularly and continuously. Capricious irregularities in the tables from age to age disturbing the orderly progression of premiums, etc., would be inconsistent with the common sense view that such figures should be reasonably regular, and would tend to arouse an entirely justifiable skepticism."* ([46], page 6)

Because of the unquestionable appeal, both theoretical and practical, of some smoothness criterion, it historically became the dominant (and sometimes only) element of prior opinion used in a graduation method. In fact it was so heavily stressed that, in the minds of many, the words "graduation" and "smoothing" were synonymous. It was this prevalent oversimplification that prompted King to make the observation quoted in Section 1.3.

We should find the tendency to this oversimplification very understandable. For the practical reasons stated above alone, the inclusion of some smoothness criterion in a graduation process is highly desirable. It is also the most obvious, and justifiable, element of our prior opinion, and the easiest to introduce into our graduation process.

No attempt is being made here to discredit the use of a smoothness criterion; in fact, precisely the opposite is true. Smoothness is so important as a characteristic of our final estimates, that in many cases *additional* smoothing, beyond that produced by a graduation process itself, may be justifiably undertaken. We can say, then, that some concept of smoothness will usually be included in our prior opinion, and built into our graduation methods somehow. Various graduation methods will then be characterized by the manner in which smoothness is defined and incorporated, as well as by the extent to which additional elements of prior opinion (if any) are included.

1.6
TESTING GRADUATED RESULTS FOR SMOOTHNESS

As indicated in the preceding section, both theoretical and practical considerations argue for some quality of smoothness in the sequence of graduated values. The degree of smoothness obtained can be observed by graphing the graduated values.

Alternatively, we can calculate a numerical measure of smoothness. This has traditionally been done by calculating several orders of finite differences* of the graduated values, and concluding that a degree of smoothness has been obtained if some order (most commonly third or fourth) of those differences is "small". A single index number to indicate smoothness can be obtained as the sum of the squares (or absolute values) of those differences. It should be emphasized that this index number has no significance in itself, but is useful to compare the relative degrees of smoothness in several graduations of the same data, and in the ungraduated data itself.

The reader will recognize that in using, for example,

$$S = \sum_i (\Delta^4 v_i)^2$$

as a measure of smoothness, where v_i is the graduated value at index i, we are implicitly considering a third degree polynomial as a standard of smoothness, since this measure will be zero if the graduated values lie on a cubic curve. Thus an effort to make S as small as possible is, in effect, an effort to constrain the graduated values toward a cubic. If the data under consideration are not thought to be in the nature of a cubic, then some measure of smoothness other than one based on fourth differences should be devised.

For example, mortality data over an extensive range of the argument age has been found to be more accurately represented by a Makeham-type exponential curve than by a cubic. In such a case, some other measure S than that defined above would be appropriate; this is further explored later in the text (see, for example, Section 4.6).

---

*See Appendix D for a summary of concepts and notation in finite differences.

1.7
CLASSIFICATION OF GRADUATION METHODS

In this text we will explore two major classes of graduation methods. Returning to our actuarial orientation of Section 1.2, we recall that our objective is to produce a survival model which is our best representation (estimate) of the true prevailing pattern of mortality. At that point we considered our model in the traditional mortality table form. Alternatively, we could construct the model in *parametric,* or *functional,* form, such as the familiar models of Gompertz and Makeham. These two possible forms for the model define our two major classes of graduation methods.

In parametric graduation, our prior opinion concerning the relation between neighboring rates is expressed by the particular functional form chosen. Note also that the smoothness criterion is automatically embraced by the chosen functional form. As a result, considerable attention can be given to the question of fit between initial and revised estimates. This approach is discussed in Chapter 6.

The prior paragraph contemplates graduation by fitting a *single* functional form over the entire range of the data. Alternatively, we can graduate by fitting separate functional forms over *subranges* of the data. One advantage of this is that generally simpler functions, such as low-degree polynomials, may be used. The fitted (graduated) data can then be summarized in this piece-wise parametric form, or in traditional tabular form. This approach includes the techniques of graduation by *splines* and graduation by *smooth-junction interpolation.* The former is discussed in Chapter 6, and the latter in Chapter 7.

In contrast to these parametric approaches, the graduation methods of Chapters 3–5 deal with initial estimates as tabular data and graduate that data to produce revised estimates that are still in tabular (or discrete) form. No functional form for the graduated data is selected, but, in some cases, a functional form is *implicitly* assumed for the true underlying values we are approximating. The significance of this will become apparent as we explore those methods. The methods in these three chapters differ from each other in their manner of incorporating the smoothness criterion and additional elements of prior opinion, and the extent to which they recognize graduation as an exercise in statistical estimation.

Chapter 3 deals with graduation by *moving-weighted-averaging,* an early method whose use is now somewhat in decline, especially in North America. Chapter 4 deals with *Whittaker's* method, a very popular one, and some variations on the traditional Whittaker method. Chapter 5 deals with the newer, and increasingly popular, method of *Bayesian* graduation. We shall see that this method, as its name implies, involves major direct use of prior opinion, and places graduation directly in the field of statistical estimation.

Chapter 8 deals with the graduation of data which is a function of two variables, such as the select and ultimate mortality model. Various methods developed in earlier chapters are adapted for use in this case.

Finally, in Chapter 9 we will analyze and compare the various graduation methods presented in the text.

1.8
SUMMARY

In this introductory chapter we have identified graduation as an exercise in statistical estimation, specifically in a situation where a sequence of estimates is to be produced, such as mortality rates by age. We indicated that the graduation process must take into account the presumed relationships that exist among the elements in the sequence under consideration, and called this our prior opinion about the data.

We believe that one element of such prior opinion is that the data sequence should show a smooth progression, and that our final graduated data should have some quality of smoothness for practical, as well as theoretical, reasons.

Finally we described, in general, types of graduation methods to be developed in this text. Before presenting these methods, however, we wish to review some basic principles of random variables and statistical estimation which will be useful in dealing with much of the graduation theory which follows.

STATISTICAL CONSIDERATIONS

2

2.1
INTRODUCTION

In this chapter we discuss some basic properties of random variables and statistical estimation. It is assumed that the reader has some familiarity with these topics from college mathematics and/or previous parts of the actuarial education program. Thus this chapter is a review of these topics, and an orientation of them to the graduation problem. The chapter is intended to reinforce and illustrate the basic principles and nature of graduation described in Chapter 1.

2.2
A SIMPLE ESTIMATION PROBLEM

Suppose we have a coin which is known to be biased such that the probability, t, of obtaining the results "heads" on a single toss is not one-half, but we have no other knowledge about the value of t. We see that t is an example of our concept of a true underlying value, as mentioned in the previous chapter.

We wish to obtain an estimate of the value of t. A very natural way to do this is by tossing the coin a number of times, n, observing the *proportion* of occurrence of heads, u. We could then take the value u as an estimate of t. In statistics it is customary to refer to an estimate of t as $\hat{t}$; thus $u = \hat{t}$, but in this text we will prefer to use the simpler notation, always keeping in mind that u is an estimate of t. If we repeated the experiment, we would not be surprised to obtain a different value of u, thus a different potential estimate of t. We recognize that this is so because the proportion of heads is a *random variable*.

Using a capital letter to denote a random variable, and a small letter to denote a realization (or observed value) of that random variable, we define the random variable H to be the *number* of heads obtained when this coin is tossed n times. Clearly H is a *binomial* random variable, with parameters n and t. Thus we see that our t, referred to above as the true underlying value of the probability of heads, is also a parameter of the underlying probability distribution. Further, we recall that the mean, or expected value, and the variance of H are given by

$$E[H] = nt \quad \text{and} \quad \text{Var}(H) = nt(1 - t).$$

Now we define the random variable U to be the *proportion* of heads obtained in n tosses of this coin. Then, clearly,

$$U = \frac{H}{n}, \tag{2.1}$$

and is referred to as a *binomial proportion,* for obvious reasons. We recall that

$$E[U] = \frac{1}{n} \cdot E[H] = t \tag{2.2}$$

and

$$\text{Var}(U) = \frac{1}{n^2} \cdot \text{Var}(H) = \frac{t(1 - t)}{n}. \tag{2.3}$$

Recall that u is an estimate of t (i.e., $u = \hat{t}$). Since the realization, u, is an *estimate* of t, then the random variable, U, of which u is a realization, is the *estimator* of t. Analogously to writing $u = \hat{t}$, we could write

$$U = \frac{H}{n} = \hat{T}. \tag{2.1a}$$

Again, to avoid a proliferation of notation, we prefer to use simply U for our estimator. Note well the distinction between an estimator, which is a random variable, and an estimate, which is a particular realization of that estimator.

Since this estimator random variable U, a binomial proportion, will receive a lot of attention in this text, we should explore it a bit further. We note the following characteristics of U:

1. We have already seen that $E[U] = t$. Thus we say that U is an *unbiased* estimator of t.

2. U is the *maximum likelihood estimator* of t (see Exercise 2–2).

3. U is also the *method of moments estimator* of t (see Exercise 2–3).

4. We have already seen that $\text{Var}(U) = \dfrac{t(1 - t)}{n}$. We note that the variance of a binomial proportion estimator is *inversely* related to sample size, an important property that gets a lot of use in graduation.

5. If n is sufficiently large, the binomial distribution of U can be adequately approximated by a normal distribution. This we will do on occasion (see Section 2.7).

We will frequently need the numerical value of the variance (or standard deviation) of our estimator. Unfortunately, the variance given by (2.3) is in terms of the unknown t, the very thing we are trying to estimate. Thus we must be content with an estimate of the variance. Although in some cases we might estimate the variance from other data, we will more commonly substitute the estimate of t, $u = \hat{t}$, which we have just produced into (2.3) to estimate the variance of the estimator. Thus we have

$$\text{est. Var}(U) = \frac{u(1 - u)}{n}. \tag{2.4}$$

Returning to our experiment with the biased coin, we have the value u, a realization of the random variable U, and can view it as an initial estimate of t. We now pose an interesting question: can we suggest any value other than u as an estimate of t which we feel is a "better" estimate? Since we began by hypothesizing "no knowledge" of t, it is rather difficult to justify any other value. We really have no logical basis to suggest another number, and u must stand, for now, as our "best" estimate of t.

2.3
ENTER GRADUATION

At this point we expand our example a bit. Suppose we have 100 different coins, and each coin has a different degree of bias. Let the coins be numbered 1 through 100. Then H_i is the random variable for the *number* of heads when coin i is tossed (we assume that the various H_i are independent), U_i is the random variable for the *proportion* of heads, and t_i is the true underlying probability of heads for coin i, thus also the parameter in the binomial distribution of H_i. As before, U_i is the *binomial proportion estimator* of t_i, and is unbiased so that $E[U_i] = t_i$. We wish to estimate the values of t_i, for $i = 1, 2, \ldots, 100$.

We toss coin i n_i times, where n_i need not be equal for all i, and observe the results $u_i = \hat{t}_i$. Now the values u_i could be taken as our estimates of t_i, but once again we ask if we can obtain "better" estimates. We have now encountered the concept of graduation. The process by which we might revise the values u_i into new values (call them v_i), *where we believe that v_i are better estimates of t_i than were u_i*, is the process of graduation. This process is not generally applicable to our *one* value u, discussed earlier; graduation normally deals with a *sequence* of estimates. (As imaginative exception to this is suggested at the end of this section.) Note that in the graduation of u_i into v_i it is not necessary that $u_i \neq v_i$ for all i. That is, some of the revised estimates can be the same as the corresponding initial estimates. But if $u_i = v_i$ for *all* i, then we have not graduated at all.

Why should we graduate u_i? How is it that our ability to produce "better" estimates of t_i than u_i happen to be is enhanced by having a sequence of values rather than just one value? The answer, as suggested in Chapter 1, is that we may be able to utilize prior opinion that we have about the relationships of the elements in the t_i sequence. We should recognize that if we know nothing about t_i *beyond the information contained in the initial estimates* u_i, then the u_i are our "best" estimates of t_i. But if we *do* have a prior opinion about t_i, beyond that contained in the observations, and fail to take it into account, then we have not done our best possible job of estimating t_i. We have "made a mistake" in our estimation exercise.

What elements of prior opinion might we possess about t_i in our biased coin model?

Suppose we know, or at least strongly believe, that the coins are numbered in increasing degree of bias towards heads. That is, t_i is an increasing function of i. Then, since the initial estimates u_i might quite plausibly not be increasing, we have a sense of direction for revising (graduating) these estimates. Actuaries have always accepted this element of prior opinion in graduating a sequence of mortality rates (except at the juvenile ages, and, in some cases, at ages in the mid-20's).

As a second example, we might have good reason to believe that the pattern of increasing bias in our coins is a fairly regular one over the range of i. That is to say, we believe that the true underlying values t_i form a *smooth* progression. The use of this element of prior opinion was considered in Chapter 1, on both theoretical and practical grounds.

More specifically, we may believe, from prior experience, that the true underlying values can be closely represented by some mathematical function of the argument. In that case, the graduation process is one of "curve fitting" the initial estimates to the assumed functional form, or estimating the parameters of the functional form directly from the data which produced the initial estimates.

As perhaps the ultimate in prior opinion, we may have some idea of the actual *numerical* values of t_i *prior to* generating the initial data, along with some way to express our prior opinion concerning the relations among the values in the t_i sequence. Our view of graduation as statistical estimation would then suggest that we blend this prior opinion with our experimental data to produce revised estimates. This is the formal Bayesian graduation process which we will explore in Chapter 5. It raises an interesting question: are we revising our numerical prior opinion in light of new experimental data, or are we revising our experimental data in light of our numerical prior opinion? (See Section 5.4.5)

Recall the statement made earlier in this section that generally we cannot graduate one element of data. We informally illustrate the Bayesian view by showing that it can produce an exception to this general rule.

Suppose you have a coin which you believe to be fair. Your prior opinion of t is thus .50. By tossing the coin 100 times you produce an observed value of .20. You are now not so sure that the coin is fair. The probability of obtaining 20 or fewer heads in 100 tosses of a fair coin is exceedingly small (being *six* standard deviations below the mean), so your observed result is not likely to be produced by randomness alone if the coin is fair. On the other hand, you don't believe that the bias toward tails is as strong as 80%, since the coin does not feel particularly imbalanced. So you conclude that t is somewhat less than .50, and the observed result is even lower than the unknown true rate due to randomness. Perhaps you arbitrarily average the two values and produce .35 as your "best estimate" of t. You have just performed an informal Bayesian graduation of one number. Congratulations! (We will formalize this totally intuitive procedure in Section 5.3.)

2.4
ANALOGY TO MORTALITY DATA

It is easy to see the analogy of the biased coin model to mortality data, changing the index from i to x (age). In this case we wish to produce an estimate of the true probability of death, rather than an estimate of the true probability of heads. For this model, standard actuarial notation would substitute q_x for t_i, θ_x for H_i, and E_x for n_i. There are two important distinctions to be made between the biased coin and mortality models, which we will now discuss.

2.4.1 EXACT VS. APPROXIMATE BINOMIAL MODELS

In the coin model, H_i was precisely binomial, and thus U_i was precisely a binomial proportion. Consequently formula (2.3) for the variance of this estimator is correct without approximation. In a mortality study, the presence of *migration* within the estimation interval means that the random variable for number of deaths (usually called θ_x) is not precisely binomial, and consequently the estimator random variable for probability of death, $U_x = \hat{Q}_x$, is not precisely a binomial proportion.

As the reader may recall from other actuarial study, the traditional approach to mortality estimation has been to approximate an "effective number of initial exposed", in the *presence* of migration, and then to proceed *as if* this number were subject to the risk of death for the *entire* interval, i.e., that there was then *no* migration in the estimation interval, so that a precise binomial model would exist. (See, for example, Elandt-Johnson and Johnson [11], pages 156–158.)

Alternatively, and more analytically, the adoption of a particular method of moments estimation procedure and the Balducci distribution assumption allows us to express our mortality estimator as

$$\hat{Q} = \frac{\theta}{E}. \tag{2.1b}$$

(See, for example, Batten [2], pages 16–27.) The analogy to (2.1a) should be obvious. The "E" in the denominator stands for "exposure" and is numerically the same as the intuitive concept "effective number of initial exposed" of the preceding paragraph. Therefore θ is not precisely binomial because E is not precisely a number of independent binomial trials, as is n in a precise binomial model. However, since

E is usually quite large compared to θ, the degree of error in acting *as if* θ were binomial (and thus *as if* $\hat{Q}$ were a binomial proportion) is small, and we would normally make this simplifying assumption. Thus we would use, for example,

$$E[\hat{Q}] = q \tag{2.2a}$$

and

$$\text{Var}\,(\hat{Q}) = \frac{q(1 - q)}{E}. \tag{2.3a}$$

Although E_x is traditionally used for the exposure at age x, in this text we prefer to reserve capital letters for random variables. Since exposure is normally used as if it represented a number of binomial trials, we will hereinafter use n_x in place of E_x for exposure. This will also avoid confusion with the error random variable E_x, defined in Section 2.6. It should be noted that the exposure n_x can be interpreted as independent binomial trials only when measured as a number of *lives*. In actuarial mortality studies, the exposure is frequently measured in *amounts of insurance*. (See, for example, Klugman [37].)

2.4.2 INDEPENDENCE

A second important distinction between the biased coin and mortality models has to do with the *independence* (or lack thereof) between the random variables in the sequence. Clearly the random variables H_i, as defined, are mutually independent, and therefore so are the random variables U_i. This follows since each coin toss can influence the estimate at only one value of the index.

In the mortality model, a particular person dying or not in the interval $[x, x+1]$ is analogous to a particular coin toss resulting in heads or not. It is generally reasonable to assume independence among the various *persons* within one estimation interval. But if the same person is a trial in each of several adjacent estimation (age) intervals, then independence *between intervals* does not exist. This is pursued in Section 5.6.

Unfortunately, in several graduation methods we find it mathematically convenient to make such an independence assumption among the variables in the sequence $\hat{Q}_x$, since this allows us to deal with Var $(\hat{Q}_x)$, but to ignore the covariance, cov $(\hat{Q}_x, \hat{Q}_y)$. In this text, we will make this assumption on occasion, and comment on the extent of its validity (or, rather, lack of validity).

2.5
SUMMARY OF NOTATION

In Section 2.4, we used the standard notation for the mortality model only for convenience. Throughout this text, the notation introduced with the coin model will be used, even for mortality data, except that we will use x for the index rather than i. Several additional symbols will be introduced as needed.

Frequently weights are used in a graduation process, and we will use w_x for these weights. Generally the weights will be some function of the sample sizes n_x, from which the associated initial estimates arose. In the formal Bayesian process of Chapter 5, t_x is itself viewed as a realization of a random variable, for which we will use T_x. Error random variables are introduced in the next section, and used extensively in Chapter 3.

To summarize our principal notation:

Symbol	Meaning
x	The index defining the sequence.
t_x	The sequence of true values to be estimated.
U_x	The estimator random variables of t_x, assumed to be unbiased binomial proportions.
n_x	The sample sizes (exposure) in these assumed binomial models.
u_x	The particular realizations of U_x, our initial estimates (or observed values) of t_x.
v_x	The revised estimates of t_x, our graduated values.
V_x	The random variables of which v_x are particular realizations.
w_x	The sequence of weights used in a graduation.
E_x	The estimation error random variables.
e_x	The particular realizations of E_x.

In several subsequent chapters, we will find it convenient to express the sequences t_x, U_x, u_x, V_x and v_x as vectors. For this we will use bold-face letters, without subscripts: **t**, **U**, **u**, **V** and **v**. The weights will be expressed in a diagonal matrix **w**.

2.6
ESTIMATION ERROR

An estimate can be viewed as being made up of the true value it is estimating plus a residual term (positive or negative) which we call the "error of estimation". For example, if you toss 10 coins and obtain .7 for the proportion of heads, a very plausible result, we can view the outcome as .5 + .2, assuming that .5 is really the true underlying value. In terms of the notation adopted in Section 2.5, we can write

$$u_x = t_x + e_x. \tag{2.5}$$

In terms of random variables we would write

$$U_x = t_x + E_x. \tag{2.5a}$$

t_x, the true underlying values, are not random variables, except in the special case of Chapter 5. The error terms, however, are random variables, defined by

$$E_x = U_x - t_x. \tag{2.6}$$

Properties of these error random variables are explored in the exercises.

Equation (2.5) suggests the following descriptive view of graduation. If G is a graduation procedure (or graduation operator), applied to the initial estimates u_x, we might take the view that G is applied to the t_x and e_x components separately, with the results added together. Schematically we are suggesting that

$$G(u_x) = G(t_x + e_x) = G(t_x) + G(e_x). \tag{2.7}$$

In order that equation (2.7) be valid, G must be a linear (or distributive) operator, and this is not always the case. It *is* the case, however, in the method of Chapter 3, in which the view expressed by equation (2.7) is directly applied.

Even if G is not linear, (2.7) still suggests a description of an ideal graduation result, namely to leave the t_x component substantially *unchanged*, while significantly *reducing* the error component e_x. Schematically we extend (2.7) to read

$$G(u_x) = v_x = G(t_x) + G(e_x) = t_x + e_x'. \tag{2.8}$$

Recall that v_x *is* the graduated result $G(u_x)$. Then (2.8) suggests that v_x is made up of the true value t_x, plus a graduated (hopefully reduced) error term e_x'. If that is true, then v_x is a "better" estimate of t_x than was u_x, in the sense of being closer to t_x, which is the purpose of graduation. This is further explored in Chapter 3.

2.7
FIT-TESTING GRADUATED RESULTS

It has always been argued that graduated values should not depart too far from the initial values; that is, there should be some degree of *fit* between the two. The initial estimates should certainly be reasonable indications of t_x (unless the sample was very small), so the revised values should be similar to the initial. The reason for departing from initial at all (i.e., for graduating), is to improve smoothness and give effect to other elements of prior opinion.

Now close fit of graduated to initial is the same as close fit of initial to graduated. Although it may appear to be a trivial point, we prefer to view it that way. Remember that the revised (graduated) value is to be our best estimate of t_x. More specifically, when our estimator random variable is a binomial proportion, then the graduated value is to be our best estimate of the expected value of that random variable. Therefore, if the graduated value deviates considerably from the initial, we are suggesting that the initial (observed) deviates considerably from the expected. Although randomness *could* produce this considerable deviation, such a result is "less probable", so we must consider the possibility that we have "misassigned" the expected value via our determination of the graduated value.

In Section 2.2 we saw from equation (2.3) that our binomial proportion random variable has a variance that is inversely related to sample size. Since variance measures the expected squared deviation of a realization of a random variable from its expected value, it follows that a realization of a random variable with a large value of n, and thus a small variance, is more likely to be a better estimate, in the expected value sense, of its own expected value than would be true if n were smaller. Therefore a graduated value should deviate less from the observed (initial estimate) for these "large n" situations, so when we graduate a sequence of such initial estimates, this statistical view suggests that "better fit" (smaller deviations) should result at those values of the argument where the initial estimates were based on larger n. (This view is qualified, however, in the illustration in Section 2.8.)

2.7.1 NUMERICAL FIT MEASURES

Numerical measures of fit can be calculated as was done for smoothness in Section 1.6. For example, we might define

$$F_1 = \sum_x w_x(v_x - u_x). \tag{2.9}$$

(Although F as defined here is a number, and not a random variable, we nonetheless prefer to use the capital letter. The same is true for S in Section 1.6.)

Fit measure (2.9) reflects sample size by weighting the deviations. Since a value of F close to 0 indicates good fit, those deviations with larger weights (sample sizes) must themselves be comparatively smaller in order to keep F small. (2.9) is an inadequate fit measure, however, since, by coincidence, positive and negative weighted deviations could cancel each other out, resulting in $F = 0$ in a situation with extremely poor fit. In light of this, we might define our fit measure as the sum of weighted squared deviations,

$$F_2 = \sum_x w_x(v_x - u_x)^2, \tag{2.10}$$

or possibly as the sum of first moments of weighted deviations,

$$F_3 = \sum_x x \cdot w_x(v_x - u_x). \tag{2.11}$$

Fit measure (2.11) has an interesting interpretation when we are dealing with mortality data if w_x is the exposure n_x, an approximation to sample size. Clearly

$w_x \cdot u_x$ is the *observed* number of deaths at age x, and $w_x \cdot v_x$ is the *graduated* number of deaths. Then

$$\sum_x x \cdot w_x \cdot u_x$$

is the total of *observed ages at death,* and, similarly

$$\sum_x x \cdot w_x \cdot v_x$$

is the total of *graduated ages at death.* Requiring (2.11) to be small is to require that total ages at death be nearly equal for observed (initial) and graduated (revised) data. Fit measure (2.9) has a similar interpretation for the total *number* of deaths, so that if both (2.9) and (2.11) are "small", the *average age at death* is nearly equal for initial and revised data.

We should repeat the observation made with respect to our smoothness measure in Section 1.6, namely that these fit measures are *index numbers,* and are mainly used to compare the fit in several graduations of the same data. To some extent, however, fit measure (2.10) is susceptible to interpretation.

2.7.2 A STANDARD FOR JUDGING FIT

We have seen (Section 2.2, Observation (5)) that the random variable U_x is approximately normal, with

$$E[U_x] = t_x \quad \text{and} \quad \text{Var}(U_x) = \frac{t_x(1 - t_x)}{n_x}.$$

If U_x is normal, then

$$\frac{(U_x - t_x)^2}{\text{Var}(U_x)}$$

has a χ^2 distribution with 1 degree of freedom. Further, if the several U_x are independent, then

$$F = \sum_x \frac{(U_x - t_x)^2}{\text{Var}(U_x)} \tag{2.10a}$$

is a random variable with a χ^2 distribution with n degrees of freedom, where there are n terms in the summation, and we know that

$$E[F] = E[\chi_{(n)}^2] = n.$$

Of course t_x is not known, but v_x is to be our best estimate of t_x. Thus we can calculate the value of fit measure (2.10) using

$$w_x = \frac{n_x}{v_x(1 - v_x)} \doteq \frac{1}{\text{Var}\,(U_x)}.$$

It must be noted however, that the degrees of freedom of such a χ^2 statistic is less than n whenever the values of v_x have been determined from the u_x data. For example, if v_x is an hypothesized functional form (see Chapter 6), with r parameters estimated from the data, then (2.10) is χ^2 with $n - r$ degrees of freedom. In non-parametric graduation methods, the appropriate reduction in degrees of freedom is less clear. This point is illustrated in Exercises 2–18, 2–19, 2–22, and 2–24.

Apart from the degrees-of-freedom issue, Taylor [55] has questioned the appropriateness of using the χ^2 test for certain graduation results, including those produced by the methods of Chapters 3 and 4. This point is also discussed by Hoem [30].

2.7.3 SIGN CHANGES

A fairly simple, but quite useful, fit measure can be defined in terms of the number and pattern of *sign changes* in the sequence of deviations between graduated and initial values. Define

$$d_x = v_x - u_x. \tag{2.12}$$

From a purely intuitive view, good fit would be indicated if the sequence of deviations showed fairly frequent changes of sign, implying that the graduated sequence interlaces with the sequence of initial data, rather than lying either above or below it throughout major subranges of x.

More analytically, if our estimator random variable is a binomial proportion, then the observed (initial) estimate u_x is *equally likely* to be above or below the median of U_x, which is approximately equal to the mean of U_x. (If U_x is assumed normal, then the median and mean are the same.) But the mean of U_x is t_x, and the revised estimate v_x is our best estimate of t_x. Thus it follows that u_x is equally likely to lie above or below v_x, so that d_x, defined by (2.12), is equally likely to be positive or negative.

Assuming independence among the various U_x implies that the sign of d_j, say, is equally likely to be the same as or different from the sign of d_{j-1}. Thus the probability of a sign *change* in moving from d_{j-1} to d_j is $\frac{1}{2}$. If there are n values of the index x, then there are $n - 1$ possible sign changes in the sequence d_x, each with probability $\frac{1}{2}$, so we see that the number of sign changes is binomially distributed with $p = \frac{1}{2}$, and the expected number of such sign changes is $\frac{1}{2}(n - 1)$.

From this rationale, we can conclude that a long run of, say, positive deviations, besides being intuitively objectionable, is quite "improbable" under the hypothesis that the sequence v_x closely represents the true sequence t_x. Thus we might adjust some of the values of v_x to obtain a "more probable" pattern of sign changes.

For a further description of fit-testing, the interested reader is referred to Chapter 11 of Benjamin and Haycocks [4], and to Seal [52].

2.8
AN ILLUSTRATIVE SUMMARY

Much of the theory of this chapter can be summarized by a numerical example, graphically illustrating the principles of graduation thus far developed. The reader will recognize that a graduation could be entirely performed by graphic means, and, indeed, many graduations have been so accomplished. The graphic method has been a popular one, and is still recommended as a quick and easy method. Its major features are illustrated in this and the following section.

The data for this illustration, given in the first four columns of Table 2.1, are taken from Miller ([46], page 11). With no other graduation methods yet available to use, we will graduate this data, with the help of a graph, to reflect our prior opinion that the true underlying pattern of mortality rates is (a) smooth, (b) increasing, and (c) more steeply increasing at the higher end of the age range. Furthermore, we will certainly attempt to obtain a reasonable fit to initial data.

In Figure 2.1, the jagged graph of u_x does tend to support both elements (b) and (c) of our prior opinion. The major graduation dilemma appears to be at ages

TABLE 2.1

Age	Sample Size	Observed Deaths	Observed Rate (Initial Estimate)	Estimated Standard Deviation
70	135	6	.044	.018
71	143	12	.084	.023
72	140	10	.071	.022
73	144	11	.076	.022
74	149	6	.040	.016
75	154	16	.104	.025
76	150	24	.160	.030
77	139	8	.058	.020
78	145	16	.110	.026
79	140	13	.093	.025
80	137	19	.139	.030
81	136	21	.154	.031
82	126	23	.183	.034
83	126	26	.206	.036
84	109	26	.239	.041

Figure 2.1

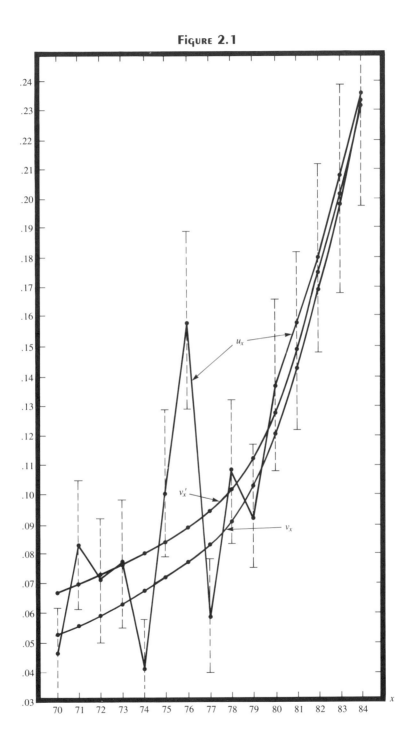

74–77. How much credence should we give to the surprisingly large value of u_{76}, and to the surprisingly small values of u_{74} and u_{77}? Some assistance in answering this is provided by the estimated standard deviation of the estimator random variable U_x at each of these ages. These standard deviations have been calculated at all ages by taking the square root of the estimated variance from equation (2.4), and are shown in the last column of Table 2.1.

To assist in our graduation decision, we have then plotted one standard deviation above and below the initial estimate at each age in Figure 2.1. As described in Section 2.7, those estimates based on larger sample size should have the smaller standard deviations. Thus the initial estimates centered in the *narrower* ranges in Figure 2.1 might be interpreted as the ones in which we have greater credence, and therefore will try to be "close" to in assigning the graduated values. If we require our graduated values to lie within the standard deviation bands, we will appear to be giving greater credence to those estimates which are based on larger sample sizes.

Specifically we see that the standard deviations at ages 74–77 are .016, .025, .030, and .020, respectively. Thus we might conclude that we have more confidence in u_{74} and u_{77} than we have in u_{75} and (especially) u_{76}, and our determination of graduated values could reflect that relative confidence.

The observed estimate at age 74 is particularly interesting, and illustrates the risk of over-reliance on the standard deviations. Intuitively it certainly appears to be "unexpectedly" small. But the random variable of which it is a realization has the *smallest* standard deviation of any in our data. This apparent paradox is easily explained, since the standard deviations are only approximate, depending on the initial estimates themselves. The small standard deviation of U_{74} has been influenced by the allegedly "undersized" estimate. This suggests that, as an alternative, we might calculate the standard deviations from the observed sample sizes and rates taken from a standard table.

The larger standard deviations at the top five ages are due, we assume, to the smaller sample sizes. Since all elements of our prior opinion are reinforced by the initial estimates in this range, our graduated values will fit the initial quite closely here. The values of v_x, read from the lower curve in Figure 2.1, are given in Table 2.2, along with the smoothness measure $\Delta^3 v_x$ and d_x defined by (2.12).

Both the graph and the Δ^3 smoothness measure would seem to indicate an adequate degree of smoothness in our graduated sequence v_x. We might, however, explore the possibility of improving our fit without sacrificing the smoothness already obtained. This can be accomplished by producing a *revised graduation* v'_x, say, which is a linear transformation of v_x. That is,

$$v'_x = av_x + b. \tag{2.13}$$

Recalling fit measures (2.9) and (2.11), and the interpretation of them for mortality data, let us solve for a and b in (2.13), and thus for v'_x, such that both fit measures will be zero. Using the sample sizes from Table 2.1 as our weights, and fit

TABLE 2.2

Age	u_x	v_x	$\Delta^3 v_x$	d_x	v_x'
70	.044	.050	.000	.006	.065
71	.084	.054	.001	−.030	.068
72	.071	.058	−.001	−.013	.072
73	.076	.062	.000	−.014	.076
74	.040	.067	.001	.027	.080
75	.104	.072	.001	−.032	.085
76	.160	.077	.002	−.083	.090
77	.058	.083	.002	.025	.095
78	.110	.091	.001	−.019	.103
79	.093	.103	.002	.010	.114
80	.139	.121	−.013	−.018	.130
81	.154	.146	.004	−.008	.153
82	.183	.180		−.003	.185
83	.206	.210		.004	.213
84	.239	.240		.001	.240

measure (2.9), we require a and b such that

$$F = \sum_{70}^{84} w_x(u_x - v_x') = \sum_{70}^{84} w_x u_x - \sum_{70}^{84} w_x(av_x + b)$$

$$= \sum_{70}^{84} w_x u_x - a \sum_{70}^{84} w_x v_x - b \sum_{70}^{84} w_x = 0,$$

or that

$$a \sum_{70}^{84} w_x v_x + b \sum_{70}^{84} w_x = \sum_{70}^{84} w_x u_x. \qquad (2.14)$$

Similarly, from fit measure (2.11), we obtain

$$a \sum_{70}^{84} x \cdot w_x v_x + b \sum_{70}^{84} x \cdot w_x = \sum_{70}^{84} x \cdot w_x u_x. \qquad (2.15)$$

This pair of equations solves for $a = .9253$ and $b = .0183$. The transformed sequence v_x' is given in Table 2.2, and is shown by the upper curve in Figure 2.1. The extent to which fit measures (2.9) and (2.11) are not precisely zero for v_x' is due to rounding.

The details of this fit-improving transformation, as well as several questions based on this illustration, are left to the exercises.

2.9
REFERENCE TO A STANDARD TABLE

One of the problems encountered in the graphic graduation of Section 2.8 is that the range of initial estimates to be plotted, from .040 to .239, creates a scaling problem. If the scale is large enough to distinguish .001, then the size of graph paper required is very large. Conversely, to fit normal graph paper, the scale may be so small as to require considerable guess-work in plotting and reading values.

2.9.1 USE OF STANDARD TABLE TO REDUCE GRAPHING RANGE

To alleviate this problem, we select a published mortality table to use as a standard, and calculate the ratio of our initial estimate (observed rate) to the standard table rate for each value of x. These ratios are given in the third column of Table 2.3 (initial ratios). The standard table used is the U.S. Life Table for White Males, 1969–71.

We again calculate the estimated standard deviation, this time for the random

TABLE 2.3

Age	Standard Table Rate	Initial Ratio	Estimated Standard Deviation	Graduated Ratio	Revised Rate
70	.049	.90	.36	.99	.049
71	.053	1.58	.44	1.00	.053
72	.057	1.25	.38	1.01	.058
73	.061	1.25	.36	1.03	.063
74	.066	.61	.24	1.04	.069
75	.072	1.44	.34	1.07	.077
76	.078	2.05	.38	1.09	.085
77	.085	.68	.23	1.12	.095
78	.091	1.21	.29	1.17	.106
79	.097	.96	.25	1.22	.118
80	.105	1.32	.28	1.28	.134
81	.113	1.36	.27	1.36	.154
82	.121	1.51	.28	1.47	.178
83	.130	1.58	.28	1.59	.207
84	.139	1.72	.29	1.73	.241

variable R_x, the mortality ratio. Since

$$R_x = \frac{U_x}{s_x},\tag{2.16}$$

where s_x is the standard table rate, then

$$\text{Var}(R_x) = \frac{\text{Var}(U_x)}{(s_x)^2} = \frac{(t_x)(1 - t_x)}{n_x(s_x)^2}.\tag{2.17}$$

We estimate the variance by using the initial estimate of t_x, which is u_x, in place of t_x, to obtain

$$\text{est. Var}(R_x) = \frac{(u_x)(1 - u_x)}{n_x(s_x)^2}.\tag{2.18}$$

(Alternatively, we could use s_x in place of t_x for our estimated variances.) The square roots of the values given by (2.18) are shown in the fourth column of Table 2.3, and plotted in Figure 2.2, above and below the initial ratios.

As in the previous section, we again notice that our extreme "outliers" at age 74 and age 77 have the smallest estimated standard deviations. But we recognize that these values are misleading, since they are highly influenced by the use of the extreme values of u_x at these ages. We thus give them little credence in drawing our graph of graduated ratios, shown in Figure 2.2 and given in the fifth column of Table 2.3.

Finally our revised estimates of the rates, v_x, are found by multiplying the graduated ratios by the standard table rates. They are given in the last column of Table 2.3. This graduation result is compared to that obtained in Section 2.8 in the exercises.

2.9.2 ANOTHER USE OF THE STANDARD TABLE

The use of ratios based on a standard table plays another role in addition to reducing our graphing range. The standard table rates introduce additional information into our graduation by expressing prior opinion about the *pattern* (if not the magnitude) of the true rates we are trying to estimate. The graduated rates will then exhibit a pattern similar to that of the standard table rates.

The standard table selected should therefore be one that is consistent with our prior opinion about the nature of the t_x sequence we wish to estimate. It should have been derived from an experience with characteristics similar to the one which produced our initial estimates being graduated. In this regard, our choice of a newer population table as a standard for graduating initial estimates based on older insurance data, may not have been entirely appropriate.

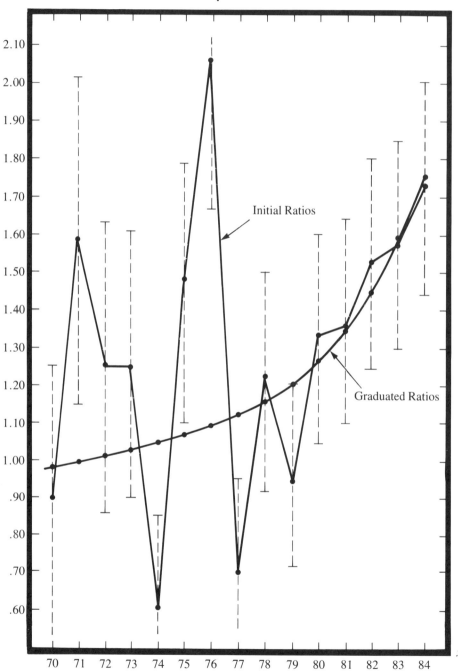

Figure 2.2

2.10
SUMMARY

In this chapter we have explored graduation in the context of multivariate statistical estimation. In particular, realizing that much of actuarial graduation deals with rates of mortality, we have mainly assumed that the estimator random variable U_x is a binomial proportion, and have made use of the properties of U_x under that assumption. This will continue in connection with most of the graduation methods which follow.

We have also given considerable emphasis to the idea that graduation inevitably involves the use of prior opinion, a feature which might be said to give graduation a Bayesian flavor through the blending of data with that opinion. We do not wish to imply that recognition of prior opinion, *per se,* constitutes a formal Bayesian process. The latter requires not just a prior opinion, but also a statement of confidence about that opinion, usually in the form of a probability distribution. Thus we will refer to the Bayesian "nature" of *all* graduation methods (by which we mean simply the use of prior opinion), and employ a formal Bayesian process in Chapter 5.

The reader should feel quite comfortable with the general graduation theory presented in these two introductory chapters before proceeding to a study of specific graduation methods in the remainder of the text.

EXERCISES

2.1   Introduction;   2.2 A Simple Estimation Problem

2–1   Verify equations (2.2) and (2.3).

2–2   Let us verify observation (2) of Section 2.2.

    a) If the probability of heads is t, write the probability of obtaining h heads in n tosses of a coin. Call this probability L.

    b) Write the natural log of L, $\ell = \ln L$.

    c) The maximum likelihood estimate (MLE) of t is that value of t, called $\hat{t}$, which maximizes the probability (likelihood) of a sample outcome. (We know that the value of t which maximizes L will also maximize $\ell = \ln L$.) Differentiate ℓ with respect to t, equate to zero, and solve for t.

    d) The equation in (c) is the ML *estimator* of t. In an experiment with 50 tosses, 20 heads were obtained. What is the *ML* estimate of t?

2–3   The method of moments estimate of t is that value which equates an actual experiment outcome to its expected value.

    a) In our coin model, what is the expected number of heads in 50 tosses?

    b) If the number actually obtained is H, what is the method of moments estimator of t?

    c) Then if the actual number in an experiment was 20, what is the method of moments estimate of t?

[Note: Exercises 2–2 and 2–3 are also intended to reinforce the distinction between and estimator and an estimate.]

2–4 Consider a coin which you *a priori* believe to be unbiased. U is the random variable for proportion of heads when this coin is tossed 100 times.

    a) What would you say, *a priori*, is $E[U]$ and Var (U)?

    b) Suppose a trial results in only 35 heads. Assuming that the probability distribution of U is approximately normal, what is the probability of obtaining a value of U this small or smaller?

    c) How confident are you now that the coin is unbiased?

2–5 Having no *a priori* idea of the value of t, you obtain 20 heads in 100 tosses of your coin. What would you estimate $E[U]$ and Var (U) to be?

2.3   Enter Graduation

2–6 What fundamental factor is used to justify the revision (graduation) of a sequence of initial estimates?

2–7 Rudy has three biased coins: a penny, nickel and dime. He states that the true probability of heads for each coin is proportional to its monetary value, and asks Kathy to estimate these probabilities, which we will call t_p, t_n, t_d. She tosses each coin a large number of times and obtains $u_p = .07$, $u_n = .32$, and $u_d = .76$.

    a) What relationship must hold among Kathy's revised estimates (v_p, v_n, v_d), in order that they satisfy her prior "knowledge"?

    b) The revised estimates are to be expressed to two decimals only. What revised estimates, satisfying prior opinion, will minimize the fit measure $F = |v_p - u_p| + |v_n - u_n| + |v_d - u_d|$?

2–8 Non-Bayesian statisticians would not approve of our arbitrary estimation procedure in the last paragraph of Section 2.3, which gave equal weight to our prior opinion and our observed data, resulting in the estimate $\hat{t} = .35$.

    a) If $t = .35$, how many standard deviations below the mean is the observed result $u = .20$?

    b) Find the greatest value for t (to two decimals) such that our result $u = .20$ is within 1.65 standard deviations below the mean.

    c) If you adopt the result in (b) as your revised estimate of t, how much weight have you given to your prior opinion?

2.4   Analogy to Mortality Data

2–9 In a mortality study, n persons, each exactly age x, are observed for one year or until prior death. Each person's chance of death is independent, and θ is the random variable for number of deaths.

a) What is the exposure?

b) What is the mortality rate estimator, $\hat{Q}_x$?

c) What is $E[\theta_x]$?

d) What is $E[\hat{Q}_x]$?

e) Why is $\hat{Q}_x$ unbiased?

2–10 In addition to the n persons of Exercise 2–9, another m persons, each exactly age $x + \frac{1}{2}$, are observed to age $x + 1$ or prior death. Each "trial" is independent. Each person subject to the risk from age $x + \frac{1}{2}$ is treated as half a person subject to the risk from age x.

a) What is the "effective number of initial exposed"?

b) What is the traditional actuarial mortality rate estimator, $\hat{Q}_x$?

c) What is the expected number of deaths, $E[\theta]$?

d) What is $E[\theta]$ under the Balducci distribution assumption?

e) Equate this $E[\theta]$ to θ and solve for the same result as in (b).

f) What is $E[\hat{Q}_x]$ under the Balducci assumption?

2–11 In Exercise 2–10, we saw that the expected deaths out of the m persons exposed from age $x + \frac{1}{2}$ was $m \cdot {}_{1/2}q_{x+1/2}$ or $\frac{1}{2}m \cdot q_x$ under the Balducci assumption.

a) If x is an age where mortality is believed to increase with age, does the Balducci assumption overstate or understate this expected number of deaths?

b) Then how does $E[\hat{Q}_x]$ really compare to q_x?

2–12 This time assume that m of the original n persons *withdraw* at age $x + \frac{1}{2}$. Then $(n - m)$ are exposed for a full year, and m for only half. Each of the m persons is treated as half a person exposed for the full year.

a) What is the effective number of initial exposed?

b) What is $\hat{Q}_x$?

c) What is $E[\theta]$?

d) What is $E[\theta]$ under the Balducci assumption?

e) What is $E[\hat{Q}_x]$ under the Balducci assumption?

f) If mortality is increasing, how does (d) compare to (c)?

g) Then how does $E[\hat{Q}_x]$ really compare to q_x?

2.5   Summary of Notation;   2.6 Estimation Error

2–13 For the error random variable defined by equation (2.6), find each of the following, assuming U_x is a binomial proportion:

a) $E[E_x]$

b) $\text{Var}(E_x)$

c) $E[(E_x)^2]$

2–14 Consider the standardized error, defined by $E_x{}^s = \dfrac{U_x - t_x}{[\text{Var}\,(U_x)]^{1/2}}$. If U_x is normally distributed, what is the distribution of $E_x{}^s$?

2.7 Fit-Testing Graduated Results

2–15 Some earlier texts suggested a ''sum of partial sums'' as a fit measure instead of our fit measures (2.10) and (2.11). Consider a column of $d_x = v_x - u_x$, ignoring weights for convenience, for $x = 1, 2, \ldots, n$. Consider

$$\sum_{x=y}^{n} d_x,$$

the sum of the d_x from the *bottom* of the column up to (and including) $x = y$. Then define

$$\uparrow\!\sum{}^2 = \sum_{y=1}^{n} \sum_{x=y}^{n} d_x.$$

Show that $\uparrow\!\sum{}^2 = \sum_{x=1}^{n} x \cdot d_x.$

2–16 Similarly, consider

$$\sum_{x=1}^{y} d_x,$$

the sum of d_x from the *top* of the column down to (and including) $x = y$. Then define

$$\downarrow\!\sum{}^2 = \sum_{y=1}^{n} \sum_{x=1}^{y} d_x.$$

Show that $\downarrow\!\sum{}^2 + \uparrow\!\sum{}^2 = (n + 1) \sum_{x=1}^{n} d_x.$

2–17 If the range of x is $[a, z]$, show that

a) $\uparrow\!\sum{}^2 = \sum_{x=a}^{z} x \cdot d_x - (a - 1) \sum_{x=a}^{z} d_x.$

b) $\downarrow\!\sum{}^2 = (z + 1) \sum_{x=a}^{z} d_x - \sum_{x=a}^{z} x \cdot d_x.$

2–18 In Exercise 2–7, we suggested the revised estimates .07, .35, .70 on the basis of least absolute departure. Suppose the respective number of tosses were 100, 80, and 120.

    a) Using $w_x = \dfrac{n_x}{v_x(1 - v_x)}$, calculate the value of fit measure (2.10).

    b) From a table of χ^2 values, what is the probability of a result this great or greater?

2–19 In Exercise 2–8, we suggested $v = .35$.

    a) Calculate $\dfrac{(u - t)^2}{\text{Var}\,(U)}$, using $v = .35$ as our estimate of t.

    b) From a table of χ^2 values, what is the probability of a result this great or greater?

2–20 Refer to Table 2.2 on page 23.

    a) How many sign changes are there in the d_x column?

    b) Under the assumptions developed in Section 2.7.3, what is the probability of this number of sign changes?

2.8 An Illustrative Summary

2–21 Consider the v_x in Table 2.2 to be our best estimate of t_x, and calculate the standard deviation of each U_x.

    a) How many of the initial estimates u_x lie within one standard deviation (above or below) their respective means?

    b) If each U_x is assumed independent and normally distributed, how many of the u_x "should" lie in these standard deviation bands?

2–22 a) Using the reciprocal of variances calculated in Exercise 2–21 as weights, calculate fit measure (2.10) for the v_x of Table 2.2.

    b) Under the assumption of independent normal for U_x, and that $v_x = t_x$, what is the expected value of fit measure (2.10)?

    c) From a table of χ^2 values, what is the probability of a result this great or greater?

*2–23 a) Verify equations (2.14) and (2.15).

    b) Verify the solution of them for a and b, and hence the column of v'_x in Table 2.2. (Care must be taken in solving for a and b, as the coefficient matrix is near-singular.)

    c) Calculate fit measures (2.9) and (2.11) for the revised graduation v'_x.

2–24 a) Using v'_x as our best estimate of t_x, calculate the reciprocals of Var (U_x), and use them as weights to calculate fit measure (2.10).

    b) From a table of χ^2 values, what is the probability of such a result?

*2–25 As an alternative to finding the a and b of (2.13) such that fit measures (2.9) and (2.11) are zero, they can be found such that fit measure (2.10) is minimized.

a) Find a and b such that $\sum\limits_{70}^{84} w_x(u_x - v_x')^2$ is minimized. (Recall that w_x is the sample size from Table 2.1)

b) Why do we not use our usual choice of $w_x = \dfrac{n_x}{v_x'(1 - v_x')}$ for the weights in part (a)?

c) Having found a and b, and hence the alternative v_x', calculate the reciprocals of Var (U_x), and use them in the calculation of fit measure (2.10). Compare this value with that obtained in Exercise 2–24, part (a).

2.9   Reference to a Standard Table

2–26 Use s_x instead of u_x in (2.18) to calculate the estimated standard deviation at ages 74 and 77.

2–77 For the graduation result given in the last column of Table 2.3, determine each of the following:

a) Number of sign changes in the deviations, $u_x - v_x$.

b) Number of initial estimates within one standard deviation of their respective means, using the revised rates as t_x.

c) The value of fit measure (2.10), using the reciprocal of variances from part (b) as weights.

2–28 Of our four graduations results, v_x and v_x' from Table 2.2, v_x from Table 2.3, and the alternative v_x' from Exercise 2–25, which do you feel is best?

MOVING WEIGHTED AVERAGE GRADUATION

3

3.1
INTRODUCTION

The graduation method described in this chapter is one of the earliest to have been developed. It is fairly easy to use, an attribute which no doubt contributed to its popularity in the days before computers. However it also has some drawbacks, which, coupled with the lessened importance of arithmetic convenience in our computer age and the development of other graduation methods, has reduced its popularity, at least in North America.

The class of M-W-A discussed in this chapter, originally called *linear-compound* formulas, was largely developed by E. L. DeForest in the 1870's. A review of his work is given by Wolfenden [63].

Another class of M-W-A formulas, called *summation* formulas, was developed in Great Britain. They were especially designed to be arithmetically convenient, by making major use of sums of values. They are little used today, and are not discussed in this text. The interested reader can find a description of them in Miller [46], Henderson [21], Elphinstone [12], and Andrews and Nesbitt [1].

Both classes together have also been referred to as *adjusted-average* in earlier texts. We prefer the name moving-weighted-average as being more descriptive and more in tune with current mathematical usage. Considerable literature exists on both classes of M-W-A. In addition to the references cited above, and others to follow, the interested reader can pursue the early development of these methods in Henderson [22] and Sheppard [54], and a modern analysis of them in Borgan [5].

3.2
THE BASIC FORMULA

The mechanics of the graduation process itself is very simple. As the name of the method implies, a graduated value is produced as a weighted average of a certain number of consecutive ungraduated values (observed values or initial estimates). In the notation adopted in Section 2.5, the basic formula is

$$v_x = \sum_{r=-n}^{n} a_r u_{x+r}. \qquad (3.1)$$

The following observations can be made of the basic formula:

1. A single graduated value (revised estimate) is produced as the weighted average of $2n + 1$ consecutive initial estimates, indexed at $x - n$ through $x + n$. The numerical value of $2n + 1$ is called the *range* of the formula.

2. The subscript of the coefficient a_r is the distance (and direction) away from x of the index of the particular initial estimate which it multiplies. Thus, a_0 multiplies u_x.

3. We consider only *symmetric* M-W-A formulas, that is, those in which

$$a_r = a_{-r}, \text{ for } r = 1, 2, \ldots, n. \qquad (3.2)$$

Although non-symmetric formulas might theoretically be derived, they are of little interest. It is safe to say that all M-W-A formulas for practical use were, and are, symmetric.

4. Because of the central nature of the averaging formula, it is apparent that we have an "end-value" problem. That is, if u_a and u_b are the lowest and highest indexed values of u_x, respectively, then the lowest and highest indexed values of v_x obtained by this formula are v_{a+n} and v_{b-n}, respectively.

The "end-value" problem of the M-W-A method is unfortunate, and is no doubt partly responsible for its lack of total popularity. Many attempts have been made to deal with this problem, as described in the several general texts on graduation listed in the bibliography. Perhaps the best approach is that of Greville, which can be found in [18], [19] and [20]. We will not pursue the problem further in this text.

It is clear at this point that the basic graduation process is easy to understand, and simple to apply. What remains is the theory and mathematics involved in the derivation of the coefficients. We present two different rationales for this derivation. The first, emphasizing reduction of statistical error, is presented in Sections 3.3 and 3.4; the second, emphasizing reduction of roughness (or increase in smoothness), is presented in Section 3.5.

3.3
REDUCTION OF ERROR

This rationale begins with the viewpoint established in Section 2.6, particularly that expressed by formula (2.5) which states that $u_x = t_x + e_x$. Substituting (2.5) into

(3.1), we obtain

$$v_x = \sum_{-n}^{n} a_r(t_{x+r} + e_{x+r}) = \sum_{-n}^{n} a_r t_{x+r} + \sum_{-n}^{n} a_r e_{x+r}. \qquad (3.3)$$

Thus we see that the M-W-A graduation operator is a linear operator (c.f., (3.3) and (2.7)). As stated in Section 2.6, we would like to feel that $G(t_x) \doteq t_x$, that is, that the assumed true value component of u_x is substantially unchanged. Thus we wish to view the first member of (3.3) as approximately reproducing t_x. Similarly, we wish to view the *residual* error in v_x, which is

$$e_x' = \sum_{-n}^{n} a_r e_{x+r}$$

as substantially smaller than e_x, the error component of u_x.

This suggests our sense of direction for deriving the coefficients: find a_r so that

1. t_x is reproduced, and
2. e_x is maximally reduced (i.e., e_x' is minimized).

3.3.1 REPRODUCING t_x

Of course we don't know the numerical values of t_x (for otherwise we don't need the graduation process at all), but we might make an assumption of a functional form for the sequence t_x, thereby introducing an element of prior opinion. Bear in mind that for one application of the M-W-A formula, we are addressing the sequence t_x over the limited range $[x - n, x + n]$ only. In light of this, it might be reasonable (and is very mathematically convenient) to assume that this limited sequence is closely represented by a low degree polynomial, such as a cubic.

Under this cubic assumption, it can be shown that the M-W-A formula will reproduce the assumed t_x, that is, that

$$\sum_{-n}^{n} a_r t_{x+r} = t_x,$$

if the coefficients satisfy the pair of conditions

$$\sum_{-n}^{n} a_r = 1 \quad \text{and} \quad \sum_{-n}^{n} r^2 a_r = 0. \qquad (3.4)$$

Equations (3.4) will be referred to as our *constraint equations*. Conditions such as

$$\sum_{-n}^{n} r a_r = 0 \quad \text{and} \quad \sum_{-n}^{n} r^3 a_r = 0 \qquad (3.5)$$

are automatically satisfied by the symmetric property expressed by (3.2). The derivation of (3.4) and the satisfaction of (3.5) by the symmetric property are left to the reader as Exercise 3–4.

Because of the symmetric property, we can write (3.4) as

$$a_0 + 2 \sum_1^n a_r = 1 \quad \text{and} \quad \sum_1^n r^2 a_r = 0. \tag{3.4a}$$

3.3.2 MINIMIZING e_x'

First we must recognize that e_x' is a number, albeit unknown; it is the residual error which makes v_x only an estimate of t_x. Thus we really can't talk of minimizing e_x', but rather the random variable E_x', of which e_x' is an (unknown) realization.

In Exercise 2–13, we showed that if U_x is a binomial proportion, then $E[E_x] = 0$. Now in terms of random variables, our M-W-A formula, from (3.1) is

$$V_x = \sum_{-n}^n a_r U_{x+r}. \tag{3.1a}$$

Then

$$E[V_x] = \sum_{-n}^n a_r E[U_{x+r}] = \sum_{-n}^n a_r t_{x+r} = t_x,$$

when conditions (3.4) hold and t_x is assumed cubic. This gives the important result that if U_x is unbiased, then V_x given by the M-W-A is also unbiased (if the cubic assumption holds), so that

$$E[E_x'] = 0.$$

This, in turn, shows that there is no merit in trying to minimize "expected residual error"; such a concept is identically zero! Instead, we consider the variance of residual error. Now

$$\text{Var}(E_x') = E[(E[E_x'] - E_x')^2] = E[(E_x')^2],$$

since $E[E_x'] = 0$. Thus we choose to minimize "expected squared residual error", which is $\text{Var}(E_x')$. But since

$$V_x = t_x + E_x',$$

it follows that $\text{Var}(E_x') = \text{Var}(V_x)$.

We recapitulate the development to this point. At the end of Section 3.2 we stated our goal of finding the coefficients for (3.1), the basic formula, so that t_x would be reproduced and e_x' would be minimized. We can now up-date that to say we seek the coefficients so that (3.4) will be satisfied and $\text{Var}(V_x)$ will be minimized, always remembering that this is based on an assumed cubic form for t_x.

Substituting (2.5a) into (3.1a), we have

$$V_x = \sum_{-n}^{n} a_r(t_{x+r} + E_{x+r}) = t_x + \sum_{-n}^{n} a_r E_{x+r}, \qquad (3.6)$$

since (3.4) is to hold, and t_x has been assumed cubic. Then

$$\text{Var }(V_x) = \text{Var} \sum_{-n}^{n} a_r E_{x+r} = \text{Var }(E'_x), \qquad (3.7)$$

since Var $(t_x) = 0$.

Now comes the key part of the derivation. If we conveniently assume that the several random variables represented by E_{x+r} are *uncorrelated*, then

$$\text{Var }(V_x) = \sum_{-n}^{n} (a_r)^2 \text{ Var }(E_{x+r}). \qquad (3.8)$$

If we further assume that each E_{x+r} has the *same* variance, σ^2, say, then we can write

$$\text{Var }(V_x) = \sigma^2 \sum_{-n}^{n} a_r^2. \qquad (3.9)$$

The pair of assumptions evolving (3.7) into (3.9) has allowed us to express Var (V_x) as a function of the yet-to-be-determined coefficients. Defining

$$R_0^2 = \sum_{-n}^{n} a_r^2, \qquad (3.10)$$

we can now say that the coefficients we seek for (3.1) are those which minimize R_0^2 and satisfy the constraint equations (3.4). An M-W-A formula with coefficients so derived is called a *Minimum-R_0* formula. The details of this constrained minimization are deferred to Section 3.6.

3.3.3 OBSERVATIONS ON THE MINIMUM-R_0 FORMULA

1. Since Var (U_x) = Var $(E_x) = \sigma^2$, then it follows that

$$R_0^2 = \frac{\text{Var }(V_x)}{\text{Var }(U_x)}. \qquad (3.11)$$

The symbol R_0^2 was chosen to suggest "ratio of variance"; the significance of the subscript, zero, will become apparent a bit later.

2. Define $y = (R_0^2)^{-1}$ to be the *weight* of our M-W-A formula. From (3.11) we see that

$$\text{Var }(V_x) = R_0^2 \text{ Var }(U_x) = \frac{\text{Var }(U_x)}{y} = \frac{t_x(1 - t_x)}{y \cdot n_x}, \qquad (3.12)$$

if U_x is approximately a binomial proportion. Now if v_x is a better estimate of t_x than was u_x, the very purpose of graduation, then e'_x should be less than e_x, which was how we specified the objective of M-W-A graduation. We measured e'_x by Var (V_x), and e_x by Var (U_x). This suggests that $R_0{}^2$ should be less than 1, or that y should exceed 1. Conversely, if $R_0{}^2$ exceeds 1, we have not achieved our goal in the graduation. Equation (3.12), in words, states that the reduction in variance of V_x from that of U_x, achieved by the graduation, is the same reduction that would be expected if the sample size n_x, which produced u_x, could have been y times as large. (See Exercise 3–9)

3. The uncorrelated assumption leading to (3.8) is somewhat questionable (but less questionable than an assumption of independence (c.f., Section 2.4.2)).

4. The validity of the equivariance assumption leading to (3.9) is perhaps even more questionable. If U_x is a binomial proportion, then

$$\text{Var } (E_x) = \text{Var } (U_x) = \frac{t_x(1 - t_x)}{n_x}, \tag{3.13}$$

where n_x is the sample size, or "exposure" which gave rise to u_x. Now t_x might not differ much over the range $[x - n, x + n]$, but n_x could differ considerably. This suggests that if Var $(E_x) = \sigma^2$ we might do better to assume that Var (E_{x+r}) relates to Var (E_x) proportionally to n_{x+r} and n_x. Thus we might take

$$\text{Var } (E_{x+r}) = \sigma^2 \cdot \frac{n_x}{n_{x+r}}. \tag{3.14}$$

Giving up the equivariance assumption will complicate our constrained minimization problem a bit, but should produce better results. The proportional variance assumption expressed by (3.14) is explored by London [41].

5. Finally, and somewhat disappointingly, it must be admitted that graduations using the Minimum-R_0 formula seldom prove to be satisfactory, frequently resulting in neither good fit nor an acceptable degree of smoothness. This is further explored in Chapter 9.

3.4
REDUCTION OF ERROR—A GENERALIZATION

Since Minimum-R_0 graduations do not prove satisfactory in practice, we will explore a modification of the Minimum-R_0 formula. We define

$$R_z{}^2 = \frac{\text{Var } (\Delta^z V_x)}{\text{Var } (\Delta^z U_x)}, \tag{3.15}$$

and recognize that (3.11) is the special case of (3.15) with $z = 0$. An M-W-A graduation formula using coefficients found by minimizing $R_z{}^2$, and satisfying the constraint equations (3.4), is called a *Minimum-R_z* formula. Empirical evidence shows that, especially for $z = 2$, 3 or 4, Minimum-R_z graduations are preferable to Minimum-R_0 graduations by the practical criteria of fit and smoothness, at least for the kind of data to which actuaries have applied the method.

We had deferred the mechanics of the constrained minimization of R_0^2 pending the development of this generalization. We can then do the constrained minimization for the general case, and the R_0^2 case will be included.

The development of R_z^2 as a function of the yet-to-be determined coefficients a_r is a bit messy, especially if we do it for z in general. We prefer to show it for $z = 2$, and it is then pursued for $z = 3$ in Exercise 3–12. We begin with

$$\Delta^2 V_x = V_{x+2} - 2V_{x+1} + V_x$$

$$= \sum_{-n}^{n} a_r U_{x+2+r} - 2 \sum_{-n}^{n} a_r U_{x+1+r} + \sum_{-n}^{n} a_r U_{x+r}.$$

We now write out each of V_{x+2}, V_{x+1} and V_x on separate lines:

$$a_{-n} \ U_{x+2-n} + \cdots + a_0 U_{x+2} + \cdots + a_{n-2} U_{x+n} + a_{n-1} U_{x+n+1} + a_n U_{x+n+2}$$
$$-2[\qquad a_{-n} \ U_{x+1-n} + a_{-n+1} U_{x+2-n} + \cdots + a_1 U_{x+2} + \cdots + a_{n-1} U_{x+n} + a_n \ U_{x+n+1} \qquad]$$
$$+ \ a_{-n} U_{x-n} + a_{-n+1} U_{x+1-n} + a_{-n+2} U_{x+2-n} + \cdots + a_2 U_{x+2} + \cdots + a_n \ U_{x+n} \ .$$

Notice how we arranged the three lines so that like values of U_x, *not* like values of a_r, are aligned. When we combine the three lines as indicated, we notice that the total coefficient of most of the U_x is some $\Delta^2 a_r$. For example, the coefficient of U_{x+2-n} is $\Delta^2 a_{-n}$, that of U_{x+2} is $\Delta^2 a_0$, and that of U_{x+n} is $\Delta^2 a_{n-2}$. The "steps" at each end of the array do not naturally produce coefficients of the $\Delta^2 a_r$ form. Clearly the terms that would be needed to "square off" the array would involve a_{n+1} (in the second line) and both a_{n+1} and a_{n+2} (in the third line) at the upper end, and a_{-n-1} (in the second line) and both a_{-n-2} and a_{-n-1} (in the first line) at the lower end. We insert these symbols, along with the appropriate U_{x+r} which they should multiply, merely as *place-holders*, specifying that they each have a value of zero. By so doing, we can now write the sum of our three lines, which is $\Delta^2 V_x$, as

$$\Delta^2 V_x = \sum_{-n-2}^{n} \Delta^2 a_r U_{x+2+r}. \qquad (3.16)$$

The reader should carefully verify (3.16), and always remember that the four coefficients a_{n+1}, a_{n+2}, a_{-n-1}, and a_{-n-2} contained in it are equal to zero. This procedure is reviewed in Exercise 3–11.

The rest of the derivation of R_z^2 is comparatively easy. Again making the assumptions of uncorrelated and equivariance as we did in Section 3.3.2, (3.16) leads to

$$\text{Var}\,(\Delta^2 V_x) = \sigma^2 \sum_{-n-2}^{n} (\Delta^2 a_r)^2. \qquad (3.17)$$

It is because we wanted to take the variance of $\Delta^2 V_x$, thus needing an expression for $\Delta^2 V_x$ as a linear combination of the various U_{x+r}, that we aligned the three lines of $\Delta^2 V_x$ with respect to like values of U_x.

By analogy, and verified in Exercise 3–13, the general case is

$$\text{Var}(\Delta^z V_x) = \sigma^2 \sum_{-n-z}^{n} (\Delta^z a_r)^2. \tag{3.18}$$

The summation in (3.18) will involve z assigned values of a_r at each end, all equal to zero.

To evaluate the denominator in (3.15), with $z = 2$, we have

$$\Delta^2 U_x = U_{x+2} - 2U_{x+1} + U_x,$$

and the uncorrelated and equivariance assumptions lead to $\text{Var}(\Delta^2 U_x) = 6\sigma^2$. Then

$$R_2^2 = \frac{1}{6} \sum_{-n-2}^{n} (\Delta^2 a_r)^2. \tag{3.19}$$

For the general case, $\text{Var}(\Delta^z U_x) = \sigma^2 \cdot$ (the sum of the squares of the binomial coefficients of order z). This quantity is shown, in Exercise 3–15, to be $\binom{2z}{z}$. Thus we can finally write

$$R_z^2 = \frac{1}{\binom{2z}{z}} \sum_{-n-z}^{n} (\Delta^z a_r)^2. \tag{3.20}$$

The constrained minimization of R_z^2 is shown in Section 3.6.

3.5
AN ALTERNATE RATIONALE

The reduction-of-error rationale, which justified the Minimum-R_0 formula, is not as satisfying when applied in the general case. Our theory of graduation would suggest a reduction of error in our graduated values, measured by $E[(E_x')^2]$, not in the zth order of differences of those values.

An alternate rationale for the constrained minimization of R_z^2 can be suggested, emphasizing the objective of smoothness in the graduated values. It produces the same graduation result, of course, using in (3.1) the coefficients obtained from the minimization of R_z^2, subject to the constraints (3.4). Thus it also makes the cubic assumption for t_x. In this rationale we deal with the realizations of the random variables U_x and V_x, not with the random variables themselves, since minimizing $\text{Var}(\Delta^z V_x)$ is not our sense of direction.

It begins with the observation that smoothness is obtained in our graduated values if $\sum_x (\Delta^z v_x)^2$ is small (c.f., Section 1.6). This measure will be small if *each* $\Delta^z v_x$ is small. Adapting (3.16) to the general case, and using realizations instead of random variables, we see that

$$\Delta^z v_x = (-1)^z \sum_{-n-z}^{n} \Delta^z a_r u_{x+r+z}, \qquad (3.21)$$

so we wish to make this quantity small. We can do nothing about the magnitude of the u_{x+r+z} values, so we turn our attention to the values of $\Delta^z a_r$. We then reason that each $\Delta^z a_r$ is made small, in some sense, if the composite measure

$$\sum_{-n-z}^{n} (\Delta^z a_r)^2 \qquad (3.22)$$

is made small. Reading it back the other way, we have reasoned that minimizing (3.22) will contribute to small values of $\Delta^z v_x$, thereby producing a smooth graduation. We describe (3.22) as a "measure of roughness" of v_x. (We choose "roughness" rather than "smoothness" since (3.22) decreases as smoothness increases, hence as roughness decreases.)

We next obtain the analogous "measure of roughness" of u_x. Now (3.22) can be described in words as "the sum of the squares of the coefficients of the several u_{x+r} in the expression for $\Delta^z v_x$"; the analogous measure for u_x would be the same phrase, ending with $\Delta^z u_x$. As already shown, this measure is the sum of the squares of the binomial coefficients of order z, which is $\binom{2z}{z}$.

Finally, the alternate rationale considers the ratio of these two measures of roughness, to obtain

$$R_z^2 = \frac{1}{\binom{2z}{z}} \sum_{-n-z}^{n} (\Delta^z a_r)^2,$$

which is (3.20). In the reduction-of-error rationale, R_z^2 stood for "ratio of variance of $\Delta^z V_x$ to that of $\Delta^z U_x$"; in the alternate rationale, R_z^2 stands for "ratio of roughness in v_x to that in u_x, as measured in the zth order of differences". As we no doubt want v_x to be smoother than u_x, we prefer to find that $R_z^2 < 1$; otherwise we would conclude that the graduation has not been satisfactory. In particular, we define

$$R_3 = \sqrt{R_3^2} \qquad (3.23)$$

to be the *smoothing coefficient* of our M-W-A formula. The smaller the value of R_3, the "less rough" is v_x compared to u_x.

In this text we are consistently trying to reveal the nature of graduation as an exercise in statistical estimation, in addition to its role of smoothing data. For this reason we have stressed the reduction-of-error rationale, and prefer to consider the reduction-of-roughness rationale as an alternate, albeit extremely relevant, rationale. We might say that the very presence of alternative rationales is a positive attribute of the M-W-A graduation approach.

3.6
THE CONSTRAINED MINIMIZATION OF R_z^2

Several approaches to the constrained minimization of R_z^2 have been advocated. We prefer an approach that we believe to be easy to understand, although not particularly elegant or compact. For an alternate treatment of this, see Chan [8]. First some preliminary observations:

1. Since R_z^2 is a sum of squares, it cannot be negative, and its absolute minimum would be zero, in the degenerative case of $a_r = 0$ for all r. This is clearly not the right answer.

2. The standard calculus technique of setting

$$\frac{\partial R_z^2}{\partial a_r} = 0, \quad \text{for all } r,$$

and solving the resulting set of simultaneous equations would produce the above result of $a_r = 0$ for all r.

3. The reason this is incorrect is because we have "forgotten" our constraint equations (3.4). The standard calculus technique assumes that R_z^2 is a function of mathematically independent variables a_r, and they are not independent, due to (3.4). (Note the distinction between *mathematical* independence used here, and *statistical* independence used earlier for our random variables U_x and E_x.)

4. Because we have two constraints, we must consider two of our variables a_r to be dependent; the remaining are independent. It doesn't matter which two we call dependent, but the most convenient pair would be a_0 and a_1.

5. The constant in R_z^2, $\dfrac{1}{\dbinom{2z}{z}}$, can be ignored in the constrained minimization.

6. The method used in this section is also given by Henderson [21].

3.6.1 MAKING R_z^2 A FUNCTION OF INDEPENDENT VARIABLES

Making use of the symmetric property (3.2), we take our constraint equations as (3.4a). From

$$\sum_1^n r^2 a_r = 0 \quad \text{and} \quad a_0 + 2a_1 + 2\sum_2^n a_r = 1,$$

we find

$$a_1 = -\sum_2^n r^2 a_r \quad \text{and} \quad a_0 = 1 + 2 \sum_2^n (r^2 - 1)a_r. \tag{3.24}$$

Using just R for $\binom{2z}{z} R_z^2$, we have

$$R = \sum_{-n-z}^n (\Delta^z a_r)^2. \tag{3.25}$$

We recall these facts about R:

1. $a_{-r} = a_r$ for $r = 1, 2, \ldots, n + z$
2. $a_r = 0$ for $r = n + 1, \ldots, n + z$
3. a_0 and a_1 are functions of the other a_r, $r = 2, 3, \ldots, n$.

Thus R can be viewed as a function of the independent variables a_r for $r = 2, \ldots, n$. The entire working process, for simple cases, is reviewed in Exercises 3–21 and 3–22.

3.6.2 DIFFERENTIATING R WITH RESPECT TO a_r

Now each a_r for $r = -n, \ldots, n$ is involved in R only in the terms $(\Delta^z a_{r-z})^2 + \cdots + (\Delta^z a_r)^2$. If all the coefficients were mathematically independent, we would have

$$\frac{\partial R}{\partial a_r} = 2(-1)^z \delta^{2z} a_r, \text{ for } r = -n, \ldots, n. \tag{3.26}$$

However, since $a_r = a_{-r}$, then when we consider only a_r for *positive* r, we find

$$\frac{\partial R}{\partial a_r} = 4(-1)^z \delta^{2z} a_r \text{ for } r = 1, 2, \ldots, n, \tag{3.26a}$$

and, as a special case,

$$\frac{\partial R}{\partial a_0} = 2(-1)^z \delta^{2z} a_0. \tag{3.26b}$$

Finally, since a_0 and a_1 are functions of the other a_r, we obtain the total derivative

$$\frac{\partial R}{\partial a_r} = 4(-1)^z \delta^{2z} a_r + \frac{\partial R}{\partial a_0} \cdot \frac{\partial a_0}{\partial a_r} + \frac{\partial R}{\partial a_1} \cdot \frac{\partial a_1}{\partial a_r}, \tag{3.27}$$

for $r = 2, \ldots, n$. (We do not find the partial with respect to a_r for $r > n$, since such $a_r = 0$, and is not a variable.) From (3.24) we find

$$\frac{\partial a_0}{\partial a_r} = 2(r^2 - 1) \quad \text{and} \quad \frac{\partial a_1}{\partial a_r} = -r^2. \tag{3.28}$$

Substituting (3.26a), at $r = 1$, (3.26b), and (3.28) into (3.27), we obtain finally

$$\frac{\partial R}{\partial a_r} = 4(-1)^z[\delta^{2z}a_r + (r^2 - 1)\,\delta^{2z}a_0 - r^2\,\delta^{2z}a_1], \qquad (3.29)$$

for $r = 2, \ldots, n$.

3.6.3 THE NATURE OF a_r

When (3.29) is equated to zero, we obtain

$$\delta^{2z}a_r = r^2\,\delta^{2z}a_1 - (r^2 - 1)\,\delta^{2z}a_0. \qquad (3.30)$$

Equation (3.30) suggests that $\delta^{2z}a_r$ is a quadratic function in r, so that a_r is a polynomial in r of degree $2z + 2$. Furthermore, since $a_r = a_{-r}$, this polynomial must contain only even power terms. This suggests that

$$a_r = \beta_0 + \beta_2 r^2 + \beta_4 r^4 + \cdots + \beta_{2z+2}r^{2z+2}. \qquad (3.31)$$

We must remember that (3.30), and hence (3.31), resulted from the symmetric nature of R, which included the place-holders $a_{n+1} = \cdots = a_{n+z} = 0$. We must also remember that the coefficients a_r given by (3.31) must satisfy (3.4a).

Now there are $z + 2$ unknown β's in (3.31). We solve for them by use of the z conditions

$$a_{n+1} = \cdots = a_{n+z} = 0$$

and the two conditions given by (3.4a). We then have a formula for producing the coefficients to use in the basic M-W-A formula (3.1).

Alternatively, we could write our even-power polynomial for a_r in factorial form as

$$a_r = [(n + 1)^2 - r^2][(n + 2)^2 - r^2] \cdots [(n + z)^2 - r^2][h + k(n^2 - r^2)]. \quad (3.31a)$$

In (3.31a), the unknown h and k are found by applying the conditions given by (3.4) or (3.4a). The conditions $a_{n+1} = \cdots = a_{n+z} = 0$ are satisfied by the factorial form of a_r. The clear advantage of using (3.31a) over (3.31) is that of solving a 2×2 set of equations instead of a $(z + 2) \times (z + 2)$ set. The purpose of writing the h and k term in factorial form as well will be revealed in Exercises 3–29 and 3–30.

3.6.4 SPECIAL CASES

The simplest special case is for $R_0{}^2$, of course. With $z = 0$, both (3.31) and (3.31a) reduce to

$$a_r = a + br^2. \qquad (3.32)$$

Applying (3.4a), we have

$$a_0 + 2\sum_{1}^{n} a_r = a(2n + 1) + 2b\sum_{1}^{n} r^2 = 1$$

and

$$\sum_1^n r^2 a_r = a \sum_1^n r^2 + b \sum_1^n r^4 = 0.$$

Solving this pair of equations for a and b, and substituting into (3.32), and simplifying, we obtain

$$a_r = \frac{3(3n^2 + 3n - 1) - 15r^2}{(2n - 1)(2n + 1)(2n + 3)}. \tag{3.33}$$

As z increases, the procedure is similar, but increasingly complex. For $z = 3$, for example, we obtain

$$a_r = \frac{315[(n + 1)^2 - r^2][(n + 2)^2 - r^2][(n + 3)^2 - r^2][3n^2 + 12n - 4 - 11r^2]}{8(n + 2)[(n + 2)^2 - 1][4(n + 2)^2 - 1][4(n + 2)^2 - 9][4(n + 2)^2 - 25]}. \tag{3.34}$$

Rather than derive these expressions for a general n, we advise using the value of n involved in any particular problem. This is illustrated in Exercises 3–29 and 3–30.

3.7
SUMMARY

In this chapter we defined the M-W-A graduation formula, and gave two alternative rationales for its derivation. We explained the mathematical steps to solve for the coefficients a_r, illustrated this solution for the $R_0{}^2$ case, and pursued the solution for other values of z in the exercises. What remains to be shown is the effect on the graduation result of different values for the parameters n and z.

In general, it has been found that a greater value of n (a greater range for the formula) will produce more smoothness, at the expense of fit. Clearly the smallest possible value, $n = 0$, leads to the one-term formula

$$v_x = a_0 u_x.$$

Since the coefficients must sum to unity, this implies that $a_0 = 1$, so that $v_x = u_x$ for all x, the no-graduation case, and the case of perfect fit. It has also been stated that $z = 3$ or $z = 4$ has been found to produce the most acceptable results in practice, for a given value of n.

This method is further analyzed in Chapter 9, and graduation results for different combinations of n and z are illustrated in Appendix C.

EXERCISES

3.1   Introduction;   3.2 The Basic Formula

3–1   Suppose we have a set of data u_x for $x = 20, 21, \ldots, 59$. We wish to graduate it with an M-W-A formula with $n = 6$.

a) What value will a_{-4} multiply when we calculate v_{42}?

b) What will be the coefficient of u_{37} when we calculate v_{34}?

c) How many terms will be used to calculate one particular v_x?

d) How many different values of u_x will be used in calculating v_x, v_{x+1}, and v_{x+2}?

e) Over what range of x will graduated values be produced?

3.3 Reduction of Error

3–2 Demonstrate that the M-W-A operator is a linear operator.

3–3 a) If t_x is a linear function, show that $t_x = \sum\limits_{-n}^{n} a_r t_{x+r}$ if

$$\sum_{-n}^{n} a_r = 1 \quad \text{and} \quad \sum_{-n}^{n} r a_r = 0.$$

b) Show that, if $a_r = a_{-r}$ for $r = 1, \ldots, n$, then, necessarily, $\sum\limits_{-n}^{n} r a_r = 0$.

3–4 Extend Exercise 3–3 to the case where t_x is cubic, thereby deriving (3.4) and (3.5).

3–5 In order to reproduce a quartic (fourth degree polynomial), $\sum\limits_{-n}^{n} r^4 a_r = 0$ must hold as well. Show that the M-W-A formula

$$v_x = u_{x-2} - 4u_{x-1} + 7u_x - 4u_{x+1} + u_{x+2}$$

will reproduce a cubic but not a quartic.

3–6 If $V_x = \delta^4 U_x$, find $E[V_x]$ and Var (V_x), assuming the several U_x are independent and have equal variance, σ^2.

3–7 If $V_x = \delta^2 U_x + \delta^4 U_x$, find Var (V_x) if the several U_x are independent and have equal variance, σ^2.

3–8 Calculate the weight of the M-W-A formula given in Exercise 3–5. Why is this formula not successful as a graduation formula?

3–9 U_1, U_2 and U_3 are all binomial proportion random variables, assumed to be independent with equal variances. t_x is assumed to be a linear function. Observed values u_1, u_2, u_3 are produced from sample sizes n_1, n_2, n_3. Ingrid decides to produce a better estimate of t_2 by reperforming the experiment and doubling n_2. Chris decides to avoid the extra work, and produces a revised estimate of t_2 as an unweighted average of u_1, u_2 and u_3. Under the stated assumptions, whose revised estimate of t_2 has the smaller variance?

3–10 The same coin is tossed n_1 times, then another n_2 times, and then another n_3 times. The proportion of tails obtained each time, u_1, u_2 and u_3 are observed. Let t be the true rate of tails. (Clearly $t_1 = t_2 = t_3 = t$.) Ingrid suggests that the best estimate of t is $v = \dfrac{u_1 n_1 + u_2 n_2 + u_3 n_3}{n_1 + n_2 + n_3}$. Chris sticks with his un-weighted average approach. Nicole wants to produce her estimate as $v = a_1 u_1 + a_2 u_2 + a_3 u_3$, where a_1, a_2, a_3 are chosen so as to minimize Var (V), but she rejects the notion of equivariance for U_1, U_2 and U_3, and adopts our formula (3.14).

a) What constraint condition must a_1, a_2, a_3 satisfy? Why? Note that the approaches of Ingrid and Chris satisfy this condition.

b) Give expressions in terms of t and n_i for Var (V) using the approaches of Ingrid and Chris. Also give Nicole's Var (V), which will involve a_i as well.

c) Show that ^{I}Var $(V) \leq {}^{C}$Var (V). Under what condition are they equal?

d) After studying Section 3.6, return to this exercise and show that Chris' result is produced by the equivariance assumption, whereas Ingrid's result is produced by the proportional variance assumption. Thus Ingrid's and Nicole's results are identical.

3.4   Reduction of Error—A Generalization

3–11 Let us derive Var $(\Delta^2 V_x)$, where $V_x = \displaystyle\sum_{-2}^{2} a_r U_{x+r}$.

a) Write out the five-term summations for V_{x+2}, V_{x+1} and V_x, aligning like values of U_x.

b) What "fillers", or place-holders, do we insert in order to "square off" the array? Specify numerical values for the place-holders.

c) Now add the top line, minus twice the middle line, plus the third line. Express the result in a summation.

d) Finally, make the independence and equivariance assumptions and write the expression for Var $(\Delta^2 V_x)$.

3–12 Rework Exercise 3–11 to derive Var $(\Delta^3 V_x)$.

3–13 By a similar approach, verify the general case given by (3.18)

3–14 Find Var $(\Delta^3 U_x)$, and hence $R_3{}^2$.

3–15 We wish to show that $\displaystyle\sum_{s=0}^{z} \binom{z}{s}^2 = \binom{2z}{z}$.

a) Note that $[(1 + x)^z]^2 = (1 + x)^{2z}$. Expand $(1 + x)^z$, square the expansion, and equate the result to the expansion of $(1 + x)^{2z}$.

b) Equate the coefficients of x^z on each side of the equation.

3.5 An Alternate Rationale

3–16 To calculate the value of $R_3{}^2$ for a given M-W-A formula, write the coefficients in a column, annex 3 zeros at each end, work out to Δ^3 in a difference table, square and sum, and remember to divide by 20.

a) Calculate $R_3{}^2$ for the M-W-A formula given in Exercise 3–5.

b) What is the smoothing coefficient of this formula?

c) Why is this formula not successful as a graduation formula under the reduction-of-roughness criterion?

3–17 We have two criteria for judging an M-W-A formula:

1. Reduction-of-variance, measured by $R_0{}^2$, and "successful" if $R_0{}^2 < 1$.

2. Reduction-of-roughness, measured by $R_z{}^2$ (most commonly $R_3{}^2$), and "successful" if $R_3{}^2 < 1$.

Consider each of the following two M-W-A formulas:

I. $v_x = \frac{1}{9}(-u_{x-2} + 4u_{x-1} + 3u_x + 4u_{x+1} - u_{x+2})$

II. $v_x = \frac{1}{35}(-3u_{x-2} + 12u_{x-1} + 17u_x + 12u_{x+1} - 3u_{x+2})$

a) First show that each formula will reproduce a cubic.

b) Calculate $R_0{}^2$ for each formula. Which is the "better" formula under the reduction-of-variance criterion?

c) Calculate $R_3{}^2$ for each formula. Which is the "better" formula under the reduction-of-roughness criterion?

3–18 The above formulas were not derived by minimizing any particular $R_z{}^2$. The coefficients given below are for the 9-term (i.e., $n = 4$) Minimum-R_0 and Minimum-R_3 formulas:

r	Min-R_0	Min-R_3
0	.25541	.33114
1	.23377	.26656
2	.16883	.11847
3	.06061	−.00987
4	−.09091	−.04072

a) Calculate $R_0{}^2$ and $R_3{}^2$ for each formula. Because of how the coefficients were derived, we know the Min-R_0 formula *must* have the smaller $R_0{}^2$, and the Min-R_3 formula *must* have the smaller $R_3{}^2$.

b) Observe from the results that, whereas the Min-R_3 formula reduces variance almost as well as the Min-R_0 formula, it reduces roughness considerably better. For this reason, Min-R_3 formulas have traditionally been preferred over Min-R_0 formulas.

3.6   The Constrained Minimization of $R_z{}^2$

3–19 Let $R = x^2 + y^2$, but where $y = 1 - x$. What values of x and y minimize R?

3–20 Verify equations (3.24).

3–21 For a simple example of the minimization mechanics, let $n = z = 2$.

    a) Express a_0 and a_1 as function of a_2.

    b) Write out $R_2{}^2$ (ignoring the ⅙), use a_r in place of a_{-r}, substitute 0 for a_r where appropriate, and substitute for a_0 and a_1 from part (a). The resulting expression for $R_2{}^2$ involves only a_2.

    c) Find a_2 to minimize this expression, and plug it back into part (a) to find a_0 and a_1.

    d) Verify that the answers satisfy the constraint conditions.

3–22 Rework Exercise 3–21 with $n = 3$ and $z = 1$. This time $R_1{}^2$ will reduce to a function of a_2 and a_3.

3–23 a) Let $z = 2$. Then $R = \cdots + (\Delta^2 a_{r-2})^2 + (\Delta^2 a_{r-1})^2 + (\Delta^2 a_r)^2 + \cdots$, and only the shown terms involve a_r. Show that $\dfrac{\partial R}{\partial a_r} = 2\, \Delta^4 a_{r-2} = 2\, \delta^4 a_r$.

    b) Let $z = 3$. In this case, the only terms in R which involve a_r will be $\cdots + (\Delta^3 a_{r-3})^2 + (\Delta^3 a_{r-2})^2 + (\Delta^3 a_{r-1})^2 + (\Delta^3 a_r)^2 + \cdots$. Show that $\dfrac{\partial R}{\partial a_r} = -2\, \Delta^6 a_{r-3} = -2\, \delta^6 a_r$.

    (This establishes (3.26) for $z = 2$ and $z = 3$, and shows how it can be verified for any other value of z.)

3–24 Verify equations (3.28) and (3.29).

3–25 Let us verify the results of our numerical approach in Exercise 3–21, with $n = z = 2$.

    a) Adapt formula (3.31) to this case.

    b) What four conditions are used to solve for our unknown β's? Give the four equations in the β's which result.

    c) The ambitious reader can then solve these four equations for the β's, plug them into part (a), and calculate a_0, a_1, a_2. The results should agree with Exercise 3–21.

3–26 Similarly, let us verify the results of Exercise 3–22, where $n = 3$ and $z = 1$.

    a) Adapt formula (3.31) to this case.

    b) What three conditions are used this time? Give the three equations in the β's which result.

    c) Solve for the three β's, plug into part (a), calculate a_0, a_1, a_2, a_3, and verify the results of Exercise 3–22.

3–27 Use formula (3.33) to verify the coefficients of the Min-R_0 formula given in Exercise 3–18.

3–28 Conditions (3.4) can be rewritten in a factorial form. Show that $(n + z + 1)^2$ times the first constraint equation, minus the second constraint equation,

results in $\displaystyle\sum_{-n}^{n} [(n + z + 1)^2 - r^2]a_r = (n + z + 1)^2$. Then $\displaystyle\sum_{-n}^{n} a_r = 1$, along

with this new second constraint, are equivalent to (3.4). Call this revised pair (3.4b).

3–29 In Exercises 3–21 and 3–22, we used a direct approach to the calculation of the desired a_r, and verified the results in Exercises 3–25 and 3–26, working from (3.31). Now we explore the use of (3.31a) to derive coefficients for the Min-R_1 formula.

a) Show that (3.31a), in this case, is

$$a_r = h[(n + 1)^2 - r^2] + k[n^2 - r^2][(n + 1)^2 - r^2].$$

b) Apply constraint equations (3.4b), from Exercise 3–28, to obtain a pair of equations in h and k.

c) Define $\displaystyle S_{n,m} = \sum_{-n}^{n} [(n + 1)^2 - r^2] \cdots [(n + m)^2 - r^2]$. (Note that, in $S_{n,m}$, the subscript n is *one less than* the constant in the first factor of the summation, and m is the number of factors.) Rewrite the equations in part (b) using this symbol for the coefficients of h and k.

d) Solve the pair of equations in part (c) for h and k, using Cramer's Rule.

e) Fortunately, we know that $S_{n,m} = (m!)^2 \left(\dfrac{2n + 2m + 1}{2m + 1} \right)$. (See Vaughan [57]) Evaluate h and k using $n = 3$. Plug these values into part (a) and calculate a_0, a_1, a_2, a_3, again verifying the results in Exercise 3–22.

3–30 a) Adapt (3.31a) for calculating the coefficients of the Min-R_2 formula.

b) Apply constraint equations (3.4b) to obtain a pair of equations for h and k, using the $S_{n,m}$ function.

c) Solve for h and k, evaluate for $n = 2$, plug into part (a), and solve for a_0, a_1, a_2, again verifying the results of Exercise 3–21.

3–31 Finally, we can now write the general case.

a) Apply constraint equations (3.4b) to obtain the pair of equations for h and k, using the $S_{n,m}$ function.

b) At this point we can see how to calculate a_r, $r = 0, 1, \ldots, n$, for any combination of n and z. As a final problem of this type, use $n = 4$ and $z = 3$ to verify the Min-R_3 coefficients given in Exercise 3–18.

3–32 Use formula (3.34) to verify the Exercise 3–18 Min-R_3 coefficients. (This also serves to verify (3.34).)

3–33 a) Show that, for the Min-R_0 formula, $R_0^2 = a_0$.

b) Show that, for the Min-R_z formula in general, $R_z^2 = \dfrac{(-1)^z \, \delta^{2z} a_0}{\dbinom{2z}{z}}$.

WHITTAKER GRADUATION

4

4.1
INTRODUCTION

The graduation method described in this chapter was developed by E. T. Whittaker in 1923 [59]. Henderson, in 1924 and 1925, [23] and [24], also contributed to the theory, and made a significant contribution in showing how the theory could be put into practice. The method has thus come to be known as the Whittaker-Henderson method, although it would appear that Whittaker was its prime mover. With no slight intended toward the contribution of Mr. Henderson, for brevity we refer in this chapter to Whittaker's method.

4.2
THE BASIC GRADUATION FORMULA

The rationale of the basic Whittaker method follows from the observations made in Chapters 1 and 2 concerning fit and smoothness. Specifically it adopts the numerical measures of fit and smoothness defined by formula (2.10) and in Section 1.6, respectively, and combines them linearly to produce

$$M = F + hS = \sum_{x=1}^{n} w_x(v_x - u_x)^2 + h \sum_{x=1}^{n-z} (\Delta^z v_x)^2. \tag{4.1}$$

The graduated values v_x, for $x = 1, 2, \ldots, n$, are then taken as those which minimize the composite measure M.

Several observations on (4.1) are in order:

1. Although x is frequently age, so that the range in (4.1) might be, say, 30 to 75, we prefer to use 1 to n for simplicity.

2. The parameter z, establishing the degree of polynomial inherently being used as a standard of smoothness, is generally taken as 2, 3, or 4.

3. By the convention used to subscript finite differences, the highest indexed value of $\Delta^z v_x$ is $x = n - z$. Thus there are z fewer terms in S than in F.

4. The weights w_x are *positive* real numbers, discussed further in Section 4.2.1.

5. The parameter h, a *positive* real number, controls the relative emphasis given to F and S in the minimization of M; it is further discussed in Section 4.2.2.

6. Historically, the minimization of (4.1) was referred to as a "Type B" Whittaker graduation; the name "Type A" was given to the special case of (4.1) in which $w_x = 1$ for all x. Different minimization procedures were used for the two types. We will use the same procedure for both types, so that Type A is contained within the more general Type B.

4.2.1 THE WEIGHTS

Since the Whittaker method is based, in part, on a minimization of fit measure (2.10), comments made in Section 2.7 concerning the weights used in (2.10) are applicable here as well. Specifically we discussed the significance of using for w_x the reciprocal of Var (U_x), approximating it by using v_x in place of t_x. This is fine for calculating a fit measure *after* the graduation has been performed. But to use

$$w_x = \frac{n_x}{v_x(1 - v_x)}$$

in (4.1) prior to determining v_x would make our minimization of M considerably more difficult. To make w_x independent of v_x, we might use the initial estimates u_x instead. This manner of estimating Var (U_x) was discussed in Section 2.2, and resulted in formula (2.4). Now we must keep in mind that the use of est. Var (U_x) is for the purpose of obtaining v_x, through the minimization of M, in the first place. Once this is done, our fit-testing can then make use of v_x exactly as described in Section 2.7.2, including the view of (2.10) as approximately a Chi-square statistic.

Frequently the weights in (4.1) will be taken as simply the sample sizes n_x. Since this makes the general magnitude of F fairly large, a sizeable value of h must then be used to avoid undue emphasis on fit at the expense of smoothness. Alternatively, we might take

$$w_x = \frac{n_x}{\bar{n}},$$

where $\bar{n}$ is the arithmetic average of n_x over all x. This procedure retains the proportional emphasis given to fit at those ages with the larger n_x, while allowing a smaller value of h to balance the attention to smoothness.

It can be shown (see Exercises 4–8 and 4–9) that the graduated values v_x which minimize (4.1) will automatically cause fit measures (2.9) and (2.11) to be zero. Thus, for mortality data with $w_x = n_x$, the total number of deaths and the total ages at death (and hence the average age at death) will be equal for the observed data and for the graduated data. Since v_x is to be our best estimate of t_x (where t_x represents q_x in the case of mortality data), then $n_x \cdot v_x$ is properly referred to as "expected" deaths, and $x \cdot n_x \cdot v_x$ is properly referred to as "expected" ages at death.

4.2.2 THE PARAMETER *h*

Considerations in the choice of *h* will be discussed when we further analyze this method in Chapter 9. For now we make only the following general observations:

1. Clearly at $h = 0$, $hS = 0$, whatever the value of S may be. Then, since $F \nless 0$, M is minimized at $F = 0$, which implies $v_x = u_x$ for all x, the no-graduation case. Thus, in general, as h approaches 0, v_x approaches u_x, and fit is emphasized over smoothness.

2. Conversely, as h is set very large, the minimization process inherently emphasizes S to overcome the influence of the large h. This, in the limiting case, constrains v_x toward the least-squares polynomial of degree $z - 1$, thereby reducing the magnitude of S, and securing a least-squares fit.

4.3
THE MINIMIZATION OF *M*

Clearly M is a function of the n unknown values of v_x. Then the v_x which minimizes M is the solution of the n equations resulting from equating the partial derivatives of M, with respect to each v_x, to zero. That is

$$\frac{\partial M}{\partial v_r} = 0, \text{ for } r = 1, 2, \ldots, n. \tag{4.2}$$

Although this standard calculus technique *does* locate the unique global minimum of M, we will present a different approach to our minimization problem, utilizing a matrix-vector formulation of M. We use bold face letters to denote vectors and matrices.

Let **u** and **v** be the vectors of the initial estimates and revised estimates (graduated values), respectively. Using $\mathbf{y}'$ to denote the transpose of **y**, we have

$$\mathbf{u}' = [u_1, \ldots, u_n] \quad \text{and} \quad \mathbf{v}' = [v_1, \ldots, v_n].$$

Let

$$\mathbf{w} = \begin{bmatrix} w_1 & & & \bigcirc \\ & \cdot & & \\ & & \cdot & \\ & & & \cdot \\ \bigcirc & & & w_n \end{bmatrix}$$

be an $n \times n$ diagonal matrix containing the weights. Let $\mathbf{k}_z$ be a special matrix containing the binomial coefficients of order z, with due regard for sign, such that the product $k_z v$ is the vector containing the values of $\Delta^z v_x$. Thus, if there are n values of v_x, so that v is an $n \times 1$ vector, then k_z will be dimension $(n - z) \times n$, and $k_z v$ will be an $(n - z) \times 1$ vector. For example, if $z = 2$ and $n = 6$, then

$$k_2 = \begin{bmatrix} 1 & -2 & 1 & 0 & 0 & 0 \\ 0 & 1 & -2 & 1 & 0 & 0 \\ 0 & 0 & 1 & -2 & 1 & 0 \\ 0 & 0 & 0 & 1 & -2 & 1 \end{bmatrix}.$$

For an odd value of z, say $z = 3$ and $n = 7$, then

$$k_3 = \begin{bmatrix} -1 & 3 & -3 & 1 & 0 & 0 & 0 \\ 0 & -1 & 3 & -3 & 1 & 0 & 0 \\ 0 & 0 & -1 & 3 & -3 & 1 & 0 \\ 0 & 0 & 0 & -1 & 3 & -3 & 1 \end{bmatrix}.$$

It is easy to see that the products $k_2 v$ and $k_3 v$ produce the desired values of $\Delta^2 v_x$ and $\Delta^3 v_x$, respectively. The reader should carefully note the pattern of the signs in k_z, especially when z is odd.

With these definitions of v, u, w, and k_z, we see that our function M, given by (4.1), can be written as

$$(v - u)' w (v - u) + h(k_z v)' k_z v = (v - u)' w (v - u) + h v' (k_z' k_z) v, \quad (4.3)$$

since $y' y$ will produce the sum of the squares of the elements of a column vector y.

The same set of equations represented by (4.2) can now be produced and represented by the matrix-vector equation

$$(w + h k_z' k_z) v = w u. \tag{4.4}$$

The reader can verify the equivalence of (4.2) and (4.4) for several choices of z and n, as suggested in Exercises 4–6 and 4–7.

In the calculus approach, one finds that special forms of the derivative equation will result for the first z and last z values of x. One major advantage of the matrix-vector approach is that these special forms are automatically taken care of.

The solution of (4.4) is an exercise in numerical methods, and it is presumed that the reader is sufficiently familiar with techniques of solving matrix equations. But one word of caution is in order. Letting $c = w + h k_z' k_z$, we write (4.4) as

$$cv = wu. \tag{4.5}$$

Now we know that the unique solution of (4.5) for v is dependent on the non-singularity of c. Fortunately c *is* non-singular, but "just barely" so. The matrix $h k_z' k_z$ is singular, and c is made non-singular by the addition of the diagonal matrix w. This condition of near-singularity implies that considerable care must be taken in order to get an accurate solution for v. In light of the special band and symmetric nature of the matrix c, the Choleski factorization method can be used to solve (4.5). This method is discussed by Kellison [34], in Section 12.7 and Appendix G, and also by Burden and Faires [6], in Section 6.7.

4.4
PROOF OF THE MINIMIZATION

We wish to show that the solution of the set of linear equations represented by (4.5) will minimize (4.1). This is the same as showing that the vector v which satisfies (4.5) will minimize (4.3). The demonstration is dependent on the result from matrix algebra which states that if a symmetric matrix c is positive definite, then it is non-singular (so that c^{-1} exists), and furthermore c^{-1} is positive definite.

We observe that our matrix c is symmetric. Now c is positive definite if $y'cy \geq 0$, and equals 0 only when $y = 0$. For our c

$$y'cy = y'wy + hy'k_z'k_zy = y'wy + h(k_zy)'(k_zy)$$

$$= \sum_1^n w_xy_x^2 + h\sum_1^{n-z} (\Delta^z y_x)^2.$$

Since h and w_x are positive, we see that $y'cy$ can be zero *only if* $y = 0$. Thus c is positive definite.

Now we write (4.3) as

$$(v - u)'w(v - u) + hv'k'kv,$$

dropping the subscript z from k for convenience. We expand $(v - u)'w(v - u)$ and combine the resulting $v'wv$ term with $hv'k'kv$ to introduce c. This produces

$$v'wv + hv'k'kv - u'wv - v'wu + u'wu$$

or

$$v'cv - u'wv - v'wu + u'wu.$$

Next we multiply each of the first three terms by the identity matrix $c^{-1}c$ (which is commutative, and, furthermore, $c' = c$ due to symmetry). We also add and subtract $u'wc^{-1}wu$. We now have

$$v'cc^{-1}cv - u'wc^{-1}cv - v'cc^{-1}wu + u'wc^{-1}wu + u'wu - u'wc^{-1}wu.$$

Because the last two terms are constant (i.e., do not involve v), they can be ignored. The remaining four terms can be written as $(v'c - u'w)c^{-1}(cv - wu)$, which is the same as $(cv - wu)'c^{-1}(cv - wu)$, due to the symmetry of c and w. Finally, since c^{-1} is positive definite, then $(cv - wu)'c^{-1}(cv - wu)$ can never be negative, and its minimum value is zero, which is obtained when $cv = wu$.

4.5
THE BAYESIAN RATIONALE

The original development of this graduation method, as given by Whittaker [59], and again by Whittaker and Robinson [60], shows that the method has a formal Bayesian rationale. A summary of this rationale is also given by Jones [33].

4.5.1 THE PRIOR PROBABILITY FOR t_x

Thus far in this text we have viewed the true values as fixed, albeit unknown, and we attempt to estimate them based on the data of an observed sample. But our prior opinion concerning t_x surely allows us to say that one possible sequence is "more likely" to represent t_x than another. For example, if t_x is the sequence of true mortality rates by age, we would consider that a smooth, increasing sequence of rates is a more probable representation of t_x than is a haphazard, irregular sequence. This expression of prior opinion has guided many of our graduation efforts thus far in this text.

Whittaker carried this descriptive extent of prior opinion a bit further (but not as far as we will carry it in Chapter 5). He proposed that one could express the probability of a given sequence being t_x in terms of the now familiar measure of smoothness

$$S = \sum_{x=1}^{n-z} (\Delta^z t_x)^2.$$

A sequence t_x which produces a smaller value of S is *a priori* more probable than one which produces a larger value. Specifically he proposed that the probability density for a given t_x sequence be taken as

$$f_T(t_x) = c_1 \cdot e^{-\lambda S}. \tag{4.6}$$

We make the following observations on formula (4.6):

1. In using $f_T(t_x)$ for the probability density of t_x, we reflect, for the first time, the view that t_x is a realization of a sequence of random variables T_x. This view characterizes Bayesian estimation.

2. λ is a constant. In our further analysis of this method in Chapter 9, we will try to give an interpretation of λ.

3. c_1 is the constant needed to make $f_T(t_x)$ integrate to unity over all possible sequences t_x.

4. Clearly $f_T(t_x)$ is larger for those t_x which produce a smaller S, hence are more smooth, and are thereby "more probable".

5. Whittaker chose this particular form for $f_T(t_x)$ "by analogy to the normal frequency law". (See [60], page 304.) This does not mean, however, that he viewed S as having a normal distribution.

We cannot stress too strongly the fact that Whittaker's concept of "more probable" was based entirely on smoothness. Note that, for example, his definition of the prior probability does not consider if a sequence is increasing. Likewise the magnitude of the t_x values has no bearing on their prior probability.

It should also be noted that, whereas he was willing to consider, *a priori*, that one sequence is "more probable" than another, he did not admit to one sequence being "most probable". This is a key point. Clearly any sequence given entirely by a polynomial of degree $z - 1$ produces $S = 0$, and maximizes $f_T(t_x)$, but Whittaker insisted that "most probable", *prior to* consideration of observed data, was undefined.

4.5.2 THE CONDITIONAL PROBABILITY FOR e_x, GIVEN t_x

Recall our error random variable defined by formula (2.6) as

$$E_x = U_x - t_x.$$

Whittaker proposed that the random variable E_x be assumed to have a normal distribution with

$$E[E_x] = 0 \quad \text{and} \quad \text{Var}(E_x) = \sigma_x^2.$$

Then for a particular value of x, say $x = y$, the conditional density for e_y, given t_y, is

$$f_{E|T}(e_y|t_y) = c_y \cdot \exp\left[-\tfrac{1}{2}(e_y/\sigma_y)^2\right], \tag{4.7}$$

or

$$f_{U|T}(u_y|t_y) = c_y \cdot \exp\left[-\tfrac{1}{2}w_y(t_y - u_y)^2\right]. \tag{4.8}$$

The conditional density for u_y, given t_y, is just a translation of the conditional density for e_y, given t_y, since $u_y = t_y + e_y$. w_y is the reciprocal of Var (U_y).

If we now assume *independence* over all x, then we can multiply (4.8) over all x, to obtain

$$f_{U|T}(u_x|t_x) = c_2 \cdot \exp\left[-\tfrac{1}{2}\sum_1^n w_x(t_x - u_x)^2\right]. \tag{4.9}$$

Some observations on Formula (4.9):

1. $c_2 = \prod_1^n c_x$ is a constant.

2. (4.9) is the "probability" of obtaining the entire sequence of initial estimates u_x, given that the sequence of true values is t_x. (4.8) expresses the same idea specifically for $x = y$.

3. w_x still represents the reciprocal of Var (E_x) which we saw is also Var (U_x). We explored this idea in Section 2.7.2.

4.5.3 THE CONDITIONAL PROBABILITY FOR t_x, GIVEN u_x

From Bayes' Theorem we know that

$$f_{U|T}(u_x|t_x) \cdot f_T(t_x) = f_{T|U}(t_x|u_x) \cdot f_U(u_x),$$

or that

$$f_{T|U}(t_x|u_x) = \frac{f_{U|T}(u_x|t_x) \cdot f_T(t_x)}{f_U(u_x)}. \qquad (4.10)$$

In (4.10), $f_{T|U}(t_x|u_x)$ is the conditional probability density for the sequence t_x, given that the sequence of initial estimates u_x has been observed. $f_U(u_x)$ is the marginal density for the sequence u_x. It is unknown, but is independent of t_x, so its unknown nature will not be a problem.

Substituting $f_T(t_x)$ from (4.6) and $f_{U|T}(u_x|t_x)$ from (4.9) into (4.10), we have

$$f_{T|U}(t_x|u_x) = \frac{c_3 \cdot \exp\left[-\lambda S - \frac{1}{2}\sum_1^n w_x(t_x - u_x)^2\right]}{f_U(u_x)}. \qquad (4.11)$$

Some observations on formula (4.11):

1. (4.11) is the *posterior* distribution of t_x, as opposed to the *prior* distribution given by (4.6).

2. $c_3 = c_1 \cdot c_2$ is a constant.

Now at this point Whittaker considers the concept of the "most probable" sequence for t_x *in light of the initial estimates* u_x. That is, the most probable t_x is defined posterior to the observed data, but not prior to it. Whittaker defined the most probable sequence to be that which maximizes (4.11). Clearly the values of t_x which maximize (4.11) is the *mode* of the posterior distribution for t_x. This mode is now adopted as the "most probable" t_x, but not necessarily the true t_x, which always remains unknown. Thus we will use the symbol v_x, rather than t_x, for this mode.

Clearly (4.11) is maximized by minimizing the quantity

$$\frac{1}{2}\sum_1^n w_x(t_x - u_x)^2 + \lambda S. \qquad (4.12)$$

Whittaker recognized the difficulty of minimizing (4.12) with w_x being the reciprocal of Var (U_x). Thus he proposed that w_x be taken as constant for all x. We may then write (4.12) as

$$wF + \lambda S, \qquad (4.12a)$$

where w represents this common weight (half of the common reciprocal variance), and $F = \sum_{1}^{n} (t_x - u_x)^2$. Finally, it is clear that the sequence which minimizes (4.12a), to be called v_x, will also minimize

$$F + \frac{\lambda}{w} S = F + hS. \tag{4.12b}$$

Thus we see that Whittaker's simplification of a common Var (U_x) leads to the Type A form, defined in Observation 6 of Section 4.2. The more general Type B, of course, does not make this simplifying assumption.

Note the elements of similarity in Whittaker's method and the M-W-A method of Chapter 3. In both cases we assumed independence of the random variables E_x over the range of x, and, for the Type A, we assumed that Var (E_x) is constant over all x. Furthermore, both methods possess alternative rationales, one based more on statistical theory and the other more on the intuitive concepts of fit and smoothness.

Whittaker's rationale has provided us with our first illustration of a formal application of Bayesian statistics to graduation, which will be further expanded in Chapter 5.

4.6
SOME VARIATIONS ON THE STANDARD WHITTAKER FORM

We have seen that Whittaker's standard form measures fit and smoothness in terms of squares of deviations and squares of $\Delta^z v_x$, respectively. In this section we explore some variations on that standard form.

4.6.1 THE GENERAL "MIXED DIFFERENCE" FORM

A more general form for M, the function of v_x to be minimized, is

$$M = \sum_{1}^{n} w_x(v_x - u_x)^2 + h_1 \sum_{1}^{n-1} (\Delta v_x)^2 + h_2 \sum_{1}^{n-2} (\Delta^2 v_x)^2 + \cdots + h_z \sum_{1}^{n-z} (\Delta^z v_x)^2.$$

$$\tag{4.13}$$

Clearly (4.13) is a generalized form of (4.1), reducing to (4.1) if $h_z > 0$ and $h_j = 0$ for all other j.

Frequently (4.13) is used with $h_2 > 0$, $h_3 > 0$, and $h_j = 0$ for all other j. Because of the linear combination of these two (or more) smoothness measures, the minimization of M is entirely analogous to the standard form, especially when cast in the matrix-vector formulation of Section 4.3. This is pursued in Exercises 4–15 and 4–16. For further reading on the mixed difference case, see Spoerl [53].

4.6.2 EXPONENTIAL FORM FOR S

We saw that the minimization of the traditional form constrains v_x toward a polynomial of degree $z - 1$. As mentioned at the end of Section 1.6, if our prior opinion about t_x is not in agreement with this polynomial form, then S should be defined so as to constrain v_x toward the form of t_x actually assumed.

For example, suppose we are graduating forces of mortality believed to follow Makeham's law. Then our prior opinion is that

$$t_x = A + Bc^x,$$

and S should be defined accordingly. Clearly

$$\Delta t_x = B(c - 1)c^x,$$

and

$$\Delta^2 t_x = B(c - 1)^2 c^x = r \, \Delta t_x,$$

where $r = (c - 1)$. Thus the quantity

$$\Delta^2 t_x - r \, \Delta t_x \tag{4.14}$$

would be zero, so we would define S as

$$S = \sum_{1}^{n-2} (\Delta^2 v_x - r \, \Delta v_x)^2. \tag{4.15}$$

The minimization of M, using (4.15) for S, would then constrain v_x toward the assumed form for t_x. Of course the parameter $r \, (> -1)$ must be specified (along with the parameters h and w_x) in the minimization.

Alternatively, we see that

$$\frac{\Delta t_{x+1}}{\Delta t_x} = c = 1 + r,$$

so that the quantity

$$\Delta t_{x+1} - (1 + r) \, \Delta t_x \tag{4.14a}$$

would be zero, and S would be defined as

$$S = \sum_{1}^{n-2} (\Delta v_{x+1} - (1 + r) \, \Delta v_x)^2. \tag{4.15a}$$

The quantities given by (4.14) and (4.14a) are equivalent (see Exercise 4–17), and therefore so are those given by (4.15) and (4.15a).

In the above example, the assumed form of t_x is a constant plus an exponential term. This is a special case of the more general situation in which t_x is assumed to be a polynomial of degree $z - 2$ plus an exponential term. In the general case, the quantity to be zero, analogous to (4.14), would be

$$\Delta^z t_x - r\,\Delta^{z-1} t_x,\qquad(4.16)$$

or its equivalent,

$$\Delta^{z-1} t_{x+1} - (1 + r)\,\Delta^{z-1} t_x,\qquad(4.16a)$$

and S would be defined accordingly. For example, if the force of mortality is assumed to follow Makeham's second law, then

$$t_x = A + Hx + Bc^x,$$

and the appropriate definition of S would be

$$S = \sum_1^{n-3} (\Delta^3 v_x - r\,\Delta^2 v_x)^2.\qquad(4.17)$$

The verification of (4.17) is left as Exercise 4–18.

The minimization of M involving an S of this type is analogous to the approach described in Section 4.3. The calculus approach is more complex due to the more complex nature of $\dfrac{\partial S}{\partial v_x}$. The matrix-vector approach is more convenient. Both approaches are pursued, step-by-step, in Exercises 4–19 through 4–21.

A nice property of this "polynomial plus exponential" form is that it may be appropriate over a greater range of x. Suppose that for part of the range of x, t_x is just a polynomial (not with an exponential term). Then, clearly, (4.16) will be zero, regardless of the value of r. Now suppose that for the rest of the range of x, t_x is just an exponential (not with a polynomial term). It will still be true that $\Delta^z t_x = r\,\Delta^{z-1} t_x$, so that (4.16) will be zero, regardless of the value of z. This will also hold if t_x is an exponential plus a polynomial of degree *less than* $z - 2$, rather than just an exponential alone.

This approach was used by Camp [7], with $z = 4$. The graduation of the Ga-1951 table [49] also used the form of S described in this section.

4.6.3 LOWRIE'S VARIATION

The variation proposed by Lowrie [42] is an interesting one in that it combines the "polynomial plus exponential" form of S with a reference to a standard table. This allows an additional input of prior opinion, as we suggested in Section 2.9.2.

Lowrie's form is

$$M = (1 - h_1) \sum_1^n w_x(v_x - u_x)^2 + h_1 \sum_1^n w_x^s(v_x - s_x)^2$$

$$+ h_2 \sum_1^{n-z} (\Delta^z v_x - r\,\Delta^{z-1} v_x)^2.\qquad(4.18)$$

In (4.18), s_x is a value from a suitably-chosen standard table, and w_x^s is the weight associated with the fit of v_x to s_x. All other symbols are as defined in this text.

Choosing h_1 ($0 \leq h_1 \leq 1$) allows for relative emphasis to be placed on fit to the standard table values vs. fit to the initial estimates. The same can be said for the choice of w_x vs. w_x^s, except that whereas a fixed value of h_1 would be used for the entire graduation, the relative sizes of w_x and w_x^s can be varied for a given value of x. Thus a particular value of u_x in which we put little credence (due to small sample size, perhaps) can carry a small w_x relative to w_x^s at that same value of x.

Lowrie goes on to show the matrix-vector formulation of his M, and the matrix equation to solve for the vector $\mathbf{v}$ of graduated values which minimize M. This procedure parallels our work in Sections 4.3 and 4.6.2, and is explored a bit further in Exercise 4–22. More detail can be obtained from the original paper [42].

Lowrie also makes the observation that a Whittaker approach can be used to *interpolate* for missing values as well as to revise given values. Suppose we seek estimates of t_x at all values of x in the range $[1, n]$. Suppose further that we have initial estimates u_x for some, but not all, of these values of x. (For the method to work, we must have values of u_x at at least z values of x.) Then, at those values of x where u_x does *not* exist, we simply take $w_x = 0$ in (4.18).

4.6.4 SCHUETTE'S VARIATION

The variation proposed by Schuette [51] is, on the surface, a very simple one. He proposed replacing the squared fit and smoothness measures in the standard Whittaker form (4.1) with absolute values. Thus Schuette's form is

$$M = \sum_{1}^{n} w_x |v_x - u_x| + h \sum_{1}^{n-z} |\Delta^z v_x|. \tag{4.19}$$

Schuette feels that the traditional squared criterion in the fit measure is appropriate whenever the error random variable E_x is normally distributed, as Whittaker assumed (recall Section 4.5.2). But if the distribution of E_x is not normal, and thus generates more "outliers" than would a normal distribution, the squared criterion is too sensitive to these outliers. That is, results using the traditional (squared criterion) Whittaker form would be more influenced by the outliers than we would wish. The alternative form, using absolute values, should be less influenced by the outliers. Such an estimation procedure is said to be *robust*. Robust estimation, particularly graduation, is explored a bit further in Chapter 9.

It should be noted that the above argument pertains more to the fit measure than to the smoothness measure. Theoretically, at least, we might contemplate using absolute values in F, but retaining the squared criterion in S. This "mixture" would further complicate the minimization of M, which is complicated enough by the use of absolute values in place of squares. Schuette deals with this very elegantly by making use of the theory of linear programming. Since our work here is in the theory of graduation, and we do not wish to presuppose a knowledge of linear programming, we will not deal with the mathematics of Schuette's method. The reader can pursue this interesting problem in [51].

Graduated results using Schuette's variation differ markedly from those produced by the standard form. The following observations summarize the characteristics of such results.

1. The method will produce $v_x = u_x$ for *at least* z values of x.

2. If $v_x = u_x$ for *exactly* z values of x, then v_x lies on a polynomial of degree $z - 1$ for all x.

3. If h is less than or equal to a certain critical value, h_L, then $v_x = u_x$ for *all* x, the no-graduation case. Recall that this happens in the standard form only when $h = 0$.

4. If h is greater than or equal to another critical value, h_U, then v_x lies entirely on a polynomial of degree $z - 1$. Recall that this happens in the standard form only as $h \to \infty$.

5. Identical values of v_x can result for different values of h within a certain range. This is a characteristic of linear programming.

A Bayesian rationale of Schuette's form, parallel to that presented in Section 4.5 for the standard form, is given by Hickman and Miller [26].

4.7
SUMMARY

In this chapter we have discussed the rationale and the mathematics of Whittaker's graduation method, and some recent variations on it. There is considerably more choice involved in using this method than was true of the M-W-A method of Chapter 3. There our choices were pretty much restricted to the parameters n and z. Here we have choices for the parameters h, z, and w_x (and r in the form of Section 4.6.2), as well as choices among the various *forms* of the method, as revealed by the variations reviewed in Section 4.6, which, in turn, may suggest even more variations.

In Chapter 9 we will pursue the discussion of parameter selection, and in Appendix C we will give illustrated graduation results for various choices of parameters.

EXERCISES

4.1   Introduction;   4.2 The Basic Formula

4–1   Consider the graduation function given by (4.1) with $z = 1$.

    a) Suppose $w_x = w$, a constant, for all x, and $h = w$. How will the values of v_x, when $w = 10$, compare to the values of v_x when $w = 1$?

b) Suppose $w_x = w$, a constant, for all x, and $h \neq w$. Let v_x be the graduated result in this case, and v_x^* be the result using $w_x = 1$ for all x and $h^* = \dfrac{h}{w}$. How will v_x compare to v_x^*?

4–2 a) Consider (4.1) with $z = 1$. Suppose the given data is $u_x = u$, a constant, for all x. What will be the values of v_x that minimize M? What will be that minimized value of M?

b) Generalize this result to the case where the u_x values lie on a polynomial of degree $d \leq z - 1$.

4.3   The Minimization of M;   4.4 Proof of the Minimization

4–3 For $z = 2$ and $n = 6$, take $\dfrac{\partial M}{\partial v_r}$ for $r = 1, 2, \ldots, 6$, expand the several Δ^2 terms in the derivatives, set each equal to zero, divide by 2, and write the resulting set of equations as linear equations in the unknown v_x. Note the symmetry between the first and last equations, and between the second and next-to-last.

4–4. Rework Exercise 4–3 for $z = 3$ and $n = 7$. Note the symmetry between the first and seventh equations, the second and sixth, and the third and fifth.

4–5 Suppose, in a Whittaker graduation, the last equation in the set $\Big($the one developed from $\dfrac{\partial M}{\partial v_n} = 0\Big)$, is $-v_{n-3} + 3v_{n-2} - 3v_{n-1} + Kv_n = u_n$. The weight $w_n = 2$. What is the value of K?

4–6 a) For $z = 2$ and $n = 6$, write the matrix $k_2'k_2$.

b) Show that the matrix-vector equation $(w + hk_2'k_2)v = wu$ represents the set of linear equations derived by calculus in Exercise 4–3.

4–7 a) For $z = 3$ and $n = 7$, write the matrix $k_3'k_3$.

b) Show that the matrix-vector equation $(w + hk_3'k_3)v = wu$ represents the set of linear equations derived by calculus in Exercise 4–4.

4–8 Let l be an $n \times 1$ vector containing all 1's. That is, $l' = [1, 1, \ldots, 1]$. Consider the equation $l'(w + hk_z'k_z)v = l'wu$.

a) What is $l'wv$?

b) What is (k_zl)?

c) Therefore what does $l'(w + hk_z'k_z)v = l'wu$ imply?

4–9 Let x be an $n \times 1$ vector containing the argument values of x. That is, $x' = [1, 2, \ldots, n]$. Consider the equation $x'(w + hk_z'k_z)v = x'wu$, where $z \geq 2$.

a) What is $\mathbf{x}'\mathbf{wv}$?

b) What is $(\mathbf{k}_z\mathbf{x})$?

c) Therefore what does $\mathbf{x}'(\mathbf{w} + h\mathbf{k}_z'\mathbf{k}_z)\mathbf{v} = \mathbf{x}'\mathbf{wu}$ imply?

4–10 Let $z = 1$, $h = 2$, $\mathbf{u}' = [2, 2, 12, 16]$ and $\mathbf{v}' = [3, 4, 10, 14]$. Find $\sum\limits_{1}^{4} w_x$.

4–11 Let $z = h = 3$, and $w_x = 2$ for all x. If $\mathbf{u}' = [1, 8, 27, 25]$, express u_4 as a linear combination of the elements of $\mathbf{v}$.

4.5 The Bayesian Rationale

4–12 Why is $f_T(t_x)$ called the *prior* probability of a given t_x sequence?

4–13 Discuss the validity of using a normal distribution for $f_{U|T}(u_y|t_y)$, in light of our view of U_y described in Chapter 2.

4–14 Explain why the unknown nature of the marginal distribution $f_U(u_x)$ does not cause a problem in the development of Whittaker's graduation method.

4.6 Some Variations on the Standard Whittaker Form

4–15 Consider the mixed difference form given by (4.13) with $h_2 > 0$, $h_3 > 0$, and $h_j = 0$ for all other j.

a) Give the linear equation resulting from $\dfrac{\partial M}{\partial v_1} = 0$.

b) Give the general form resulting from $\dfrac{\partial M}{\partial v_r} = 0$, where v_r is not near either end of the range.

c) Express M in matrix-vector notation [c.f., equation (4.3)]

d) State the matrix equation to be solved for the vector $\mathbf{v}$ which minimizes M [c.f., equation (4.4)]

e) Show that the results of Exercises 4–8 and 4–9 also hold in this case.

4–16 A set of five values, represented by the vector $\mathbf{u}$, is to be graduated by minimizing the function

$$M = \sum_{1}^{5} w_x(v_x - u_x)^2 + h\left[\frac{1}{2} \sum_{1}^{3} (\Delta^2 v_x)^2 + \frac{1}{2} \sum_{1}^{4} (\Delta v_x)^2 \right].$$

The vector of graduated values $\mathbf{v}$ is obtained by solving the matrix equation $(\mathbf{w} + \frac{1}{2}h\mathbf{b})\mathbf{v} = \mathbf{wu}$.

a) Find the matrix $\mathbf{b}$.

b) Let $\mathbf{c} = \mathbf{w} + \frac{1}{2}h\mathbf{b}$. If a Type A graduation is being performed with $h = 2$, find the matrix $\mathbf{c}$.

4–17 Show that $\Delta^2 t_x - r\,\Delta t_x = \Delta t_{x+1} - (1+r)\,\Delta t_x$.

4–18 Verify equation (4.17).

4–19 Let $M = \sum\limits_{1}^{n} w_x(v_x - u_x)^2 + h\sum\limits_{1}^{n-2}(\Delta^2 v_x - r\,\Delta v_x)^2$, as would be appropriate according to Makeham's force of mortality law.

a) Show that $\dfrac{\partial M}{\partial v_3} = 0$, which is the lowest value of x to produce the general form, results in $w_3 v_3 + h(\delta^4 v_3 + r\,\delta^4 v_3 - r^2\,\delta^2 v_3) = w_3 u_3$.

b) Find the first special equation, resulting from $\dfrac{\partial M}{\partial v_1} = 0$, as a linear equation in v_1, v_2, and v_3.

c) Find the second special equation, resulting from $\dfrac{\partial M}{\partial v_2} = 0$.

d) Find the last special equation, resulting from $\dfrac{\partial M}{\partial v_n} = 0$. Unfortunately, it is *not* symmetric with the first equation (from part (b)) as was true in the standard Whittaker form.

e) Find the next-to-last special equation, resulting from $\dfrac{\partial M}{\partial v_{n-1}} = 0$. Unfortunately, it is not symmetric with the second.

f) The results from parts (a)–(e) allow us to write the set of linear equations for the case $z = 2$ and, say, $n = 6$. These equations, as before, can be represented by the matrix equation $(\mathbf{w} + h\mathbf{g}_2'\mathbf{g}_2)\mathbf{v} = \mathbf{wu}$. Summarize this exercise by writing the matrix $\mathbf{g}_2'\mathbf{g}_2$.

4–20 In the spirit of Section 4.3, we would like to be able to reach the result of $(\mathbf{w} + h\mathbf{g}_2'\mathbf{g}_2)\mathbf{v} = \mathbf{wu}$ without resorting to the approach of Exercise 4–19, especially as z grows larger so that more special equations result (and we can't benefit from symmetry as we did before.)

a) For our $z = 2$, $n = 6$ case, define $\mathbf{k}_2$ as before. $\mathbf{k}_2$ is a 4×6 matrix.

b) Define $\mathbf{r}_2$ to be the 4×6 matrix

$$\mathbf{r}_2 = \begin{bmatrix} r & -r & 0 & 0 & 0 & 0 \\ 0 & r & -r & 0 & 0 & 0 \\ 0 & 0 & r & -r & 0 & 0 \\ 0 & 0 & 0 & r & -r & 0 \end{bmatrix}$$

Notice how the last row of $\mathbf{r}_2$ has one final zero.

c) Now define $\mathbf{g}_2 = \mathbf{r}_2 + \mathbf{k}_2$, and show that $\mathbf{g}_2'\mathbf{g}_2$ agrees with the one implied by the linear equations in Exercise 4–19, part (f).

4–21 Let us generalize the results of Exercises 4–19 and 4–20 for other values of z. For $z = 3$, we have

$$M = \sum_1^n w_x(v_x - u_x)^2 + h \sum_1^{n-3} (\Delta^3 v_x - r\,\Delta^2 v_x)^2.$$

Now in the standard Whittaker form we saw that (for the $z = 2$ case)

$$M = (\mathbf{v} - \mathbf{u})'\mathbf{w}(\mathbf{v} - \mathbf{u}) + h\mathbf{v}'(\mathbf{k}_2'\mathbf{k}_2)\mathbf{v},$$

and the solution vector $\mathbf{v}$ was given by $(\mathbf{w} + h\mathbf{k}_2'\mathbf{k}_2)\mathbf{v} = \mathbf{w}\mathbf{u}$. In our exponential form above we saw that (for the $z = 2$ case)

$$M = (\mathbf{v} - \mathbf{u})'\mathbf{w}(\mathbf{v} - \mathbf{u}) + h\mathbf{v}'(\mathbf{g}_2'\mathbf{g}_2)\mathbf{v},$$

and the solution vector $\mathbf{v}$ was given by $(\mathbf{w} + h\mathbf{g}_2'\mathbf{g}_2)\mathbf{v} = \mathbf{w}\mathbf{u}$. (Here we are defining $\mathbf{g}_2\mathbf{v}$ to be the vector whose elements are squared and summed in S.)

a) Now by analogy, write the first three elements, and the last element, of the vector $\mathbf{g}_3\mathbf{v}$.

b) Hence deduce the $(n - 3) \times n$ matrix $\mathbf{g}_3$, writing the first two rows and the last row.

c) Then if $\mathbf{g}_3 = \mathbf{r}_3 + \mathbf{k}_3$, write the first two rows and the last row of $\mathbf{r}_3$.

d) Finally, we notice that it is *almost* true that $\mathbf{r}_z = -r\mathbf{k}_{z-1}$. Why is this not completely true?

4–22 By the same approach used in Exercise 4–21, write, in vector notation, for Lowrie's variation

a) The function M given by (4.18).

b) The equation for the solution vector $\mathbf{v}$.

BAYESIAN GRADUATION

5

5.1
INTRODUCTION

The moving-weighted-average method (Chapter 3), dating from the last century, is a grandparent among graduation methods. Whittaker's method (Chapter 4), being born around 1920, is of mature middle-age. The formal Bayesian approach of this chapter is a teen-ager by comparison, but one with a promising future.

The word "formal" is attached here to separate the approach of this chapter from other graduation methods which, it might be said, have a Bayesian "flavor", imparted by their use of prior opinion. This chapter will discuss both the formal Bayesian process, and specific methods consistent with that process. The method of Kimeldorf and Jones may be viewed as a standard Bayesian method, but we will recognize that variations on that model exist. We will also see that Whittaker's method, our first example of a Bayesian approach, was not as thorough in its specification of prior opinion as it is possible to be.

The literature on Bayesian graduation is comparatively sparse, as is to be expected from its newness. The principal works are those of Jones [33], Kimeldorf and Jones [35], and Hickman and Miller [27], including the excellent discussions submitted on those papers. The presentation in this chapter is based mainly on these works; they are recommended as further reading for those who develop an interest in Bayesian graduation.

5.2
THE BAYESIAN PROCESS

The standard Bayesian approach to our graduation problem may be described in four steps, listed below and then discussed in separate subsections of this section. The reader will surely recognize how these steps correspond to Whittaker's rationale presented in Section 4.5.

1. Formulate a prior probability distribution for t_x, the sequence we wish to estimate.

2. Select the model for the experiment; that is, an expression for the conditional distribution of observed data u_x, given the sequence t_x.

3. Use Bayes' Theorem to solve for the posterior distribution of t_x, given the obtained data u_x.

4. Select the graduated values v_x from the posterior distribution, in light of the objective of the graduation problem.

Because, in graduation, we are always dealing with estimation of a sequence of values, the vector notation, introduced in Section 4.4, will be convenient, and will be used throughout the presentation. Bold face letters denote vectors and matrices.

5.2.1 THE PRIOR DISTRIBUTION FOR t_x

As mentioned earlier, in a Bayesian approach to graduation the true values are viewed as random variables.* Thus we will use T_x for the name of these variables. In our vector notation we use simply **T** for this *random vector*, and **t** for the vector of realizations of **T**. Since **T** is a vector of continuous random variables, we are seeking to establish the prior density function $f_{\mathbf{T}}(\mathbf{t})$, which is, of course, a multivariate function.

We have already seen an example of this. Formula (4.6) in Section 4.5.1 is the prior density for **T** suggested by Whittaker, and motivated by considerations of smoothness. In the Bayesian methods which follow in this chapter, prior densities for **T** will be based on other considerations in addition to smoothness. That is, our prior distributions will be more completely specified.

How will we formulate our prior density for **T**? In theory, we should construct such a density so as to reflect accurately all of our prior opinion about **T**. This is much easier said than done. In practice we might approximate such an ideal density by adopting a member of a convenient family of distributions. In addition to being an adequate approximation to our ideal density, the adopted density might be chosen to possess certain convenient mathematical properties. Whittaker's prior density, although not a complete one, did at least reflect his prior opinion of smoothness, and did possess convenient mathematical properties.

5.2.2 THE MODEL FOR THE EXPERIMENT

This is the conditional density for the data, given **t**. For our graduation problem we use the notation $f_{\mathbf{U}|\mathbf{T}}(\mathbf{u}|\mathbf{t})$. Here we are likely to find less subjectivity than that

---

*Many people are not comfortable with this view, and prefer to say that t_x is fixed (not random), albeit unknown. Then they select a prior density for t_x (or for the multivariate **t**) as a way of characterizing, or summarizing, their uncertainty about t_x. The posterior density which results is then seen as a revised summarization of uncertainty about t_x, in light of the data. The mathematics is identical in either case, whether or not t_x is viewed as a random variable in the usual sense.

involved in the selection of $f_T(t)$. As discussed in Chapter 2, we might feel that the appropriate model, that is, the appropriate distribution of the random variable U_x, is binomial with parameters t_x and n_x. Of course we really wish to deal with the distribution of the random vector U, and furthermore, we will find it convenient to presume a continuous distribution for each U_x, rather than the discrete binomial. We will return to these issues later.

5.2.3 THE POSTERIOR DISTRIBUTION FOR t

As in Whittaker's rationale of Section 4.5, we next use Bayes' Theorem to find

$$f_{T|U}(t|u) = \frac{f_{U|T}(u|t) \cdot f_T(t)}{f_U(u)}. \tag{4.10a}$$

Equation (4.10a) is really equation (4.10), in terms of our vector notation. We recognize that $f_{T|U}(t|u)$ is multivariate.

Equation (4.10a) should cause us to think about our earlier determinations of $f_T(t)$ and $f_{U|T}(u|t)$. Since we are going to multiply them together, it will be nice if they were chosen such that their product is a convenient expression. This can be accomplished by making use of conjugate distributions, defined as follows:

> *If the prior, $f_T(t)$, is a member of a family of distributions which is* conjugate *for the model of the experiment, then the posterior, $f_{T|U}(t|u)$, will be a member of that same family, and consequently, will possess the same properties as possessed by the prior.*

Although the use of conjugate distributions is not absolutely necessary in our Bayesian approach to graduation, it is certainly an excellent way to obtain a convenient result from the multiplication, and thereby facilitates the analysis of the posterior distribution in the final step. Note the convenient multiplication in Whittaker's rationale. Examples of conjugate distributions will be illustrated in the Bayesian methods that follow.

5.2.4 SELECTING THE GRADUATED VALUES v_x

We recognize that the posterior distribution contains our current information about T, reflecting our prior opinion as now modified by our knowledge of the data contained in u. The vector of graduated values v is selected from the information contained in $f_{T|U}(t|u)$ to reflect our graduation objective.

If we choose to define graduated values to be the expected value of T, in light of the observed vector u, then we would take v to be the *mean* of $f_{T|U}(t|u)$. On the other hand, throughout this text we have referred to the graduated values as the "most likely" or "most probable" values of T. This suggests that we take v to be the *mode* of $f_{T|U}(t|u)$, as did Whittaker, following the suggestion of King (see page 3). Other choices, such as the median of the posterior distribution, might also be appropriate, and will be discussed further in Section 5.7.

5.3
AN ILLUSTRATION

As a simple illustration of the Bayesian process, we return to the intuitive Bayesian graduation of one number which we did at the end of Section 2.3. There we suggested that our prior opinion of the binomial parameter t, the true rate of heads for our coin, was ½. A formal Bayesian process requires that we express our prior opinion about t in a probability distribution, rather than as a point estimate. We are then expressing our confidence, as a probability density, in any particular specific value of t.

For this problem, a natural distribution for the prior density of the random variable T is the Beta distribution. Thus

$$f_T(t) = \frac{\Gamma(a + b)}{\Gamma(a) \cdot \Gamma(b)} \, t^{a-1}(1 - t)^{b-1}, \ 0 \le t \le 1, \tag{5.1}$$

where $a > 0$ and $b > 0$ are parameters. That $\int_0^1 f_T(t) \, dt = 1$ is easily verified, since $\int_0^1 t^{a-1}(1 - t)^{b-1} \, dt$ is the Beta function, $B(a, b) = \dfrac{\Gamma(a) \cdot \Gamma(b)}{\Gamma(a + b)}$.

Now the model for the experiment is clearly binomial. Letting H be the random variable for the number of heads in n tosses, we have

$$p_{H|T}(h|t) = \frac{n!}{h!(n - h)!} \, t^h(1 - t)^{n-h}, \ 0 \le t \le 1, \ h = 0, 1, \ldots, n. \tag{5.2}$$

The marginal distribution $p_H(h)$ is found from

$$p_H(h) = \int_0^1 p_{H|T}(h|t) \cdot f_T(t) \, dt,$$

and is

$$\frac{\Gamma(a + b)n!}{\Gamma(a) \cdot \Gamma(b)h!(n - h)!} \cdot \frac{\Gamma(a + h) \cdot \Gamma(b + n - h)}{\Gamma(a + b + n)} \quad \text{(see Exercise 5–2).} \tag{5.3}$$

The posterior distribution, given by (4.10), is

$$f_{T|H}(t|h) = \frac{\Gamma(a + b + n)}{\Gamma(a + h) \cdot \Gamma(b + n - h)} \, t^{a+h-1}(1 - t)^{b+n-h-1}, \tag{5.4}$$

which is again a Beta distribution, with a replaced by $a + h$, and b replaced by $b + n - h$. Thus we see that the Beta distribution is conjugate to the binomial, which is part of our reason for choosing it for our prior.

Now we are ready to analyze our posterior distribution. In our little intuitive problem, we suggested that our prior "best estimate" of t was ½. By that we perhaps meant that $E[T] = \frac12$. Since $E[T] = \dfrac{a}{a + b}$ (see Exercise 5–3), then our prior opinion that $E[T] = \frac{1}{2}$ implies that $a = b$. On the other hand, as has already been suggested, perhaps we meant that $\frac{1}{2}$ was our "most likely" value of T, that is, the mode of $f_T(t)$. Conveniently, if $E[T] = \frac{1}{2}$, then the mode is $\frac{1}{2}$ as well, but it is not true that the mode and mean of the Beta distribution are, in general, equal (see Exercise 5–4).

Let us define our graduated value to be the mean of the posterior distribution,

$$v = E[T|H] = \frac{a + h}{a + b + n}.$$ (5.5)

For insight, we write (5.5) as

$$v = \frac{a}{a + b} \cdot \frac{a + b}{a + b + n} + \frac{h}{n} \cdot \frac{n}{a + b + n}.$$ (5.6)

Now recall that our prior mean of T was $E[T] = \frac{1}{2}$, which implies $a = b$. Recall also from Section 2.3 that our experiment used $n = 100$, and resulted in $h = 20$. Then (5.6) becomes

$$v = .50 \cdot \frac{2a}{2a + 100} + .20 \cdot \frac{100}{2a + 100}.$$ (5.7)

Our intuitive graduation, which we did before learning the formal Bayesian process, concluded with an unweighted average of .50, our prior mean, and .20, our experimental result, to produce our graduated value $v = .35$. What does this unweighted average decision imply? We can clearly see that v, given by (5.7) is a *weighted* average of these two inputs. For our formal Bayesian procedure to reproduce our intuitive, arbitrary result, the weights must be equal, which implies $a = 50$. This, in turn, means that we must have had equal confidence in our prior opinion and our experimental data. The purpose of this illustration is to explain the Bayesian process; we do not mean to suggest that the conclusion is a proper one (recall Exercise 2–8). If a coin believed to be unbiased produced only 20 heads in 100 tosses, is it realistic to place equal confidence in the prior opinion and the data? If not, then how do we decide the relative confidence to place? This is a major stumbling block in applying the Bayesian process. Exercises 5–5 and 5–6 provide some practice with the mathematics of this illustration, but do not answer the question of how we determine our degrees of confidence in the two inputs. Such a question is open to analysis, but is beyond the scope of this text.

This example is extended to its multivariate counterpart in Section 5.6.

5.4
THE KIMELDORF-JONES METHOD

Historically, we have seen that Whittaker's method was really the first Bayesian graduation. The Kimeldorf-Jones method [35], however, more thoroughly specifies the prior distribution for **T**, and, consequently, more broadly applies the Bayesian process to graduation. In this section, we will describe this method, referring to it as the K-J method, showing how each of the four steps in the standard Bayesian process are accomplished. (We will use the same notation as in [35], except that, where we use $\mathbf{T}$, the original paper uses $\mathbf{W}$.)

5.4.1 THE PRIOR DISTRIBUTION FOR T

The K-J method begins by adopting $f_{\mathbf{T}}(\mathbf{t})$ from the family of multinormal distributions. This appears to be a good choice on several grounds. It will prove to have mathematically convenient consequences, and the family is broad enough to permit an expression of prior opinion about $\mathbf{T}$ through the specification of the parameters.

The reader who is not totally familiar with the multinormal may wish to review it in a textbook on mathematical statistics. Here we might provide at least a minimum description of it by analogy to the univariate normal (see also Exercise 5–7). The univariate normal has parameters m and a, the mean and variance, respectively. The multinormal has parameters $\mathbf{m}$ and $\mathbf{A}$, the mean *vector* and covariance *matrix,* respectively. (We abandon our notational rule of reserving capital letters for random variables.)

The density function for the univariate normal is

$$f_T(t) = (2\pi a)^{-1/2} \exp\left[-\tfrac{1}{2}a^{-1}(t-m)^2\right].$$

For the multinormal, a is replaced by the matrix $\mathbf{A}$, and $(t - m)$ is replaced by the column vector $(\mathbf{t} - \mathbf{m})$. The matrix-vector counterpart of $a^{-1}(t - m)^2$ is

$$(\mathbf{t} - \mathbf{m})'\mathbf{A}^{-1}(\mathbf{t} - \mathbf{m}),$$

where, as usual, prime denotes transpose. Finally, the constant factor becomes $[(2\pi)^n|\mathbf{A}|]^{-1/2}$, where n is the number of elements in our vectors $\mathbf{T}$ and $\mathbf{m}$.

Therefore, our multinormal prior density for $\mathbf{T}$ is

$$f_{\mathbf{T}}(\mathbf{t}) = k_1 \cdot \exp\left[-\tfrac{1}{2}(\mathbf{t} - \mathbf{m})'\mathbf{A}^{-1}(\mathbf{t} - \mathbf{m})\right], \qquad (5.8)$$

and is completely specified by assigning values to $\mathbf{m}$ and $\mathbf{A}$. This specification is really the heart of the method, and is deferred to the next section so that we can present the method without disruption. For the moment, it is clear that $\mathbf{A}$ is symmetric, from its definition as a covariance matrix. In order for $\mathbf{T}$ to be multinormal, $\mathbf{A}$ must be positive definite, and hence non-singular. $\mathbf{A}$ is of dimension $n \times n$. The constant is called simply k_1 in (5.8); we will continue to use k_i for constants, increasing the subscript whenever the constant changes.

5.4.2 THE MODEL FOR THE EXPERIMENT

We have already mentioned that an appropriate conditional distribution for U_x, given t_x, is the binomial (or, rather, the binomial proportion). In the K-J method, the multivariate conditional distribution for $\mathbf{U}$, given $\mathbf{t}$, is taken to be multinormal.

(The approximation of the binomial proportion by the normal is quite common.) Since $E[U_x] = t_x$, it follows that the mean vector for our conditional multinormal is **t**. If we assume mutual independence of the U_x variables, the covariances are all zero, so the covariance matrix, **B**, for the conditional distribution becomes a diagonal $n \times n$ matrix, containing only the variances of the variables U_x. The specification of **B** is also deferred to the next section.

The above decisions lead us to the conditional density

$$f_{U|T}(\mathbf{u}|\mathbf{t}) = k_2 \cdot \exp\left[-\tfrac{1}{2}(\mathbf{u} - \mathbf{t})'\mathbf{B}^{-1}(\mathbf{u} - \mathbf{t})\right], \tag{5.9}$$

where **B** is the above-mentioned diagonal, positive definite matrix, and the constant is $k_2 = [(2\pi)^n|\mathbf{B}|]^{-1/2}$.

5.4.3 THE POSTERIOR DISTRIBUTION FOR T

We next use equation (4.10a), which is Bayes' Theorem, to develop $f_{T|U}(\mathbf{t}|\mathbf{u})$, by multiplying $f_{U|T}(\mathbf{u}|\mathbf{t})$ and $f_T(\mathbf{t})$, given by (5.9) and (5.8), respectively. We first note that $f_U(\mathbf{u})$ is constant with respect to **t**, so it can be combined with k_1 and k_2. We let

$$k_3 = f_U(\mathbf{u}) \quad \text{and} \quad k_4 = \frac{k_1 \cdot k_2}{k_3}.$$

We then see that equation (4.10a) produces our posterior density as

$$f_{T|U}(\mathbf{t}|\mathbf{u}) = k_4 \cdot \exp\left\{-\tfrac{1}{2}[(\mathbf{t} - \mathbf{m})'\mathbf{A}^{-1}(\mathbf{t} - \mathbf{m}) + (\mathbf{u} - \mathbf{t})'\mathbf{B}^{-1}(\mathbf{u} - \mathbf{t})]\right\}. \tag{5.10}$$

Now a bit of matrix algebra is required to rearrange this exponent. In our interest of a smooth presentation, this is deferred to Exercise 5–9, with hints. There we will see that (5.10) can be rearranged to read

$$k_6 \cdot \exp\left[-\tfrac{1}{2}(\mathbf{t} - \mathbf{v})'\mathbf{C}^{-1}(\mathbf{t} - \mathbf{v})\right], \tag{5.11}$$

where 1. k_6 does not involve **t**,
2. $\mathbf{v} = (\mathbf{A}^{-1} + \mathbf{B}^{-1})^{-1}(\mathbf{B}^{-1}\mathbf{u} + \mathbf{A}^{-1}\mathbf{m})$, and
3. $\mathbf{C} = (\mathbf{A}^{-1} + \mathbf{B}^{-1})^{-1}$.

This is a very nice result. We see that $f_{T|U}(\mathbf{t}|\mathbf{u})$ is also a multinormal distribution, with mean vector **v** and covariance matrix **C**. Thus we see that the multinormal (as the prior) is conjugate to itself (as the model for the experiment), so that the posterior is multinormal as well, which will facilitate the last part of the Bayesian process. This convenience might have been part of our reason for choosing a multinormal prior in the first place, but, in theory, the prior is really to be selected to reflect our prior opinion about **T**, as accurately as possible.

5.4.4 SELECTING THE GRADUATED VALUES

In Section 5.2.4, we suggested that either the mean, mode, or median of $f_{T|U}(\mathbf{t}|\mathbf{u})$ might logically be taken as the vector of graduated values. In the K-J method, since the posterior is multinormal, these three are all the same. This common vector, which we have already called $\mathbf{v}$, is therefore selected as the vector of graduated values, a very logical choice. Thus our graduated values are

$$\mathbf{v} = (\mathbf{A}^{-1} + \mathbf{B}^{-1})^{-1}(\mathbf{B}^{-1}\mathbf{u} + \mathbf{A}^{-1}\mathbf{m}). \tag{5.12}$$

5.4.5 INTERPRETATION

Equation (5.12), our Bayesian graduation formula, has a nice interpretation. The vector $\mathbf{m}$ is part of our prior opinion about $\mathbf{T}$ ($\mathbf{A}$ being the other part), and the vector $\mathbf{u}$ contains our observed data. Clearly $\mathbf{v}$, given by (5.12), is a weighted average of $\mathbf{m}$ and $\mathbf{u}$, each weighted by the inverse of the appropriate covariance matrix, the multivariate counterpart of inverse variance in a univariate case. (5.12) reflects the general view of graduation as a blending of the two inputs, prior opinion and observational data.

Equation (5.12) can be rearranged (see Exercise 5–11) to read

$$\mathbf{v} = \mathbf{u} + (\mathbf{I} + \mathbf{A}\mathbf{B}^{-1})^{-1}(\mathbf{m} - \mathbf{u}), \tag{5.13}$$

where $\mathbf{I}$ is the identity matrix of order n. Since $\mathbf{B}$ is diagonal, it is easily inverted, so (5.13) requires only one difficult matrix inversion, whereas (5.12) requires two.

An alternate rearrangement of (5.12) (see Exercise 5–12) would result in

$$\mathbf{v} = \mathbf{m} + (\mathbf{I} + \mathbf{B}\mathbf{A}^{-1})^{-1}(\mathbf{u} - \mathbf{m}). \tag{5.14}$$

Clearly (5.14) is not as computationally practical as is (5.13). Together they represent an interesting pair of views, however. (5.13) suggests that $\mathbf{v}$ results from modifying $\mathbf{u}$, the observed data, in light of our prior opinion given by $\mathbf{m}$. (5.14) suggests that $\mathbf{v}$ results from modifying $\mathbf{m}$, our prior opinion, in light of our observed data given by $\mathbf{u}$. This supplies the answer to the riddle posed in Section 2.3.

5.5
SPECIFYING THE ELEMENTS OF m, A, AND B

The elements of $\mathbf{m}$, $\mathbf{A}$, and $\mathbf{B}$ are the parameters of the graduation method, and must be specified in order to perform the graduation. This is true for any method. In some methods, however, such as the M-W-A, we have very little guidance in fixing the parameters (n and z) a priori. We frequently tend to graduate the data, using various combinations of parameters, and then select the graduated result which is most pleasing. Thus the parameters are specified a posteriori.

This approach is largely due to a lack of understanding about the role of the parameters. But in the K-J method, we have an interpretation of these parameters. We know what they represent. Although this certainly does not imply unique values for them, it does guide the selection of them to some extent, as will now be discussed.

5.5.1 THE ELEMENTS OF m

Since the prior distribution for **T** is normal, **m** is the mean (expected value), mode ("most probable" value), and median (equal chance of being above or below) of **T**. It represents our best estimate of **t** in absence of experimental data.

Suppose we needed mortality rates for making pension calculations for a large group of employees, but had no data derived from the recent experience of this group. We would be likely to choose rates from a published table which was based on the experience of another group, with characteristics as similar to our group as possible. If then, a few years later, we did a study of mortality in our group, and chose to graduate it by the K-J method, these standard table rates would be logical candidates for the prior mean vector **m**.

5.5.2 THE ELEMENTS OF A

Without doubt, this is the most difficult aspect of the K-J method. Despite an understanding of the role played by the matrix **A**, considerable subjectivity is still involved in specifying its elements. Fortunately we do have some guidance. Let us see how far this can take us; where it stops, subjectivity (or personal preference) must take over to complete the task.

The first bit of guidance comes from the very nature of graduation and the role of **A** as the covariance matrix of the random vector **T**. We laid the theoretical basis for this earlier in the text, particularly in Section 1.4, where we quoted Elphinstone's description of graduation as the theory of "relations between neighboring rates". Let us attempt to represent these "relations" by the correlation coefficients between each pair of rates.

Clearly the diagonal elements of **A** are the variances of the random variables **T**. Thus if we can satisfactorily select, for all i, our prior variance of T_i, which is the element a_{ii} of the matrix **A**, and the correlation coefficient c_{ij} between T_i and T_j, then the covariance between T_i and T_j, which is the element a_{ij} of **A**, is

$$a_{ij} = c_{ij}\sqrt{a_{ii} \cdot a_{jj}}. \qquad (5.15)$$

It appears that we have merely avoided the hard problem of selecting a_{ij} by substituting for it the hard problem of selecting c_{ij}. But we may find that the correlation coefficient is more intuitively meaningful to us than is the covariance, so this would be a step in the right direction.

A second bit of guidance is our intuition. We might agree that all $c_{ij} \geq 0$, which implies that all $a_{ij} \geq 0$. We might also agree that the correlation between T_i and T_j decreases as the distance between i and j increases. Thus, if j is closer to i than is k, we are suggesting that $c_{ij} > c_{ik}$. This does not imply that $a_{ij} > a_{ik}$, but rather that

$$\frac{a_{ij}}{\sqrt{a_{jj}}} > \frac{a_{ik}}{\sqrt{a_{kk}}}, \qquad (5.16)$$

and we would require the elements of **A** to be constrained by (5.16).

A third bit of guidance is provided by a desire for simplicity and computational convenience. Since we must invert the matrix $\mathbf{A}$, (or the matrix $(\mathbf{I} + \mathbf{AB}^{-1})$ if we use (5.13) for computing $\mathbf{v}$), we will simplify the computations if $\mathbf{A}$ contains some elements equal to zero. Clearly $a_{ij} = 0$ implies $c_{ij} = 0$. Thus we might decide that T_i and T_j are not (appreciably) correlated for i and j "sufficiently" far apart. Here we reach one of our several points where subjectivity must take over.

As an example of simplicity in specifying the elements of $\mathbf{A}$, we might select a formula for a_{ij}, in terms of relatively few parameters. Of course we have once again made a substitution for the problem: instead of selecting each a_{ij} numerically, we must select the parameters of the chosen formula for a_{ij}.

One such simple formula, suggested by Kimeldorf and Jones and defined by them as matrix class a_1, is

$$a_{ij} = p^2 r^{|i-j|}, \quad p > 0, \quad 0 \le r < 1. \tag{5.17}$$

Some observations on (5.17):

1. It satisfies the condition given by (5.16).
2. The matrix $\mathbf{A}$ which it defines is positive definite, and clearly symmetric.
3. p^2 is the variance of T_i for all i.
4. r is the correlation coefficient between T_i and T_j where $|i - j| = 1$.
5. Similarly, if $|i - j| = 2$, the correlation coefficient between T_i and T_j is taken to be r^2, etc.

At this point, personal preference again intervenes. Are we content with a matrix given by (5.17) as a satisfactory approximation to our "true" prior covariance matrix for $\mathbf{T}$? If we don't like the idea of a constant $c_{i,i+1}$ for all i, then we might (somehow) develop $c_{i,i+1}$ for each i separately. That is, determine our correlation coefficients between every pair of adjacent random variables in $\mathbf{T}$, and then build the correlation between more distant random variables by multiplication. Thus if we determine $c_{1,2} = r_1$, $c_{2,3} = r_2$, and $c_{3,4} = r_3$, then $c_{1,3} = r_1 r_2$, $c_{2,4} = r_2 r_3$, $c_{1,4} = r_1 r_2 r_3$, etc. Combining this with the above assumption of equal variance for all T_i leads to

$$a_{ij} = p^2 r_i r_{i+1} \ldots r_{j-1}. \tag{5.18}$$

Kimeldorf and Jones call all matricies given by (5.18) the matrix class a_2. (Class a_1 is contained within class a_2.) As for class a_1, $p > 0$ and $0 \le r_k < 1$ for all k. We have stated (5.18) assuming that $i < j$, which only defines the upper right triangle of $\mathbf{A}$. The lower left triangle is defined by the symmetry of $\mathbf{A}$. Any matrix in class a_2 also satisfies condition (5.16), and is positive definite.

Finally, if we are not content with the assumption of equal variance for all T_i, we must (somehow) determine the variance for each T_i separately. Suppose the correlation assumption of class a_1 is acceptable to us. Then, if p_i is our standard deviation of T_i, we could define our matrix **A** by

$$a_{ij} = p_i p_j r^{|i-j|}. \tag{5.19}$$

A matrix given by (5.19) satisfies condition (5.16), and is positive definite.

In summary, in this subsection, which is perhaps the most elusive in the entire text, we have tried to give some guidance to the hard problem of selecting the elements of the prior covariance matrix **A**, noting that ultimately some expression of personal preference must enter in. This should not be surprising, however, when one recalls that the entire subject of graduation is ultimately based on some degree of subjectivity and judgment. If this were not so, we would be entertaining the notion of the "correct" graduation, a creature as mythological as the Loch Ness Monster.

5.5.3 THE ELEMENTS OF B

In contrast with our difficulty in specifying the elements of **A**, the elements of **B** for the K-J method are naturally suggested.

Recall that **B** is diagonal (reflecting the independence assumption), and the element b_{ii} is the variance of U_i in the conditional distribution for **U**, given **t**. As we established in Chapter 2, and have used several times since, if U_i is approximately a binomial proportion, then

$$\text{Var}(U_i) = \frac{t_i(1 - t_i)}{n_i}.$$

But in the K-J method, **B** must be free of **t**, so we might instead take

$$b_{ii} = \frac{m_i(1 - m_i)}{n_i}, \tag{5.20}$$

since **m** is our prior "best estimate" of **T**. Compare this with a similar problem described in the first paragraph of Section 4.2.1.

5.5.4 A VARIATION ON THE KIMELDORF-JONES METHOD

In a sequel paper to that of Kimeldorf and Jones, Hickman and Miller [27] suggest that use of an appropriately selected transformation of the random vectors **T** and **U** will facilitate the specification of the elements of **A** and **B**, and provide some other advantages as well. Exploration of this idea will not be pursued in this text, and the interested reader is referred to [27].

In addition, Hickman and Miller point out that, in using mortality rates for financial calculations, we might want to use something "safer" than the "most probable" rates given by the mode of the posterior distribution. For example, we might want to use a rate at each age, such that the probability of the true rate being greater than our chosen rate is only .25, say. In order to make such probability statements, we have to know, with some confidence, the nature of our distribution. The use of an appropriate transformation can result in a posterior that is more nearly multinormal than is the posterior in the standard (untransformed) K-J model.

5.6
ANOTHER EXAMPLE OF THE BAYESIAN GRADUATION PROCESS

In the K-J method, it was assumed that the random variables of the vector U were mutually statistically independent. We should note that the K-J method does not *require* this independence, which, we recall, implied a diagonal matrix for B. Abandoning the assumption would make the specification of B more involved, and would make the computation of v by equation (5.12) more difficult, by requiring the inversion of a non-diagonal B. In this section, we explore an example in which an independence assumption would not be valid.

Suppose, as frequently happens with clinical data, we wish to estimate the survival rates of patients following a particular operation. Age might be an insignificant factor, so our primary variable of interest is duration since operation. Suppose we have d such patients, and we conduct a follow-up study to observe these d patients until all die. This model is the multivariate generalization of Section 5.3.

Let D_i be the random variable for the number of deaths occurring in the ith time interval, with the last death occurring in the nth interval. Then, clearly,

$$\sum_1^n D_i = d,$$

and the several D_i cannot be independent. The appropriate model for this experiment is multinomial, with

$$p_{D|T}(d|t) = \frac{d!}{\prod\limits_1^n d_i!} \cdot \prod_1^n t_i^{d_i}, \quad 0 \le t_i \le 1. \tag{5.22}$$

Some observations on formula (5.22):

1. We use p (rather than f) for the conditional distribution of D, given t, since it is discrete.

2. In this case, the true rate for the ith interval, t_i, is $_{i-1|}q_0$, in standard actuarial notation.

3. $\sum\limits_1^n d_i = d.$

4. $\sum_{1}^{n} t_i = 1$, so that $t_n = 1 - \sum_{1}^{n-1} t_i$.

How shall we express our prior distribution $f_{\mathbf{T}}(\mathbf{t})$? Recall our discussion of conjugate distributions. In order to obtain a convenient posterior distribution, we express $f_{\mathbf{T}}(\mathbf{t})$ as a Dirichlet distribution, since it is conjugate to the multinomial, and thus the posterior will also be Dirichlet. The Dirichlet is a generalization of the Beta distribution (see Wilks [62]), and, of course, the multinomial is a generalization of the binomial; therefore this model is a generalization of Section 5.3. Thus our prior distribution is

$$f_{\mathbf{T}}(\mathbf{t}) = \frac{\Gamma\left(\sum_{1}^{n} a_i\right)}{\prod_{1}^{n} \Gamma(a_i)} \cdot \prod_{1}^{n} t_i^{a_i - 1}, \quad a_i > 0, \quad 0 \le t_i \le 1. \tag{5.23}$$

The values of a_i are the parameters of the distribution. Let $a = \sum_{1}^{n} a_i$. For this distribution (see Exercise 5–21),

$$E[T_i] = \frac{a_i}{a}. \tag{5.24}$$

To specify our prior completely, we might again select our vector of prior means for $\mathbf{T}$, again calling it $\mathbf{m}$, as we did for the K-J method. (This time, however, $\mathbf{m}$ is not the mode as well.) We must also fix the value of a; some guidance for doing this will be provided later. Then with a and each m_i specified, each a_i is found from (5.24).

As mentioned, the posterior distribution is again Dirichlet, with

$$f_{\mathbf{T}|\mathbf{D}}(\mathbf{t}|\mathbf{d}) = \frac{\Gamma\left(\sum_{1}^{n} (a_i + d_i)\right)}{\prod_{1}^{n} \Gamma(a_i + d_i)} \cdot \prod_{1}^{n} t_i^{(a_i + d_i) - 1}. \tag{5.25}$$

Let us define our vector of graduated values to be the mean vector of the posterior distribution for $\mathbf{T}$, given the vector of observations $\mathbf{d}$. Following from (5.24), we have

$$v_i = E[T_i|d_i] = \frac{a_i + d_i}{a + d}, \tag{5.24a}$$

so that

$$\mathbf{v} = \frac{\mathbf{a} + \mathbf{d}}{a + d}. \qquad (5.26)$$

Additional insight into (5.24a) can be obtained by writing it as

$$v_i = \frac{a_i}{a} \cdot \frac{a}{a + d} + \frac{d_i}{d} \cdot \frac{d}{a + d}. \qquad (5.27)$$

In equation (5.27), we see that $\frac{d_i}{d}$ is our estimate of t_i based on the observed data alone. We have already stated that $\frac{a_i}{a} = m_i$ is our prior estimate of t_i, in that it is $E[T_i]$. Then, clearly, (5.27) is a weighted average of our prior opinion and our experimental data, in the true Bayesian spirit (c.f., equation (5.6)). Note also that for a fixed value of a, greater weight is given to the experimental value $\frac{d_i}{d}$ as d increases, as we should expect.

On the other hand, for a fixed value of d, greater weight is given to our prior opinion value m_i as a increases. This allows us to interpret a as a measure of the degree of confidence which we have in our prior opinion values, in the same sense that d is a similar measure for our experimental values. As a benchmark for a, given d, suppose we consider $a = d$. Then, clearly, m_i and $\frac{d_i}{d}$ are weighted equally. Can we somehow establish the value of d for which we would place equal confidence in our prior opinion and our experimental data? The answer to this obviously subjective issue establishes the value of a. The reader should compare this analysis to the parallel case, with $n = 2$, in Section 5.3; the comments made there regarding subjectivity are equally applicable in this case.

The example presented in this section was suggested by Hickman [25].

5.7
SUMMARY

In this chapter we have explored the application of Bayesian methods to the graduation problem, giving two quite different examples of the Bayesian process. The Bayesian approach graphically demonstrates the nature of graduation as a blending of prior opinion with experimental, or observed, data. At the risk of oversimplification, it appears that the Bayesian process reverses the traditional order of considering these two inputs.

Traditionally, the actuarial view has been to first obtain the data (which we have called initial estimates) from a study, and to scrutinize the data, possibly with the aid of a graph, to see how consistent it is with prior opinion (which might be only a concept of smoothness). Then, to the extent that the initial data deviates from prior opinion, it is revised (or graduated) to be made more consistent with that prior opinion, while still retaining some resemblance (fit) to the original data. The revised data is then tested for an acceptable balance between these two objectives. If it is not found to be acceptable in some regard, it may be further revised.

The Bayesian approach appears to reverse the order. Prior opinion is expressed, in the form of the prior distribution $f_T(t)$, *before* seeing the observed data. (This suggests that the prior estimate is really the ''initial'' estimate, rather than the observed value!) This prior opinion is then revised by the experimental data, whereas the traditional actuarial view is that the observed data is revised by prior opinion. This is the dichotomy of views suggested by formulas (5.13) and (5.14).

Without question, the Bayesian approach to graduation is a controversial one, due largely to the degree of subjectivity inherent in it. Furthermore, the use of normal distributions for the prior and the data, as in the K-J method, has been criticized on theoretical grounds which are beyond the scope of this text. (See Leamer [40].)

The example presented in Section 5.6 was motivated by the inappropriateness of the independence assumption made in the K-J method. This suggests a basic connection between the design of the study which produced the experimental data and the method chosen to graduate that data. It is submitted that this connection has not always been recognized, and graduation methods, and their parameters, have perhaps therefore been inappropriately chosen. The need for compatibility of study design and graduation method is nicely illustrated in the Bayesian approach.

Finally, In Section 1.7 we mentioned that a statistical model, such as mortality data, could be summarized in either tabular form or functional form. Now a third possibility has been suggested: the model can be summarized in the form of a probability distribution, with any number of distinct ''mortality tables'' obtainable from it, as suggested in Section 5.5.4. This approach might well see greater use in the future.

EXERCISES

5.1   Introduction;   5.2 The Bayesian Process

5–1   London's Chocolates of Punxsutawney, Pennsylvania, makes solid chocolate bunnies for Easter. In a standard batch of bunnies, the number which are defective due to ''milk spots'' is a random variable, Y, with a Poisson distribution. The Poisson parameter $m = E[Y]$ is related to the outside temperature (the plant not being air-conditioned), having an exponential distribution with parameter $\lambda = \dfrac{1}{c}$, where c is the outside Celsius temperature.

a) What is our prior distribution for M, $f_M(m)$?

b) What is our conditional distribution for Y, given $M = m$, $p_{Y|M}(y|m)$?

c) What is the marginal distribution for Y, $p_Y(y)$?

$$\left[\text{Hint:} \int_0^\infty x^n e^{-ax} \, dx = \frac{n!}{a^{n+1}} \right]$$

d) Verify that your $p_Y(y)$ satisfies $\sum_{y=0}^\infty p_Y(y) = 1$.

e) On a certain day, the temperature is $10°$ Celsius. How many "milk spot" bunnies do we expect that day?

f) What is the posterior distribution for M, given $Y = y$, $f_{M|Y}(m|y)$?

g) On a certain day our thermometer is broken, but we found 15 "milk spot" bunnies. What is the expected outside temperature?

5.3   An Illustration

5–2   a) Verify that $p_H(h)$ is given by (5.3).

      b) Verify that $f_{T|H}(t|h)$ is given by (5.4).

5–3   Prove that the mean of the prior distribution is $E[T] = \dfrac{a}{a+b}$. [Hint: recall that $\Gamma(\alpha) = (\alpha - 1)\Gamma(\alpha - 1)$]

5–4   Find the mode of the Beta distribution. Show that the mode and the mean are equal only when they are both $\frac{1}{2}$.

5–5   In the coin exercise of Section 5.3, we again take our prior mean to be $\frac{1}{2}$. We toss the coin 10 times and obtain 7 heads. Because of the small number of tosses, we express twice as much confidence in our prior opinion as in our experimental result. In light of the experimental outcome, what is our revised "expected value" of T (i.e., our posterior mean)?

5–6   Linda has tossed a coin 100 times and observed 45 heads. She states that, in absence of further evidence, .45 is the "most probable" value for T. Frank decides to provide further evidence, and spends a rainy afternoon tossing the same coin 1000 times, obtaining 600 heads. Linda concedes that his result should be more reliable, but thinks he may have miscounted. She is willing to give his result four times the weight of hers. What is Linda's "most probable" value for T in light of the further evidence (i.e., her posterior mode)? What does this imply for the values of a and b in the Beta distribution?

5.4   The Kimeldorf-Jones Method

5–7   To gain some familiarity with the multinormal distribution, let us examine the bivariate case. Hoel [29] defines the bivariate normal density for the random variables T_1 and T_2 as

$$f(t_1, t_2) = \frac{\exp\left\{-\dfrac{1}{2(1-\rho^2)}\left[\left(\dfrac{t_1 - \mu_1}{\sigma_1}\right)^2 - 2\rho\left(\dfrac{t_1 - \mu_1}{\sigma_1}\right)\left(\dfrac{t_2 - \mu_2}{\sigma_2}\right) + \left(\dfrac{t_2 - \mu_2}{\sigma_2}\right)^2\right]\right\}}{2\pi\sigma_1\sigma_2(1-\rho^2)^{1/2}},$$

where μ_i and σ_i are the mean and standard deviation of T_i, and the correlation coefficient between T_1 and T_2 is

$$\rho = \frac{\text{cov}_{12}}{\sigma_1\sigma_2}.$$

We wish to show that our (5.8), with $n = 2$, is the same as Hoel's $f(t_1, t_2)$.

a) Write our matrix $\mathbf{A}$ using the above notation.

b) What is $|\mathbf{A}|$?

c) Show that our k_1^{-1} equals Hoel's denominator.

d) What is $\mathbf{A}^{-1}$, in terms of σ_1, σ_2, and ρ?

e) Finally, multiply out $-\frac{1}{2}(\mathbf{t} - \mathbf{m})'\mathbf{A}^{-1}(\mathbf{t} - \mathbf{m})$ to obtain the exponent in Hoel's numerator.

5–8 In our (5.9), the diagonal matrix $\mathbf{B}$ contains the variances of U_i for $i = 1, \ldots, n$. Let $b_i = \text{Var}(U_i)$.

a) What is $|\mathbf{B}|$?

b) What is $\mathbf{B}^{-1}$?

c) Express the exponent of (5.9) in a summation.

d) Compare this with the definition of F in Whittaker's method, and the discussion concerning weights in Section 4.2.

5–9 Here we will do the algebra to rearrange (5.10) into (5.11).

a) Multiply out the exponent of (5.10), recalling that $(\mathbf{t} - \mathbf{m})' = \mathbf{t}' - \mathbf{m}'$. Remember that commutativity does not always hold, so be careful to keep your terms in the same order. Check your result.

b) Factor out the two terms which do not involve $\mathbf{t}$. Combine them with k_4 and call the result k_5. What is k_5?

c) Rearrange the six remaining terms, doing some factoring to the left, or right, or both, to obtain

$$k_5 \cdot \exp\{-\tfrac{1}{2}[\mathbf{t}'(\mathbf{A}^{-1} + \mathbf{B}^{-1})\mathbf{t} - \mathbf{t}'(\mathbf{B}^{-1}\mathbf{u} + \mathbf{A}^{-1}\mathbf{m})$$
$$- (\mathbf{u}'\mathbf{B}^{-1} + \mathbf{m}'\mathbf{A}^{-1})\mathbf{t}]\}.$$

d) Define $\quad\quad\quad \mathbf{C}^{-1} = (\mathbf{A}^{-1} + \mathbf{B}^{-1})$
and $\quad\quad\quad\quad\; \mathbf{v} = \mathbf{C}(\mathbf{B}^{-1}\mathbf{u} + \mathbf{A}^{-1}\mathbf{m}),$
so that $\quad\quad\quad \mathbf{C}^{-1}\mathbf{v} = (\mathbf{B}^{-1}\mathbf{u} + \mathbf{A}^{-1}\mathbf{m}),$

and substitute these into our result in part (c) to obtain

$$k_5 \cdot \exp\{-\tfrac{1}{2}[\mathbf{t}'\mathbf{C}^{-1}\mathbf{t} - \mathbf{t}'\mathbf{C}^{-1}\mathbf{v} - (\mathbf{u}'\mathbf{B}^{-1} + \mathbf{m}'\mathbf{A}^{-1})\mathbf{t}]\}.$$

e) Since $\mathbf{C}^{-1}\mathbf{v} = (\mathbf{B}^{-1}\mathbf{u} + \mathbf{A}^{-1}\mathbf{m})$, then

$$(\mathbf{C}^{-1}\mathbf{v})' = \mathbf{v}'(\mathbf{C}^{-1})' = (\mathbf{B}^{-1}\mathbf{u})' + (\mathbf{A}^{-1}\mathbf{m})' = \mathbf{u}'(\mathbf{B}^{-1})' + \mathbf{m}'(\mathbf{A}^{-1})'.$$

Then $\mathbf{v}'\mathbf{C}^{-1} = \mathbf{u}'\mathbf{B}^{-1} + \mathbf{m}'\mathbf{A}^{-1}$. Why is $(\mathbf{X}^{-1})' = \mathbf{X}^{-1}$ for $\mathbf{X} = \mathbf{A}, \mathbf{B}, \mathbf{C}$?

f) Substitute $\mathbf{v}'\mathbf{C}^{-1}$ for $\mathbf{u}'\mathbf{B}^{-1} + \mathbf{m}'\mathbf{A}^{-1}$ into our result in part (d). Add and subtract $\mathbf{v}'\mathbf{C}^{-1}\mathbf{v}$ inside the bracket to obtain

$$k_5 \cdot \exp\{-\tfrac{1}{2}[\mathbf{t}'\mathbf{C}^{-1}\mathbf{t} - \mathbf{t}'\mathbf{C}^{-1}\mathbf{v} - \mathbf{v}'\mathbf{C}^{-1}\mathbf{t} + \mathbf{v}'\mathbf{C}^{-1}\mathbf{v} - \mathbf{v}'\mathbf{C}^{-1}\mathbf{v}]\}.$$

g) Factor out the term $-\mathbf{v}'\mathbf{C}^{-1}\mathbf{v}$, defining $k_6 = k_5 \cdot \exp[\tfrac{1}{2}\mathbf{v}'\mathbf{C}^{-1}\mathbf{v}]$. The remaining four terms are the expansion of $(\mathbf{t} - \mathbf{v})'\mathbf{C}^{-1}(\mathbf{t} - \mathbf{v})$. We have established (5.11). Wasn't that fun?

5-10 Suppose T_1, T_2 and T_3 are assumed to be *independent* normal random variables with prior means and variances given by

$$\mathbf{m}' = [2, 6, 16] \quad \text{and} \quad \mathbf{A} = \begin{bmatrix} \tfrac{1}{4} & 0 & 0 \\ 0 & 1 & 0 \\ 0 & 0 & 2 \end{bmatrix}.$$

An experiment produces a set of observations given by $\mathbf{u}' = [1, 4, 18]$, with Var $(\mathbf{U}|\mathbf{T})$ given by

$$\mathbf{B} = \begin{bmatrix} \tfrac{1}{5} & 0 & 0 \\ 0 & \tfrac{3}{4} & 0 \\ 0 & 0 & \tfrac{3}{2} \end{bmatrix}.$$

Using the K-J method, find the vector of graduated values $\mathbf{v}$.

5-11 Derive (5.13) from (5.12). The approach is to add $\mathbf{u}$ and subtract it as $(\mathbf{A}^{-1} + \mathbf{B}^{-1})^{-1}(\mathbf{A}^{-1} + \mathbf{B}^{-1})\mathbf{u}$. Find a pair of terms to cancel, factor $(\mathbf{m} - \mathbf{u})$ to the right, and simplify.

5-12 Derive (5.14) from (5.12) by an analogous approach.

5-13 a) Show that $(\mathbf{A}^{-1} + \mathbf{B}^{-1})^{-1} = \mathbf{A}(\mathbf{A} + \mathbf{B})^{-1}\mathbf{B} = \mathbf{B}(\mathbf{A} + \mathbf{B})^{-1}\mathbf{A}$.

b) Use the results in part (a) to derive the following expressions for $\mathbf{v}$, which are alternative forms for (5.12), (5.13), and (5.14), respectively.

   i. $\mathbf{A}(\mathbf{A} + \mathbf{B})^{-1}\mathbf{u} + \mathbf{B}(\mathbf{A} + \mathbf{B})^{-1}\mathbf{m}$

   ii. $\mathbf{u} + \mathbf{B}(\mathbf{A} + \mathbf{B})^{-1}(\mathbf{m} - \mathbf{u})$

   iii. $\mathbf{m} + \mathbf{A}(\mathbf{A} + \mathbf{B})^{-1}(\mathbf{u} - \mathbf{m})$

c) We know that $\mathbf{v}$ is the particular value of $\mathbf{t}$ that will maximize the posterior density of $\mathbf{T}$, because it is the mode of $\mathbf{T}$. Therefore it must minimize the exponent of $f_{\mathbf{T}|\mathbf{U}}(\mathbf{t}|\mathbf{u})$, given in (5.10). Show that this is true.

5.5 Specifying the Elements of **m**, **A**, and **B**

5–14 Doug and Jean are engaged in the exciting pastime of specifying the prior covariance matrix **A** for a K-J graduation of mortality data. Doug has selected for m_i the value of q_i from a large study of a few years ago. "My prior mean is .005," he says, "but I have no idea what to use for a prior variance." "How much confidence do you have in .005?" Jean asks. "Pretty much," says Doug. "That's no answer," Jean replies. "Look, would you say there's a 50-50 chance that T_i lies between, say, .0049 and .0051?" "No, I need a wider interval for that. I'd say T_i has a 50-50 chance to lie between .0048 and .0052." "O.K.," says Jean. "There's your answer, and don't forget the ⅔ rule." What does Doug use for his prior variance of T_i?

5–15 Verify expression (5.16).

5–16 Doug and Jean are still working on their matrix **A**. They have completed the principal diagonal, and are busy selecting covariances. "How many of these pairs are really correlated?" Doug asks. Jean replies, "Look, if you selected a value for T_{31}, and then I told you the real value of T_{30}, could that affect your degree of confidence in your T_{31}?" "Sure it could." "Well, would my telling you T_{30} affect your degree of confidence in your T_{35}?" "Yeah, but not as much." "Well, what is your first T_i for which your confidence is *not* affected by my telling you T_{30}?" "T_{40}; 10 or more apart, and my confidence is not affected." Doug's matrix **A** is 20 × 20. How many zeros will it contain?

5–17 For a certain vector of normal random variables, T_i for $i = 1, 2, \ldots, 6$, the following have been selected.

   i.   The mean vector $\mathbf{m}' = [.314, .329, .345, .360, .376, .392]$.

   ii.   The variance of each T_i is to be calculated from

$$\text{Var}(T_i) = \frac{m_i(1 - m_i)}{n_i}, \text{ where } \mathbf{n}' = [100, 70, 50, 30, 20, 10].$$

   iii.   Each adjacent pair T_i, T_{i+1} is correlated by $r = .9$; each pair T_i, T_{i+2} is correlated by $r = .4$; each pair T_i, T_{i+3} is correlated by $r = .1$; all other pairs are uncorrelated.

Complete the matrix **A** to four decimal places.

5.6 Another Example of the Bayesian Graduation Process

5–18 Show that, when $n = 2$, (5.22) reduces to (5.2).

5–19 Show that, when $n = 2$, (5.23) reduces to (5.1).

5–20 We wish to show that the Dirichlet distribution (5.23) integrates to unity. Consider the case with $n = 3$ (we already did $n = 2$ in Section 5.3). The integral is

$$\int_a^b \int_c^d f_{\mathbf{T}}(\mathbf{t})\, dt_2\, dt_1.$$

a) Why is there no integral with respect to t_3?

b) How is t_3 represented in the integrand?

c) What are the limits $[c, d]$ on the inside integral?

d) What are the limits $[a, b]$ on the outside integral?

e) Complete the integration. You might find it useful to make the variable change $s = \dfrac{t_2}{1 - t_1}$.

f) How would you write the integrand and limits for the general case?

g) Can you visualize the complexity of the variable changes to carry out the integral in part (f)?

5–21 Verify formula (5.24) for $E[T_i]$, $i = 1, 2, 3$, in the case with $n = 3$. Note the similarity to Exercise 5–20.

5–22 a) Find the mode of the Dirichlet distribution when $n = 3$. (Remember that t_3 is not a variable.)

b) In what case does the mode equal the mean?

5–23 a) What is the marginal distribution, $p_{\mathbf{D}}(\mathbf{d})$, for $n = 3$?

b) What is the marginal in the general case?

PARAMETRIC GRADUATION

6

6.1
INTRODUCTION

The graduation methods of Chapters 3, 4 and 5 were characterized by taking a sequence of observed values, which we called initial estimates of the true sequence t_x, and modifying that sequence of values to produce a sequence of revised estimates which purported to be, in some sense, better estimates of t_x. Our modification, or revision, was guided by our prior opinion about t_x, which, for the most part, was expressed as a concept of smoothness. In Chapter 5 we expressed our prior opinion about t_x in the form of a prior probability distribution.

The revised sequence, represented by the vector **v**, was necessarily expressed in numerical form. This characteristic of all graduation methods considered heretofore is the basic distinction between those methods and the methods to be explored in this chapter.

In this chapter we shall express the revised sequence as a mathematical function of the argument x. Thus the symbol for the graduated values, v_x, represents a function of x, involving parameters which must be determined from the data. Of course the resulting function can then be evaluated at all desired values of x, and the graduated values can be written numerically in tabular form, if desired.

The approach we are describing here is certainly within our definition of graduation, which is to revise a sequence of initial estimates in light of our prior opinion about the vector **t**. Here our prior opinion is expressed by the particular *functional form* which is chosen to represent v_x. The ever-present opinion of smoothness is implicit in this form, as is an opinion of the *shape* of the t_x sequence. We recognize that prior opinion regarding the shape of t_x did not play a major role in the methods thus far considered, except for the Bayesian method of Chapter 5.

The technique we are describing here, although certainly a graduation method, is not unique to graduation, or to actuarial applications. The reader has no doubt encountered such an exercise in other statistical study, and has called it *regression*.

To summarize:

1. The shape and smoothness of the revised sequence v_x are determined by the functional form selected.

2. The magnitude of the v_x values are determined from the initial estimates u_x, through the determination of the parameters by regression, or other techniques.

3. Since our information about the magnitude of t_x is contained solely in u_x, we strive for good fit between v_x and u_x, pulling away from u_x to the extent necessary to obtain the desired functional form. Thus the parameters of v_x are chosen so as to achieve this good fit.

Thus the general nature of this graduation method has been established, and it remains for us to describe techniques by which we accomplish our objective. Since, as stated above, these techniques are somewhat familiar, we will concentrate on adapting them to situations of special interest to actuaries. In this regard, a degree of similarity to Chapter 7 of Elandt-Johnson and Johnson [11] is noted.

Several variations on the standard problem are discussed in Sections 6.4 and 6.5.

6.2
THE FUNCTIONAL FORMS

We see that our estimation problem has been reduced to a curve-fitting problem. A widely used curve-fitting technique is that of least-squares, which we will emphasize in this chapter. In turn, least-squares fitting is facilitated whenever the functional form being fit is a polynomial, especially a first-degree polynomial. In many actuarial applications, our prior opinion about t_x does not suggest a polynomial form; then some adaptation is required in order to fit by a least-squares technique, with an increased amount of computation.

In this section we review three functional forms which have commonly been used to express mortality data. It is anticipated that the actuarial reader, at least, is familiar with these forms (or "laws" of mortality). We will use standard actuarial notation for them, departing, where necessary, from our convention in this text of reserving capital letters for random variables.

In choosing a functional form to be fit to our u_x data, we might do some preliminary testing of the data to help guide our selection of a form. Alternatively, we might fit the data to several different forms, and choose our preferred graduated sequence from among the results.

6.2.1 GOMPERTZ' FORM

The simplest form we will consider is the one suggested by Gompertz in 1825 [14]. In dealing with mortality data, we have a choice among several mortality *measures,* and then among functions of that measure by the use of transformations. With Gompertz' form, the natural choice is to start with the force of mortality (the hazard rate), which is

$$\mu_x = Bc^x, \quad B > 0, \quad c > 1 \tag{6.1}$$

and, in turn, to use a log transformation, producing

$$\log \mu_x = \log B + x \log c, \tag{6.2}$$

where either natural or common log can be used.

This assumes that our initial estimates u_x are forces of mortality. If the study was designed to produce probabilities (q_x) instead, they may be converted to forces using, perhaps, the popular relationship

$$\mu_{x+1/2} \doteqdot \frac{q_x}{1 - \frac{1}{2} \cdot q_x}. \tag{6.3}$$

Preliminary testing of the data for compatibility with a Gompertz form is thus suggested, in that a graph of $\log u_x$ against x should be approximately linear. If this is not obtained, it suggests that a form other than Gompertz should be considered. Incidently, the calculation of $\log u_x$ is made unnecessary by the use of semi-log paper for our test graph.

If the conversion to forces of mortality is not made, we can work with the survival probability p_x. Then the Gompertz form is

$$p_x = g^{c^x(c-1)}. \tag{6.4}$$

Clearly the log transform is again useful, resulting in

$$\log p_x = (c - 1)(\log g)c^x. \tag{6.5}$$

Now we see that our functional form is exponential. The appropriate preliminary test of the data would be to examine the sequence

$$\frac{\log u_{x+1}}{\log u_x}, \tag{6.6}$$

for $x = 1, 2, \ldots, n - 1$, for near-constancy.

Since (6.5) is not a polynomial, further adaptation is required for least-squares fitting, as discussed in Section 6.3.4. Since we have the option of fitting (6.2), however, that will be our preferred choice.

6.2.2 WEIBULL'S FORM

A second form we will consider is the Weibull. In terms of the force of mortality (hazard rate) we have

$$\mu_x = k(x - a)^n, \quad x \geq a, \quad k > 0, \quad n > 0. \tag{6.7}$$

A special case, which we consider for simplicity, with $a = 0$, results in

$$\mu_x = k \cdot x^n. \tag{6.7a}$$

The log transform produces

$$\log \mu_x = \log k + n \cdot \log x. \tag{6.8}$$

This suggests that a preliminary test of the data would be to graph $\log u_x$ against $\log x$. If a Weibull fit is appropriate, the test graph should be nearly linear. The graphing is facilitated by the use of log–log paper.

In terms of the survival probability p_x, we have

$$p_x = \exp\left\{-\frac{k}{n+1}[(x+1)^{n+1} - x^{n+1}]\right\}, \tag{6.9}$$

and

$$\ln p_x = -\frac{k}{n+1}[(x+1)^{n+1} - x^{n+1}] = -\frac{k}{n+1}\Delta x^{n+1}, \tag{6.10}$$

where the natural log, denoted by ln, is used.

If n were an integer (which it is *not* constrained to be), then

$$\Delta^n \ln p_x = -\frac{k}{n+1}\Delta^{n+1}x^{n+1} = -\frac{k}{n+1}(n+1)! = -k \cdot n! \tag{6.11}$$

is constant. This suggests that a preliminary test of the data would be to construct a difference table on $\ln u_x$, looking for near-constancy in some order of differences. Finding this would imply a preliminary value of n.

Clearly the log-linear (6.8) is a much better choice for least-squares fitting than is (6.10).

6.2.3 MAKEHAM'S FORM

Perhaps the most popular form used for mortality data is Makeham's modification of Gompertz, suggested in 1860 [43]. Here

$$\mu_x = A + Bc^x \tag{6.12}$$

and

$$p_x = s \cdot g^{c^x(c-1)}. \tag{6.13}$$

In this case, $\log \mu_x$ is neither linear nor log-linear, and an adaptation for least-squares fitting is required (see Section 6.3.4).

For preliminary testing of the data, we can see that

$$\log \Delta\mu_x = \log [B(c - 1)] + x \log c, \tag{6.14}$$

so that a graph of $\log \Delta u_x$ against x should be nearly linear. Again semi-log paper will facilitate the graphing. Similarly,

$$\log p_x = \log s + (c - 1)(\log g)c^x, \tag{6.15}$$

suggests that the sequence

$$\frac{\Delta \log u_{x+1}}{\Delta \log u_x}, \quad \text{for } x = 1, 2, \ldots, n - 2, \tag{6.16}$$

should show near-constancy in order that the data be judged compatible with the Makeham form. [c.f., Section 4.7.2]

In summary, in this section we have looked at three functional forms possibly suitable for mortality data. We have noted appropriate tests of the given data, to guide our selection of a form, in both the case where u_x is a sequence of forces of mortality (μ_x), and where u_x is probabilities of mortality (q_x), and hence survival probabilities (p_x). For all three forms we saw that the μ_x measure was the easiest to work with for our curve-fitting exercise.

6.3
TECHNIQUES OF CURVE-FITTING

We have stated that least-squares fitting will be our preferred approach. The discussion in Section 6.2 concerning preliminary testing of the u_x data suggests other approaches as well, which are briefly described here and reviewed in the exercises.

6.3.1 GRAPHIC TECHNIQUES

Consider the test graph of $\log u_x$ against x. Suppose this results in a very nearly straight line, so that a Gompertz fit is suggested. From (6.2) we see that the slope of our line is $\log c$, and the intercept is $\log B$. Then B and c can be deduced from the graph.

Alternatively, if semi-log paper is used, we can proceed as follows:

1. Pick any value of the argument x. Note the value of the ordinate $\log u_x$.
2. Find the value of the argument x', such that the ordinate $\log u_{x'}$ is in the corresponding position, in the second cycle of the graph, as $\log u_x$ is in the first cycle.
3. Then, assuming common log paper,

$$u_{x'} = 10 \cdot u_x,$$

so that

$$\log u_{x'} = \log B + x' \log c = \log 10 + \log B + x \log c.$$

Since log 10 = 1, this implies

$$\log c = \frac{1}{x' - x},\qquad(6.17)$$

from which c may be obtained. Then B is obtained by noting the value of the ordinate at any value of x.

If we obtain a nearly straight line in a graph of log Δu_x against x, suggesting a Makeham fit from (6.14), the same procedure can be used to obtain B and c, but not A. Alternatively, since

$$\mu_x - A = Bc^x,$$

we could perhaps find a straight line for the graph of log $(u_x - A)$, with A determined by trial and error. The successful straight-line result gives the value of A, and B and c are then obtained as above.

If we obtain a nearly straight line in a graph of log u_x against log x, suggesting a Weibull fit from (6.8), then the slope is n and the intercept is log k. Using log-log paper, the procedure described above for the Gompertz form will yield

$$n = \frac{1}{\log x' - \log x}.\qquad(6.17a)$$

6.3.2 COLLOCATION

We illustrate this technique for the case where u_x is observed values of p_x, to which we fit Makeham's form.

Select three equally-spaced values of the argument, say, x, $x + r$, and $x + 2r$. From (6.16), we see that

$$\frac{\Delta_r \log u_{x+r}}{\Delta_r \log u_x} = c^r,\qquad(6.16a)$$

from which c is determined; then from

$$\Delta_r \log u_x = (c - 1)(c^r - 1)(\log g)c^x\qquad(6.18)$$

g is determined; finally from (6.15) itself,

$$\log u_x = \log s + (c - 1)(\log g)c^x$$

s is determined.

This is reviewed and expanded in the exercises.

In a fit by collocation, the parameters are totally dependent on the particular values of u_x which are chosen. In the above example, only three values of u_x are used to determine v_x; if a different set of three had been selected, different parameters (and thus a different v_x) would have resulted. This property makes fit by collocation less desirable than fit by regression.

6.3.3 LEAST-SQUARES (SIMPLE LINEAR REGRESSION)

Consider any case of the form

$$u_x^* = a + bx^*. \tag{6.19}$$

We note that our (6.2) is of this form with $u_x^* = \log u_x$ and $x^* = x$. Similarly, our (6.8) is of this form with $u_x^* = \log u_x$ and $x^* = \log x$. In all cases, the weighted sum of squares

$$SS = \sum_{x=1}^{n} w_x (u_x^* - a - bx^*)^2, \tag{6.20}$$

viewed as a function of a and b, is to be minimized. The partial derivatives of SS with respect to a and b, equated to zero, produce the normal equations

$$a \sum_1^n w_x + b \sum_1^n x^* w_x = \sum_1^n w_x u_x^*$$
$$a \sum_1^n x^* w_x + b \sum_1^n (x^*)^2 w_x = \sum_1^n x^* w_x u_x^* \tag{6.21}$$

from which the least-squares estimates, $\hat{a}$ and $\hat{b}$, are obtained. In turn, $\hat{a}$ and $\hat{b}$ imply estimates of the parameters in the original function (before the log transform). It must be noted, however, that these implied estimates are *not* the least-squares estimates of the parameters of the original function. (See also Burden and Faires [6], Section 7.1.) True least-squares estimates can be obtained as in Section 6.3.4.

It is interesting to compare (6.20) to the Whittaker form given by (4.1). There we also sought to minimize the weighted sum of squares of deviations of observed values from the revised values, but that least-squares fit was modified by our attempt to minimize a smoothness measure as well. Here we have built our smoothness requirement directly into the form of v_x.

Appropriate selection of the weights is similar to the same issue for Whittaker's method. Again the reciprocal of the approximate variance of U_x should be considered. An unweighted sum of squares (i.e., $w_x = 1$ for all x), could also be considered, and would be analogous to the Whittaker Type A.

Finally, (6.20) and (6.21) can be considered in matrix-vector notation, as we did for Whittaker's method. This is pursued in the exercises.

6.3.4 NON-LINEAR REGRESSION

We see that Makeham's form is not directly accommodated by simple linear regression, since the linear form of $\log \Delta \mu_x$, given by (6.14), will not produce a value for A, and the linear form

$$\log (\mu_x - A) = \log B + x \log c$$

requires a pre-determination of A. Thus we must modify the regression approach to handle Makeham's non-linear form.

We begin by approximating $\mu_x = A + Bc^x$ by a Taylor series. Let

$$\mu_x = \mu_x^0 + (A - A_0)\frac{\partial \mu_x}{\partial A}\bigg|_0 + (B - B_0)\frac{\partial \mu_x}{\partial B}\bigg|_0 + (c - c_0)\frac{\partial \mu_x}{\partial c}\bigg|_0 + \cdots. \quad (6.22)$$

The method requires initial estimates of A, B, c, which we call A_0, B_0, c_0. These might be obtained by one of the methods discussed in Section 6.3.1 or Section 6.3.2. In (6.22), the notation $|_0$ means that the indicated partial derivative of μ_x is evaluated at A_0, B_0, c_0. Since $\mu_x = A + Bc^x$, the indicated partials are

$$\frac{\partial \mu_x}{\partial A} = 1, \quad \frac{\partial \mu_x}{\partial B} = c^x, \quad \frac{\partial \mu_x}{\partial c} = Bxc^{x-1}.$$

Letting $A - A_0 = d_A$, $B - B_0 = d_B$, $c - c_0 = d_c$, we have

$$SS = \sum_1^n w_x(u_x - \mu_x^0 - d_A - d_B c_0^x - d_c B_0 x c_0^{x-1})^2, \quad (6.20a)$$

where u_x represents observed values of μ_x, $\mu_x^0 = A_0 + B_0 c_0^x$, and where we have approximated μ_x by the Taylor series as far as the first derivative term only in (6.22). Then the derivatives of SS with respect to d_A, d_B and d_c, equated to zero, produce the normal equations

$$(6.23)$$

$$d_A \sum_1^n w_x + d_B \sum_1^n w_x c_0^x + d_c \sum_1^n w_x B_0 x c_0^{x-1} = \sum_1^n w_x(u_x - \mu_x^0)$$

$$d_A \sum_1^n w_x c_0^x + d_B \sum_1^n w_x(c_0^x)^2 + d_c \sum_1^n w_x B_0 x c_0^{2x-1} = \sum_1^n w_x c_0^x(u_x - \mu_x^0)$$

$$d_A \sum_1^n w_x B_0 x c_0^{x-1} + d_B \sum_1^n w_x B_0 x c_0^{2x-1} + d_c \sum_1^n w_x(B_0 x c_0^{x-1})^2 = \sum_1^n w_x B_0 x c_0^{x-1}(u_x - \mu_x^0).$$

Equations (6.23) are then solved for d_A, d_B, d_c. When added to A_0, B_0, c_0, respectively, we obtain, say, A_1, B_1, c_1, which could be taken as our estimates of A, B, c. However, they are not the true least-squares estimates of A, B, c, since (6.22) is only an approximation. Therefore, we consider A_1, B_1, c_1 to be improved estimates from A_0, B_0, c_0. We use them in place of A_0, B_0, c_0 in (6.23) to solve again for d_A, d_B, d_c, and hence other estimates called A_2, B_2, c_2. Continued use of this iterative approach will show a convergence of the successive estimates to the least-squares estimates $\hat{A}, \hat{B}, \hat{c}$. Since d_A, d_B, d_c represent the refinements, or corrections, in each successive approximation, the process can be halted whenever all of d_A, d_B, d_c become less than some predetermined value, such as 10^{-6}.

This process was first suggested to this writer in an unpublished work by Nesselle [48], and is also described in Section 7.6 of Miller and Wichern [47]. It is reviewed and illustrated in the exercises.

6.4
AN INTERESTING VARIATION

It is possible to obtain v_x as a parametric estimate of t_x directly from the basic data, *without* first obtaining an initial sequence of estimates u_x. If we were to take literally our definition of graduation as a *revision* of initial estimates, then we might say that the approach of this section is not a graduation method, *per se,* but rather is an alternative to graduation. It by-passes the need for the graduation step in the process of model construction.

On the other hand, if we take a broader definition of graduation, such as "estimation of the sequence of true values t_x in light of prior opinion and experimental data", then we *are* considering a graduation method here, one that differs from those previously considered in that the determination of initial estimates is unnecessary. This would appear to be the view of Chan and Panjer [9].

Tenenbein and Vanderhoof [56] argue that this approach is preferable to traditional mortality model construction involving orthodox graduation techniques. They feel that efforts should be made to refine the functional forms for the "law" of mortality, as originally suggested by Makeham and Gompertz, to reflect modern knowledge of biology and gerontology, and then to continually revise our opinion about those forms, and the values of their parameters, as emerging data would indicate. The issue of refined functional forms is beyond the scope of this text, but the special graduation method which we have described will now be examined further.

The fundamental approach is to write the likelihood of the basic sample data as a function of the parameters of the assumed functional form. Estimates of those parameters are then obtained by maximizing this likelihood, a statistical estimation procedure with which the reader is assumed to have some familiarity. Some similarity to Section 7.8 of Elandt-Johnson and Johnson [11] can be seen. We will not assume any specific functional form here, but will pursue several very elementary examples in the exercises.

The construction of the likelihood function to be maximized will depend on certain characteristics of the sample data. Restricting our attention to mortality data, we can distinguish between cases of complete data (where each person in the sample is observed to die), and incomplete data (where persons withdraw from the sample prior to death). We can also distinguish between cases where the exact age at death (or withdrawal) is known, and those where death (or withdrawal) is only known to occur in a certain age interval. This produces quite a number of combinations, but only a selected few will be explored here. The interested reader can pursue this further in Elandt-Johnson and Johnson [11] and Chan and Panjer [9]. The latter also discusses the solution of the likelihood equations for more complex functional forms.

6.4.1 COMPLETE DATA, EXACT AGE AT DEATH

Using standard actuarial notation, consider person i who enters the study at age x_i and dies at age y_i. Neither x_i nor y_i need be integral. The probability (likelihood) of this is

$$L_i = {}_{y_i-x_i}p_{x_i} \cdot \mu_{y_i} = \exp\left[-\int_{x_i}^{y_i} \mu_s\,ds\right] \cdot \mu_{y_i}, \tag{6.24}$$

where L_i means the likelihood of the event actually performed by person i. Assuming independence, the overall likelihood of the entire sample data is

$$L = \prod_{i=1}^{n} L_i, \tag{6.25}$$

where there are n persons in the sample.

Following the usual procedure for maximum likelihood estimation, we take

$$\ell_i = \ln L_i = -\int_{x_i}^{y_i} \mu_s\,ds + \ln \mu_{y_i}, \tag{6.26}$$

and thus

$$\ell = \ln L = \sum_{i=1}^{n} \ell_i = \sum_{i=1}^{n}\left[\ln \mu_{y_i} - \int_{x_i}^{y_i} \mu_s\,ds\right]. \tag{6.27}$$

We then take the partial derivative of ℓ with respect to each parameter in the assumed form of μ, equate to zero, and solve for the maximum likelihood estimates of those parameters. Frequently the derivative equations will not solve explicitly for those parameters, and numerical methods must be employed.

6.4.2 INCOMPLETE DATA, EXACT AGE AT DEATH OR WITHDRAWAL

In this case we consider a person i who enters at age x_i and withdraws alive at age z_i. The likelihood of this is simply ${}_{z_i-x_i}p_{x_i}$. Note that we are not interested in estimating the rate of withdrawal. The survival of person i from age x_i to z_i, at which point withdrawal occurs, is known to have happened, but the likelihood of it must be included in the overall likelihood. When we consider all who withdraw and all who die, the overall likelihood is

$$L = \prod_{\mathcal{D}} \exp\left[-\int_{x_i}^{y_i} \mu_s\,ds\right] \cdot \mu_{y_i} \cdot \prod_{\mathcal{W}} \exp\left[-\int_{x_i}^{z_i} \mu_s\,ds\right], \tag{6.28}$$

where the first product considers all who died, and the second considers all who withdrew. (6.28) can be written more compactly as

$$L = \prod_{i=1}^{n} \exp\left[-\int_{x_i}^{w_i} \mu_s \, ds\right] \cdot (\mu_{w_i})^{a_i}, \tag{6.28a}$$

where w_i is either y_i or z_i, as appropriate, and the indicator variable a_i is 1 if person i died, and 0 if person i withdrew.

Then

$$\ell = \ln L = \sum_{i=1}^{n} \left[a_i \ln \mu_{w_i} - \int_{x_i}^{w_i} \mu_s \, ds\right], \tag{6.29}$$

and we would proceed to solve (6.29) for the maximum likelihood estimates of the parameters of μ.

6.4.3 INCOMPLETE DATA, GROUPED DEATHS, EXACT AGE AT WITHDRAWAL

As a final example, let us explore a case commonly encountered by actuaries in a mortality study of individual life insurance policyholders. Using terminology given by Batten [2], we assume an observation period from policy anniversaries in calendar year Z to those in year $Z + M$. We use insuring ages, so that all entrants into the study do so at an integral age, and we further assume that all withdrawals occur on policy anniversaries, hence integral ages. Deaths are recorded as to the insuring age last anniversary at death.

Let n_x be the number of entrants into the study at age x, including those who enter when the study begins (the so-called "starters"). Let w_x be the number of withdrawals at age x, and let θ_x be the number of deaths in the interval $[x, x + 1]$. Most of the w_x are "enders", i.e., those alive when the study closes. a is the lowest age at which there is any recorded data, and h is the highest such age.

Our approach in this example will be to consider the likelihood of the result for the interval $[j, j + 1]$, and then combine all intervals for the overall likelihood, rather than the individual person approach of the two previous examples. The number of persons entering the interval $[j, j + 1]$ is

$$A_j = \sum_{x=a}^{j} (n_x - w_x - \theta_{x-1}) = \sum_{x=a}^{j} (n_x - w_x - \theta_x) + \theta_j,$$

so that

$$A_j - \theta_j = \sum_{x=a}^{j} (n_x - w_x - \theta_x).$$

The likelihood of θ_j deaths in this interval, out of A_j entering the interval, is proportional to the binomial probability for this event, the constant involved in the probability being unnecessary in maximum likelihood estimation. Thus

$$L_j = (q_j)^{\theta_j}(1 - q_j)^{A_j - \theta_j}. \tag{6.30}$$

The overall likelihood is

$$L = \prod_{j=a}^{h} L_j = \prod_{j=a}^{h} (q_j)^{\theta_j}(1 - q_j)^{A_j - \theta_j}, \tag{6.31}$$

and the log likelihood is

$$\ell = \sum_{j=a}^{h} \theta_j \ln q_j - \sum_{j=a}^{h} (A_j - \theta_j) \int_{j}^{j+1} \mu_s \, ds. \tag{6.32}$$

Since $q_j = 1 - \exp\left[-\int_{j}^{j+1} \mu_s \, ds\right]$, the first term does not simplify very much, and the resulting likelihood equations will have to be solved numerically. Alternatively, (6.32) can be maximized directly by computer subroutine.

The examples presented in this section are reviewed in the exercises.

6.5
PIECE-WISE PARAMETRIC GRADUATION (SPLINES)

In all cases considered so far in this chapter, a *single* functional form has been used to estimate t_x over the entire range of the data under consideration. In many applications, if the range of the data is broad, it is not possible to achieve a satisfactory graduation with a single functional form. In such cases, functions can be fit over subranges of the data, with special attention paid to the manner in which adjacent fitted functions meet each other. The general name for this approach is graduation by *splines*.

A fundamental characteristic of graduation by splines is that the subrange fitted functions can be of simpler mathematical form than would be the case for a function fitted over the entire range. We will consider only third degree polynomial functions, and will fit our cubic spline to the initial estimates u_x by least squares.

The interested reader can pursue spline theory in general, and its application to graduation, in DeBoor [10], Greville [17], and McCutcheon [44] and [45].

We make the following preliminary observations on this graduation method:

1. The sequence of revised estimates v_x is given by a function of x which is called a spline.

2. The spline is composed of two or more successive cubic curves, or *arcs*, which will join each other smoothly.

3. It will not be required that $v_x = u_x$ at any particular value of x.

4. Values of u_x need not be available at all values of x for which v_x is desired. If this is the case, then the spline is an *interpolant,* as well as a revision of initial estimates.

5. The parameters of the spline will be determined by a least-squares fit to the initial estimates u_x.

6.5.1 THE LEAST-SQUARES CUBIC

The extension from linear least-squares fit to fitting a least-squares cubic is quite easy. Since we will be making use of this technique, we will now briefly review it.

Suppose we have initial estimates u_x for values of x in the range $[a, b]$, and our prior opinion about t_x suggests that the revised estimates v_x be expressed as the cubic which best fits u_x in the least-squares sense. Then we define

$$SS = \sum_{x=a}^{b} w_x(u_x - v_x)^2 = \sum_{x=a}^{b} w_x(u_x - c_1 - c_2x - c_3x^2 - c_4x^3)^2, \qquad (6.33)$$

where, as before, w_x is a suitably chosen weight, possibly the reciprocal of the approximate variance of U_x. The four partial derivatives of SS, with respect to c_1, c_2, c_3, c_4, equated to zero, produce the normal equations which solve for the least-squares estimates $\hat{c}_1$, $\hat{c}_2$, $\hat{c}_3$, $\hat{c}_4$. We will review these equations again in the exercises, and show that they are represented by the matrix equation

$$\mathbf{x'wxc} = \mathbf{x'wu}. \qquad (6.34)$$

6.5.2 A TWO-ARC CUBIC SPLINE

Now suppose we find that a single cubic does not adequately represent our prior opinion about t_x over the range $[a, b]$, but that an adequate representation can be obtained by using *two* cubics which join at $x = k$. k is called a *knot,* and need not be a value of x for which a value of u_x exists. Then our two-arc spline v_x, expressing the graduated values, is

$$v_x = \begin{cases} p_0(x) & \text{for } a \leq x \leq k \\ p_1(x) & \text{for } k \leq x \leq b \end{cases} \qquad (6.35)$$

and (6.33), adapted to this case, is

$$SS = \sum_{a}^{b} w_x(u_x - v_x)^2 = \sum_{a}^{h} w_x[u_x - p_0(x)]^2 + \sum_{h+1}^{b} w_x[u_x - p_1(x)]^2, \qquad (6.36)$$

where h is the greatest value of x less than (or equal to) k at which a value of u_x exists.

To obtain the desired smooth junction of $p_0(x)$ and $p_1(x)$, we will require that they meet with equal ordinates and equal first and second derivatives. That is

$$p_0(k) = p_1(k), \tag{6.37a}$$

$$p_0'(k) = p_1'(k), \tag{6.37b}$$

and
$$p_0''(k) = p_1''(k). \tag{6.37c}$$

Since $p_0(x)$ and $p_1(x)$ are cubics, they are internally twice differentiable; conditions (6.37) assure that the entire spline is twice differentiable.

We let

$$p_0(x) = c_1 + c_2 x + c_3 x^2 + c_4 x^3 \tag{6.38a}$$

and

$$p_1(x) = c_1 + c_2 x + c_3 x^2 + c_4 x^3 + c_5 (x - k)^3. \tag{6.38b}$$

That (6.38a) and (6.38b) satisfy conditions (6.37) is easily verified, and is left to the exercises.

Substituting (6.38a) and (6.38b) into (6.36) produces

$$SS = \sum_a^h w_x [u_x - c_1 - c_2 x - c_3 x^2 - c_4 x^3]^2$$

$$+ \sum_{h+1}^b w_x [u_x - c_1 - c_2 x - c_3 x^2 - c_4 x^3 - c_5 (x - k)^3]^2. \tag{6.39}$$

6.5.3 THE THREE-ARC CASE

Let the range $[a, b]$ be divided into three subranges by two internal knots, at $x = k_1$ and $x = k_2$. Then

$$v_x = \begin{cases} p_0(x) & \text{for } a \leq x \leq k_1 \\ p_1(x) & \text{for } k_1 \leq x \leq k_2 \\ p_2(x) & \text{for } k_2 \leq x \leq b. \end{cases} \tag{6.40}$$

In addition to conditions (6.37), with k replaced by k_1, we also have

$$p_1(k_2) = p_2(k_2),$$

$$p_1'(k_2) = p_2'(k_2), \tag{6.41}$$

and
$$p_1''(k_2) = p_2''(k_2).$$

With $p_0(x)$ already given by (6.38a), and $p_1(x)$ given by (6.38b), with k replaced by k_1, we now define

$$p_2(x) = c_1 + c_2x + c_3x^2 + c_4x^3 + c_5(x - k_1)^3 + c_6(x - k_2)^3. \quad (6.38c)$$

That $p_1(x)$ and $p_2(x)$ satisfy conditions (6.41) is again clear. Now we have

$$SS = \sum_{a}^{h_1} w_x[u_x - p_0(x)]^2 + \sum_{h_1+1}^{h_2} w_x[u_x - p_1(x)]^2 + \sum_{h_2+1}^{b} w_x[u_x - p_2(x)]^2, \quad (6.42)$$

where h_1 is the greatest value of x less than (or equal to) k_1 at which a value of u_x exists, and h_2 is similarly defined with respect to k_2. Substituting our expressions for $p_0(x)$, $p_1(x)$ and $p_2(x)$ into (6.42), we obtain

$$SS = \sum_{a}^{h_1} w_x[u_x - c_1 - c_2x - c_3x^2 - c_4x^3]^2$$

$$+ \sum_{h_1+1}^{h_2} w_x[u_x - c_1 - c_2x - c_3x^2 - c_4x^3 - c_5(x - k_1)^3]^2 \quad (6.43)$$

$$+ \sum_{h_2+1}^{b} w_x[u_x - c_1 - c_2x - c_3x^2 - c_4x^3 - c_5(x - k_1)^3 - c_6(x - k_2)^3]^2.$$

6.5.4 THE GENERAL CASE

Let the range $[a, b]$ be divided into $(n + 1)$ subranges by n internal knots, at $x = k_1$, $k_2, \ldots, k_n$. Let $h_1, h_2, \ldots, h_n$ be defined as above. Then

$$v_x = \begin{cases} p_0(x) & \text{for } a \le x \le k_1 \\ \vdots \\ p_i(x) & \text{for } k_i \le x \le k_{i+1} \\ \vdots \\ p_n(x) & \text{for } k_n \le x \le b. \end{cases} \quad (6.44)$$

The total conditions imposed on the $p_i(x)$ are

$$p_{i-1}(k_i) = p_i(k_i),$$
$$p'_{i-1}(k_i) = p'_i(k_i), \quad (6.45)$$

and

$$p''_{i-1}(k_i) = p''_i(k_i),$$

for $i = 1, 2, \ldots, n$.

Analogous to (6.38c) for the three-arc case, we have, in general,

$$p_i(x) = p_0(x) + c_5(x - k_1)^3 + \cdots + c_{i+4}(x - k_i)^3, \quad (6.46)$$

for $i = 1, 2, \ldots, n$.

Finally, the least-squares function to be minimized is

$$SS = \sum_{a}^{h_1} w_x[u_x - c_1 - c_2 x - c_3 x^2 - c_4 x^3]^2$$

$$+ \sum_{h_1+1}^{h_2} w_x[u_x - c_1 - c_2 x - c_3 x^2 - c_4 x^3 - c_5(x - k_1)^3]^2 + \cdots \qquad (6.47)$$

$$+ \sum_{h_n+1}^{b} w_x[u_x - c_1 - \cdots - c_5(x - k_1)^3 - \cdots - c_{n+4}(x - k_n)^3]^2.$$

6.5.5 THE LEAST-SQUARES EQUATIONS

In Section 6.5.1 (and Exercise 6–25), we saw that the equations which solve for the parameters of v_x that minimize SS are represented by

$$\mathbf{x'wxc} = \mathbf{x'wu}, \qquad (6.34)$$

where the matrix $\mathbf{x}$ was $(m \times 4)$, there being m values of u_x, at $x = a, \ldots, b$.

Now (6.34) can stand as the general representation of the least-squares normal equations, with $\mathbf{x}$ being appropriately defined. For the two-arc case, we can see that $\mathbf{x}$ is $(m \times 5)$, specifically

$$\begin{bmatrix} 1 & a & a^2 & a^3 & 0 \\ \vdots & \vdots & \vdots & \vdots & \vdots \\ 1 & h & h^2 & h^3 & 0 \\ 1 & h+1 & (h+1)^2 & (h+1)^3 & (h+1-k)^3 \\ \vdots & \vdots & \vdots & \vdots & \vdots \\ 1 & b & b^2 & b^3 & (b-k)^3 \end{bmatrix}. \qquad (6.48)$$

The normal equations for the two-arc case come from differentiating (6.39) with respect to each c_i, equating each such derivative to zero. In the exercises, we will show that these equations are indeed represented by (6.34) with $\mathbf{x}$ defined by (6.48).

Similarly, the normal equations for the three-arc case come from differentiating (6.43) with respect to c_i, for $i = 1, 2, \ldots, 6$, equating each such derivative to zero. Again these equations are represented by (6.34), this time with $\mathbf{x}$ given by

$$\begin{bmatrix} 1 & a & a^2 & a^3 & 0 & 0 \\ \vdots & \vdots & \vdots & \vdots & \vdots & \vdots \\ 1 & h_1 & h_1^2 & h_1^3 & 0 & 0 \\ 1 & h_1+1 & (h_1+1)^2 & (h_1+1)^3 & (h_1+1-k_1)^3 & 0 \\ \vdots & \vdots & \vdots & \vdots & \vdots & \vdots \\ 1 & h_2 & h_2^2 & h_2^3 & (h_2-k_1)^3 & 0 \\ 1 & h_2+1 & (h_2+1)^2 & (h_2+1)^3 & (h_2+1-k_1)^3 & (h_2+1-k_2)^3 \\ \vdots & \vdots & \vdots & \vdots & \vdots & \vdots \\ 1 & b & b^2 & b^3 & (b-k_1)^3 & (b-k_2)^3 \end{bmatrix}. \qquad (6.49)$$

The extension to the general case should now be clear.

6.5.6 THE KNOTS

We should discuss briefly the issue of the number and location of the knots used in a spline graduation. There are really no fixed rules for determining this, so an element of judgment must inevitably enter in. Scrutinizing a graph of u_x for major changes of shape should give some indication.

Intuitively, as the number of knots increases, the fitted spline v_x will approach u_x. Certainly if there are only four values of u_x in the subrange $[k_i, k_{i+1}]$, then $p_i(x) = u_x$, the no-graduation case. Conversely, too few knots might not produce an acceptable graduation.

Since our objective is to minimize SS, which can be interpreted as a χ^2 statistic (see Section 2.7.2), the resulting value of SS can be used as a comparative measure of the success of the graduation. It is interesting to note that judicious relocation of the knots can sometimes be more effective in reducing the magnitude of SS than would be obtained by adding another knot. An interesting possibility is to consider SS as a function of the knot values, as well as the parameters of v_x, and make the selection of the knots part of the minimization process, with it understood that the knots are constrained to lie in the interval $[a, b]$.

6.6
SUMMARY

In this chapter we have explored the types of functional forms that have been used to model mortality data, and have examined approaches to determining the parameters of those forms. In particular, we have found a way of applying the standard linear regression technique to the non-linear Makeham form.

The approach of Section 6.4 is of special interest. This method produces a parametric estimate of the sequence t_x without the preliminary determination of a sequence of initial estimates. The approach embraces the philosophy mentioned in Section 5.8 of coordinating the estimation procedure with the characteristics of the original sample data. In addition, this approach renders unnecessary the making of simplifying assumptions, such as the exponential, uniform, or Balducci distributions, during the estimation process. With the computing facilities that we have at our disposal, this approach could well see greater use in the future. We have given only a brief description in this text, with references for those who wish to investigate it further.

The spline method is presented as an alternative to fitting a single function over the entire range of the data.

In all methods of this chapter, the graduated values v_x are given by a continuous function of x. Thus they are available at all x, even if only desired at, say, integral values. A characteristic of these methods, therefore, is that graduated values can be obtained at more values of x than those for which u_x values were given.

In many studies, especially general population studies, the u_x initial estimates are sometimes available only at quinquennial values of x. In such cases, the methods of this chapter interpolate for additional estimates, as well as revise the initial ones. Interpolation methods of graduation, similar to our cubic spline method but embodying different assumptions and expressed in different forms, have long been used. Because of their popularity in actuarial graduations, they are explored in depth in the following chapter.

EXERCISES

6.1 Introduction; 6.2 The Functional Forms

6–1 The following data are taken from a mortality table graduated to the Gompertz form. Determine the values of c and g, to three decimal places.

x	q_x	x	q_x
65	.02875	68	.03598
66	.03099	69	.03876
67	.03339		

6–2 Convert the rates in Exercise 6–1 to forces of mortality by formula (6.3), and calculate c from these forces.

6–3 Derive (6.9) from (6.7a).

6–4 The following data is taken from a table graduated to the Weibull form, with $a = 0$. Determine the values of n and k.

x	μ_x	x	μ_x
30	.00065	33	.00104
31	.00076	34	.00121
32	.00089		

6–5 The following values of $\ln p_x$ fit the Weibull form with integral n. Find the values of n and k.

x	$\ln p_x$	x	$\ln p_x$
20	−.001261	23	−.001657
21	−.001387	24	−.001801
22	−.001519		

6–6 The following values of u_x are observed forces of mortality. On the same paper, graph $\log u_x$ and $\log \Delta u_x$ against x. Is this data more compatible with a Gompertz or a Makeham form?

x	u_x	x	u_x
20	.00267	50	.01374
30	.00374	60	.03245
40	.00653		

6–7 Makeham's Second Law is $\mu_x = A + Hx + Bc^x$, or $p_x = sw^{2x+1}g^{c^x(c-1)}$.

   a) What function of μ_x is a linear function of x?

   b) What function of p_x, analogous to (6.16), is constant? What is that constant?

6.3 Techniques of Curve-Fitting

6–8 For a certain value of A in Makeham's form, it is found that log $(\mu_x - A)$ is linear, and that $\mu_{20} - A = .001$ and $\mu_{40} - A = .010$. Find the value of log B.

6–9 A graph of log μ_x against log x is found to be linear. If $\mu_{20} = .001$ and $\mu_{70} = .010$, find the Weibull constant k, using the approximate values of log $2 = .3$, log $3 = .4$, log $7 = .8$.

6–10 Determine the Makeham constants by a collocation fit to the following values:

$$p_{30} = .998 \quad p_{45} = .994 \quad p_{60} = .977$$

6–11 To the data of Exercise 6–10, add the value $p_{75} = .881$. Solve by collocation for the parameters s, w, g, and c in Makeham's Second Law, given in Exercise 6–7.

6–12 The following data are initial estimates of forces of mortality, to which we wish to fit the Gompertz form by unweighted simple linear regression.

x	u_x	x	u_x
51.5	.00462	56.5	.00697
52.5	.00508	57.5	.00758
53.5	.00552	58.5	.00829
54.5	.00598	59.5	.00910
55.5	.00645	60.5	.00998

   a) From equations (6.21), what are $\hat{a}$ and $\hat{b}$?

   b) What are the implied estimates of the Gompertz parameters B and c? (Remember these are not the least-squares estimates.)

6–13 Fit the data of Exercise 6–12 to the Weibull form by the same method.

   a) What are $\hat{a}$ and $\hat{b}$?

   b) What are the implied estimates of the Weibull parameters n and k?

6–14

$$\text{Let } \mathbf{u}^* = \begin{bmatrix} u_1^* \\ \vdots \\ u_n^* \end{bmatrix}, \ \mathbf{w} = \begin{bmatrix} w_1 & & \bigcirc \\ & \ddots & \\ \bigcirc & & \ddots \\ & & w_n \end{bmatrix}, \ \mathbf{b} = \begin{bmatrix} a \\ b \end{bmatrix}, \text{ and } \mathbf{x}^* = \begin{bmatrix} 1 & 1 \\ 1 & 2 \\ \vdots & \vdots \\ \vdots & \vdots \\ 1 & n \end{bmatrix}.$$

a) Write the matrix $\mathbf{x}^*\mathbf{b}$.

b) Express (6.20) in the above matrix-vector notation. Note that this is for the case when $x^* = x$.

6–15 a) Show that the right hand sides of equations (6.21) are given by the vector $\mathbf{x}^{*\prime}\mathbf{w}\mathbf{u}^*$.

b) Show that the four coefficients of a and b on the left side of (6.21) are given by the matrix $\mathbf{x}^{*\prime}\mathbf{w}\mathbf{x}^*$.

c) Hence express (6.21) as a matrix equation.

6–16 If $x^* = \log x$, as in the case of a Weibull fit, what changes must be made in order that the results of Exercises 6–14 and 6–15 will be correct?

6–17 What is the vector $\mathbf{x}^*$ for Exercise 6–12?

6–18 What is the vector $\mathbf{x}^*$ for Exercise 6–13?

6–19 Verify the normal equations given by (6.23).

*6–20 Let us use the data of Exercise 6–12, and the initial estimates $A_0 = .002$, $B_0 = .00005$, $c_0 = 1.08$, to fit Makeham's form by the method of Section 6.3.4. Let $w_x = 1$ for all x.

a) Calculate the needed values of c_0^x, c_0^{x-1}, and c_0^{2x-1}.

b) Calculate the matrix of coefficients for the left side of equations (6.23).

c) Calculate the vector of constants for the right side of (6.23).

d) Solve for d_A, d_B and d_c, and hence A_1, B_1 and c_1.

e) Repeat the process recursively to obtain the least-squares estimates of A, B and c.

6.4   An Interesting Variation

6–21 Suppose the force of mortality is assumed to be a linear function of age, $\mu_x = bx$. Consider a sample of n persons all coming under observation at age x. Each is observed to die while under observation, with person i dying at age y_i.

a) Evaluate the log likelihood, given by (6.27).

b) What is the maximum likelihood estimate of b?

6–22 a) Evaluate (6.29) assuming a Gompertz form for μ.

b) Derive the equations to be solved for the maximum likelihood estimates of B and c. Note that a numerical solution will be required.

6–23 Suppose that $\mu_x = \dfrac{b}{x}$, a decreasing force of mortality, which is believed to be appropriate for male lives in the late 20's.

a) Derive the expression for q_j.

b) Show that ℓ, as defined by (6.32), as a function of b, can be written as

$$\ell = \sum_{j=a}^{h} \left\{ \theta_j \{ \ln [(j+1)^b - j^b] \} + (A_j - \theta_j) \ln j^b - A_j \ln (j+1)^b \right\}.$$

c) Find $\dfrac{d\ell}{db}$. Note that a numerical solution of $\dfrac{d\ell}{db} = 0$ is again required.

6.5 Piece-Wise Parametric Graduation

6–24 a) Take the derivative of (6.33) with respect to c_1, and equate to zero. This is the first normal equation.

b) Similarly, with respect to c_2.

c) Similarly, with respect to c_3.

d) Similarly, with respect to c_4.

6–25 Define the matrix $\mathbf{x}$ and the diagonal matrix $\mathbf{w}$ as follows:

$$\mathbf{x} = \begin{bmatrix} 1 & a & a^2 & a^3 \\ 1 & a+1 & (a+1)^2 & (a+1)^3 \\ \vdots & \vdots & \vdots & \vdots \\ 1 & b & b^2 & b^3 \end{bmatrix} \qquad \mathbf{w} = \begin{bmatrix} w_a & & & \bigcirc \\ & w_{a+1} & & \\ & & \ddots & \\ \bigcirc & & & w_b \end{bmatrix}$$

a) Show that the vector $\mathbf{x}'\mathbf{wu}$ contains the four constants on the right sides of the normal equations.

b) Show that the matrix $\mathbf{x}'\mathbf{wx}$ contains the coefficients of the four c_i on the left sides of the normal equations.

c) Thus show that the normal equations are represented as $\mathbf{x}'\mathbf{wxc} = \mathbf{x}'\mathbf{wu}$.

6–26 Show that $p_0(x)$ and $p_1(x)$, as defined by (6.38a) and (6.38b), satisfy (6.37).

6–27 Show that $p_1(x)$, defined by (6.38b) with k replaced by k_1, and $p_2(x)$, defined by (6.38c), satisfy conditions (6.41).

6–28 For the general case, with n internal knots, how many parameters are there to be determined?

6–29 Suppose we wish to fit a *quadratic* spline over the range [20, 89], with three internal knots at $x = 29.7$, 62.5 and 80.6. For a quadratic spline, we require arcs to join with equal ordinates and first derivatives.

a) How should we define $p_1(x)$?

b) How should we define $p_3(x)$?

c) Write the expression for SS, in a form analogous to (6.47).

6–30 The first four normal equations to yield the least squares estimates of (6.39), the two-arc case, are obtained as in Exercise 6–24.

a) What is the fifth normal equation?

b) Now repeat Exercise 6–25 to show that these equations are represented by (6.34), with $\mathbf{x}$ defined by (6.48).

6–31 Repeat Exercise 6–30 for the three-arc case. Again the first four normal equations are obtained as in Exercise 6–24.

a) What is the fifth normal equation?

b) What is the sixth normal equation?

c) Show that these equations are represented by (6.34), with $\mathbf{x}$ defined by (6.49).

6–32 For our four-arc quadratic spline of Exercise 6–29,

a) Define the matrix $\mathbf{x}$.

b) For the final time, show that the normal equations obtained from your SS given by part (c) of Exercise 6–29 are represented by (6.34), with $\mathbf{x}$ defined by part (a).

SMOOTH-JUNCTION INTERPOLATION

7

7.1
INTRODUCTION

In the spline method of Chapter 6, we considered the case of u_x values available at, say, quinquennial values of x only, so that the fitted function v_x interpolated for intermediate values. A characteristic of our method of determining the spline v_x was that *all* values of u_x were used in the least-squares fit.

As an alternative, the interpolating arc could be determined by considering only a limited number of consecutive u_x values. This property distinguishes the interpolation method of this chapter from that of Chapter 6. In addition, different derivation approaches will be used; in particular, least-squares fitting is not used.

We presume that the reader is somewhat familiar with polynomial interpolation from a study of numerical methods. In particular, the central-difference approach, described in Chapter 4 of Kellison [34], is used here. More specifically, we use the Everett form of such interpolation formulas, discussed by Kellison in Section 4.7.

A characteristic of smooth-junction interpolation is that a separate interpolating arc is used for each subrange defined by the sequence of initial estimates u_x. Thus, in the terminology of Section 6.5, each u_x is a knot for this method. As in the general spline method, adjacent arcs will be made to join smoothly, justifying the name of this method. In some cases, however, only ordinates and first derivatives of adjacent arcs will be equal; in other cases, equal second derivatives will also be required.

To summarize the nature of graduation by smooth-junction interpolation:

1. Graduated values v_x are desired at arguments intermediate to those for which u_x is available.

2. An interpolating arc is determined in Everett form for the subrange $[x, x + 1]$, where a change of scale has been made, based on a certain (even) number of initial estimates, called *pivotal points*. (Section 7.2.1)

3. Adjacent arcs will join with equal ordinates and (at least) first derivatives. (Section 7.2.2)

4. It may or may not be true that $v_x = u_x$. (Section 7.2.3)

5. An important concept in the derivation of these formulas is the idea of degree of exactness. (Section 7.2.4)

6. In most cases, a preliminary problem is the determination of the pivotal points. (Section 7.5)

The discussion of these formulas in the remainder of the chapter is largely drawn from the work of Boom (see Greville, *et. al.* [16]).

7.2
PROPERTIES OF SMOOTH-JUNCTION INTERPOLATION FORMULAS

In this section we will expand on the general description of these formulas summarized in the preceding section.

7.2.1 THE FORM OF THE FORMULAS

All the interpolation formulas which we consider can be written in the general Everett form

$$v_{x+s} = F(s)u_{x+1} + F(t)u_x, \quad 0 \le s \le 1; \quad t = 1 - s \tag{7.1}$$

where

$$F(s) = A(s) + B(s)\,\delta^2 + C(s)\,\delta^4 + \cdots. \tag{7.2}$$

The sequence of given values, $\ldots, u_{x-1}, u_x, u_{x+1}, \ldots$, are equally spaced, and may be regarded (after a change of scale, if necessary) as occurring at unit intervals; v_{x+s} denotes the interpolated (graduated) value for the argument $x + s$. We use different letters for the given values and the interpolated values, since the formulas we shall consider will include some for which $v_x \ne u_x$. Such formulas smooth (graduate) the given values, as well as interpolate for intermediate values.

Whereas $A(s)$, $B(s)$, etc. are ordinary functions of s, it should be noted that $F(s)$ is not a function, but rather an *operator* on u_x, having functions of s as coefficients of the various powers of δ.

Note that, if $F(s)$ ends with the term containing δ^{2m}, the formula gives, within the interval $[x, x + 1]$, values of a function v_{x+s} in terms of s and the $2m + 2$ values $u_{x-m}, u_{x-m+1}, \ldots, u_{x+m+1}$; it is then called a "$(2m + 2)$-point interpolation formula".

Writing the interpolation formula in the general Everett form involves the assumption that the formula is *symmetrical*. By a symmetrical interpolation formula we mean one that gives the same interpolated value for any given argument whether we interpolate forwards or backwards. In other words, merely reversing the order of the given values u_x does not change the results obtained. Any interpolation formula in which the interpolated value is expressible as some linear combination of neighboring given values (as is the case with all of the formulas that we shall consider) can be written in the general Everett form if and only if it is symmetrical. Since all interpolation formulas commonly used by actuaries are symmetrical, we are justified in assuming this general form.

The familiar two-point formula for linear interpolation is the simplest example of an interpolation formula in Everett form. In this case, $F(s) = s$, so that

$$v_{x+s} = su_{x+1} + tu_x, \quad 0 \le s \le 1, \quad t = 1 - s.$$

Whereas $A(s)$, $B(s)$, etc., could, in theory, be any continuous functions of s having the required number of derivatives, it is usual to take them as polynomials in s, typically polynomials of low degree. In practice, the interpolation formula is required to satisfy certain conditions, as described in the remainder of this section, and we shall see that these conditions severely restrict the choice of these polynomials. To the extent that each polynomial is not completely determined, it is usual to take it as the polynomial of lowest degree satisfying the conditions imposed. This will become clearer as we consider some particular cases.

7.2.2 THE SMOOTH-JUNCTION PROPERTY

The use of the general Everett form terminating with a specified order of differences (usually second or fourth), and choosing polynomials for the functions $A(s)$, etc., imply that v_{x+s} is itself some polynomial in s, which, in effect, we use to calculate interpolated values in the interval $[x, x + 1]$. It is useful to denote $x + s$ by the single letter y, and to consider v_y as a function of y. In this case, v_y is a piece-wise polynomial function, or a spline, as we called it in Chapter 6. Then

$$\vdots$$
$$v_y = \begin{array}{ll} p_{x-1}(y) & \text{for } x - 1 \le y \le x \\ p_x(y) & \text{for } x \le y \le x + 1 \end{array}. \tag{7.3}$$
$$\vdots$$

In general, $p_{x-1}(y)$ is a different polynomial from $p_x(y)$.

We may thus think of the graph of v_y as being composed of a number of polynomial arcs laid end to end, joining at the integers. Of course the ordinates of adjacent arcs must be equal at the argument x, i.e., $p_{x-1}(x) = p_x(x)$, for otherwise v_y would have a discontinuity at $y = x$. To assure that $p_{x-1}(x) = p_x(x)$, we require that

$$v_{x-1+s}|_{s=1} = v_{x+s}|_{s=0}. \tag{7.4}$$

In terms of the general Everett formula, we have

$$v_{x-1+s|s=1} = A(1)u_x + B(1)\,\delta^2 u_x + C(1)\,\delta^4 u_x + \cdots$$
$$+ A(0)u_{x-1} + B(0)\,\delta^2 u_{x-1} + C(0)\,\delta^4 u_{x-1} + \cdots$$

and

$$v_{x+s|s=0} = A(0)u_{x+1} + B(0)\,\delta^2 u_{x+1} + C(0)\,\delta^4 u_{x+1} + \cdots$$
$$+ A(1)u_x + B(1)\,\delta^2 u_x + C(1)\,\delta^4 u_x + \cdots .$$

Equating these two expressions, and cancelling terms that are common to both, gives

$$A(0)u_{x-1} + B(0)\,\delta^2 u_{x-1} + C(0)\,\delta^4 u_{x-1} + \cdots$$
$$= A(0)u_{x+1} + B(0)\,\delta^2 u_{x+1} + C(0)\,\delta^4 u_{x+1} + \cdots . \tag{7.5}$$

This equality will hold for *all* values of u_x if and only if

$$A(0) = B(0) = C(0) = \cdots = 0. \tag{7.6}$$

Thus the conditions given by (7.6) must be satisfied by our eventual $A(s)$, $B(s)$, etc.

To achieve the desired overall smoothness for v_y, we require matching of first derivatives of adjacent arcs, as well as matching of ordinates. In other words, we require that $p'_{x-1}(x) = p'_x(x)$. We might also require that $p''_{x-1}(x) = p''_x(x)$. If ordinates and first derivatives *only* are matched, the resulting formulas are said to be *tangential,* as suggested by Beers [3]. If second derivatives, as well as ordinates and first derivatives, are matched, the resulting formulas are said to be *osculatory.*

To assure the matching of first derivatives, we require that

$$v'_{x-1+s|s=1} = v'_{x+s|s=0}, \tag{7.7}$$

where the differentiation is with respect to s. We use $F'(s)$ to denote differentiation of the operator $F(s)$ with respect to s, obtaining

$$F'(s) = A'(s) + B'(s)\,\delta^2 + C'(s)\,\delta^4 + \cdots . \tag{7.8}$$

Note carefully that, since $t = 1 - s$, then

$$\frac{d}{ds}F(t) = -F'(t). \tag{7.9}$$

Now we substitute the general Everett form given by (7.1) into (7.7), being careful to negate each $F'(t)$. Then (7.7) gives

$$F'(1)u_x - F'(0)u_{x-1} = F'(0)u_{x+1} - F'(1)u_x, \tag{7.10}$$

or

$$2F'(1)u_x = F'(0)(u_{x+1} + u_{x-1}) = F'(0)(2 + \delta^2)u_x,$$

making use of the identity $\delta^2 u_x = u_{x+1} - 2u_x + u_{x-1}$. Thus the interpolation formula will be tangential if and only if

$$2F'(1) = F'(0)(2 + \delta^2). \tag{7.11}$$

Similarly, we assure matching of second derivatives by requiring that

$$v''_{x-1+s|s=1} = v''_{x+s|s=0}, \tag{7.12}$$

which implies that

$$F''(1)u_x + F''(0)u_{x-1} = F''(0)u_{x+1} + F''(1)u_x, \tag{7.13}$$

or

$$F''(0)(u_{x+1} - u_{x-1}) = 0. \tag{7.14}$$

Thus the interpolation formula will be osculatory if and only if $F(s)$ satisfies both condition (7.11) and the additional condition $F''(0) = 0$ (i.e., $A''(0) = B''(0) = \cdots = 0$), implied by (7.14).

7.2.3 THE SMOOTHING VS. REPRODUCING PROPERTY

In Observation (4) of Section 7.1, we remained flexible on the issue of whether or not our formulas would produce $v_x = u_x$ at integral x (where, in our model, u_x is assumed to exist). Formulas which do have this property are called *reproducing;* those which do not have this property are called *smoothing,* since the principal reason for having $v_x \neq u_x$ is to improve the smoothness of the overall v_x sequence. (In older texts, smoothing formulas were called ''modified'', and reproducing formulas were called ''unmodified''.) Since (7.6) must be satisfied to assure continuity, we have

$$v_x = v_{x+s|s=0} = A(1)u_x + B(1)\,\delta^2 u_x + C(1)\,\delta^4 u_x + \cdots . \tag{7.15}$$

For a formula to be reproducing, $v_x = u_x$, regardless of the values of u_x (and their differences). (7.15) shows that this will be true if and only if

$$A(1) = 1 \quad \text{and} \quad B(1) = C(1) = \cdots = 0, \tag{7.16}$$

along with (7.6), of course. In all formulas which we consider, we will use $A(1) = 1$. Clearly the values $B(1), C(1)$, etc., will play a role in determining the departure (if any) of v_x from u_x. For greater simplicity, we will use the notation

$$L = B(1) \quad \text{and} \quad M = C(1).$$

7.2.4 THE DEGREE-OF-EXACTNESS PROPERTY

An important characteristic of an interpolation formula is the degree of polynomials that it interpolates exactly. Thus we say that a formula is exact for degree z if it invariably gives exact results when used to interpolate values of a polynomial of degree z (or less). Note that this has nothing to do with the highest order of differences appearing in $F(s)$, defined by (7.2), but depends instead on the choice of the functions $A(s)$, $B(s)$, etc.

By simple algebraic manipulation, and the identity $\Delta^{2m}u_{y+1} = \Delta^{2m}u_y + \Delta^{2m+1}u_y$, the general Everett form can be expressed as

$$v_{x+s} = [A(s) + A(t)]u_x + A(s)\,\Delta u_x + [B(s) + B(t)]\,\Delta^2 u_{x-1}$$

$$+ B(s)\,\Delta^3 u_{x-1} + [C(s) + C(t)]\,\Delta^4 u_{x-2} + C(s)\,\Delta^5 u_{x-2} + \cdots \tag{7.17}$$

Now (7.17) is in the form of the Gauss forward formula (see Kellison [34], Section 4.3). Therefore our v_{x+s} will be exact for polynomials of degree z or less if and only if it agrees with the Gauss formula up to and including the term involving z^{th} differences. This observation gives us the following table of conditions, with an Everett-form formula being exact for the tabulated degree z if and only if the conditions in the table up to and including the one corresponding to degree z are satisfied.

TABLE OF DEGREE-OF-EXACTNESS CONDITIONS _____

Degree	Condition
0	$A(s) + A(1 - s) = 1$
1	$A(s) = s$
2	$B(s) + B(1 - s) = \frac{1}{2}s(s - 1)$
3	$B(s) = \frac{1}{6}s(s^2 - 1)$
4	$C(s) + C(1 - s) = \frac{1}{24}s(s^2 - 1)(s - 2)$
$\vdots$	$\vdots$

The above table has the interesting property that, whenever a condition corresponding to an odd degree is satisfied, the one corresponding to the preceding even degree is automatically satisfied, and is therefore redundant.

7.3
DERIVATION OF FOUR-POINT FORMULAS

We illustrate the theory developed to this point by deriving some interpolation formulas. As we have seen, a formula will be determined by specifying the properties that we wish it to have. Let us derive four-point formulas to have the following properties:

1. One degree of exactness, i.e., exact for linear functions,

2. Tangential, and

3. A parameter to control the smoothing property.

In light of property (3), we will be deriving a *family* of formulas, with each member of the family defined by the value of its smoothing parameter.

7.3.1 DERIVING THE GENERAL FAMILY

Having decided to derive four-point formulas in Everett form, we have at once $v_{x+s} = F(s)u_{x+1} + F(t)u_x$, with, in this case, $F(s) = A(s) + B(s) \delta^2$. $A(s)$ and $B(s)$ are to be determined.

$A(s) = s$ is immediately determined by the requirement of one degree of exactness; therefore we consider only $B(s)$.

To assure matching of ordinates, (7.6) tells us that we need $B(0) = 0$. Our requirement (3) can be stated as $B(1) = L$.

To assure matching of first derivatives, we evaluate (7.11), with $F(s)$ limited to $A(s) + B(s) \delta^2$, and $A(s) = s$. This results in the two conditions

$$B'(0) = 0 \quad \text{and} \quad B'(1) = \tfrac{1}{2},$$

which are derived in Exercise 7–17.

We now see that the general $B(s)$ for our formulas must satisfy the four conditions

$$B(0) = 0$$
$$B(1) = L$$
$$B'(0) = 0$$
$$B'(1) = \tfrac{1}{2}.$$

(7.18)

We choose for $B(s)$ the polynomial of minimum degree which will satisfy these conditions. Thus $B(s)$ will be of third degree. Applying conditions (7.18) produces

$$B(s) = (3L - \tfrac{1}{2})s^2 + (\tfrac{1}{2} - 2L)s^3,$$

(7.19)

which is verified in Exercise 7–18.

7.3.2 SPECIAL MEMBERS OF THE FAMILY

A formula of special interest is the reproducing member of the family, which, from (7.16), results from setting $L = B(1) = 0$. The resulting $B(s)$ is

$$B(s) = \tfrac{1}{2}s^2(s - 1),$$

(7.20)

and is called the Karup-King formula. In Exercise 7–19 it is shown that this formula also has two degrees of exactness.

Another interesting special case results from setting $L = \tfrac{1}{4}$. The resulting $B(s)$ is

$$B(s) = \tfrac{1}{4}s^2,$$

(7.21)

the only member of the family that is quadratic rather than cubic.

A companion to formula (7.21) would be the formula resulting from $L = \frac{1}{6}$, thereby eliminating the quadratic term in the general $B(s)$, and producing

$$B(s) = \frac{1}{6}s^3. \tag{7.22}$$

This formula is the only member of the family that is osculatory (see Exercise 7–20.)

7.4
DERIVATION OF SIX-POINT FORMULAS

In a manner totally parallel to that of Section 7.3, we now derive a family of six-point formulas to have the following properties:

1. Three degrees of exactness,

2. Osculatory, and

3. A parameter to control the smoothing property.

7.4.1 DERIVING THE GENERAL FAMILY

Because this is completely analogous to the four-point case already considered, we will merely present the results, which the reader should carefully verify.

1. By our decision to use six points, it follows that

$$F(s) = A(s) + B(s)\, \delta^2 + C(s)\, \delta^4.$$

2. The degree-of-exactness requirement determines

$$A(s) = s \quad \text{and} \quad B(s) = \frac{1}{6}s(s^2 - 1).$$

3. Only $C(s)$ must be derived:

   a) The matching ordinate requirement implies $C(0) = 0$.

   b) The smoothness parameter requirement implies $C(1) = M$.

$$\tag{7.23}$$

   c) Matching of first derivatives implies $C'(0) = 0$ and $C'(1) = -\frac{1}{12}$ (see Exercise 7.22).

   d) Matching of second derivatives implies $C''(0) = 0$.

Since we have five specific conditions on $C(s)$, we let it be a fourth degree polynomial. Applying these five conditions given by (7.23), we obtain

$$C(s) = (4M + \tfrac{1}{12})s^3 - (3M + \tfrac{1}{12})s^4, \tag{7.24}$$

which is verified in Exercise 7–23.

7.4.2 SPECIAL MEMBERS OF THE FAMILY

Again the reproducing member of the family can be found from setting $M = 0$ in (7.24), resulting in

$$C(s) = \frac{1}{12}s^3(1 - s).$$ (7.25)

The only member of the family that is cubic rather than quartic is found by setting $M = -\frac{1}{36}$ in (7.24), resulting in

$$C(s) = -\frac{1}{36}s^3,$$ (7.26)

a formula developed by Jenkins [32], and generally considered to produce good results.

The six-point analogy to formula (7.22) would be the formula resulting from $M = -\frac{1}{48}$, thereby eliminating the cubic term in the general $C(s)$, and producing

$$C(s) = -\frac{1}{48}s^4.$$ (7.27)

7.5
DETERMINATION OF THE PIVOTAL POINTS

We have assumed that the given u_x values, the pivotal points in the interpolation formulas, were available at, say, every fifth value of the argument. In this section we briefly describe the determination of these pivotal points.

In some experience mortality studies, particularly general population studies, deaths and "exposures" are tabulated in quinquennial age groups. If the data are available at individual ages, and the interpolation method is to be used, then preliminary grouping is a first step. From this grouped data, pivotal points can then be obtained. One popular method of doing this is to use King's pivotal value formula.

When applied to mortality data, it is usual to develop pivotal values for the deaths and "exposures" separately, dividing the latter into the former to obtain pivotal rates of mortality, upon which the interpolation would then be based. The reason for this is that King's method utilizes quinquennial sums of data; the sum of five mortality *rates* is not a meaningful concept.

Thus we let u_x represent the sequence of data (deaths or exposures), available at all integral x. Let w_x represent the sum of five consecutive values of u_y, centered at x. That is

$$w_x = \sum_{x-2}^{x+2} u_y.$$ (7.28)

King's formula, correct to fifth differences, is

$$u_x^P = .2w_x - .008(w_{x-5} - 2w_x + w_{x+5})$$
$$+ .000896(w_{x-10} - 4w_{x-5} + 6w_x - 4w_{x+5} + w_{x+10}).$$ (7.29)

Generally only the first two terms are used, so the formula is correct to third differences, and becomes

$$u_x^P = .2w_x - .008(w_{x-5} - 2w_x + w_{x+5}). \tag{7.30}$$

(For a derivation of King's pivotal point formula, see Miller [46], page 64.)

We note that (7.30), having a central nature, would not produce a pivotal point corresponding to the first available quinquennial sum, w_a, say. In that case, the advancing formula (correct to second differences only)

$$u_a^P = .2w_a - .008(w_a - 2w_{a+5} + w_{a+10}) \tag{7.31}$$

can be used. Similarly, for the pivotal value corresponding to the last available quinquennial sum, w_b, say, we could use the backward formula (correct to second differences)

$$u_b^P = .2w_b - .008(w_b - 2w_{b-5} + w_{b-10}). \tag{7.32}$$

(For a derivation of (7.31) and (7.32), as well as a derivation of (7.30) adapted to other than quinquennial sums, see Greville, *et. al.* [16], pages 49–50.)

7.6
SUMMARY

In this chapter we have reviewed the popular graduation method of smooth-junction interpolation, deriving entire families of four-point and six-point Everett form interpolation formulas. We saw that such formulas are determined by specifying the properties that we would like them to have, translating those properties into conditions which must be satisfied by the $A(s)$, $B(s)$, etc., functions. These conditions in turn determine the $A(s)$, etc., functions.

Thus the process can be applied to other combinations of properties than those which we illustrated. Several such examples are pursued in the exercises.

EXERCISES ■

7.1   Introduction;   7.2 Properties of Smooth-Junction Interpolation Formulas

7–1   Let us review ordinary central-difference interpolation.

a) If $\delta^4 u_{x+7} = \Delta^4 u_y$, what is y?

b) The Gauss forward formula is

$$v_{x+s} = u_x + c_1 \Delta u_x + c_2 \Delta^2 u_{x-1} + c_3 \Delta^3 u_{x-1} + c_4 \Delta^4 u_{x-2} + \cdots .$$

What are c_1, c_2, c_3, c_4?

c) Everett's formula is

$$v_{x+s} = A(s)u_{x+1} + B(s) \delta^2 u_{x+1} + C(s) \delta^4 u_{x+1} + \cdots$$
$$+ A(1 - s)u_x + B(1 - s) \delta^2 u_x + C(1 - s) \delta^4 u_x + \cdots .$$

What are $A(s)$, $B(s)$, $C(s)$?

7–2 If an Everett form interpolation formula is said to be a ten-point formula, what is the highest power of δ involved in the formula?

7–3 $F(s)$ is said to be an *operator* on u_x. If $u_{x-1} = 4$, $u_x = 7$, and $u_{x+1} = 15$, what is the result of the operation $F(0)u_x$?

7–4 Using the values of u_{x-1}, u_x, and u_{x+1} given in Exercise 7–3, show that, for the familiar two-point formula $v_{x+s} = su_{x+1} + tu_x$,

a) $v_{x-1+s}|_{s=1} = v_{x+s}|_{s=0}$

b) $v'_{x-1+s}|_{s=1} \neq v'_{x+s}|_{s=0}$

7–5 If a polynomial in s, say, $B(s)$, must satisfy five specific (non-redundant) conditions, what is the minimum possible degree that $B(s)$ can be?

7–6 Suppose we have given values u_x at $x = 20, 24, 28, 32, 36, \ldots$ We desire graduated values at all integral x. What values of s will be used in the interpolation?

7–7 Verify equation (7.5).

7–8 Suppose $u_{x-2} = 2$, $u_{x-1} = 5$, $u_x = 7$, $u_{x+1} = 15$, and $u_{x+2} = 22$. Let $A(s) = s$ and $B(s) = \frac{1}{4}(1 - s)$, in a four-point interpolation formula.

a) Show that $v_{x-1+s}|_{s=1} = v_{x+s}|_{s=0}$.

b) What is $B(0)$?

c) How is it that part (a) can be true when $B(0) \neq 0$?

7–9 If an interpolation formula has the properties that

$$v_{x-1+s}|_{s=1} = v_{x+s}|_{s=0},$$

$$v'_{x-1+s}|_{s=1} \neq v'_{x+s}|_{s=0},$$

and $\qquad v''_{x-1+s}|_{s=1} = v''_{x+s}|_{s=0},$

is the formula osculatory?

7–10 Verify equation (7.10), and hence (7.11).

7–11 a) For the two-point formula $v_{x+s} = A(s)u_{x+1} + A(t)u_x$ to be tangential, what specific conditions must $A(s)$ satisfy?

b) Show that it is not possible to find a quadratic $A(s)$ which satisfies these conditions.

c) Find a cubic $A(s)$ which will satisfy these conditions.

7–12 Consider the two-point formula with $A(s) = 4s^3 - 3s^4$.

a) Is the formula tangential or osculatory?

b) Is the formula smoothing or reproducing?

7–13 Can a four-point formula produce $v_x = u_x$ even if $B(1) \neq 0$?

7–14 Let us verify the degree-of-exactness table in Section 7.2.4.

a) Write out v_{x+s} defined by (7.1) and (7.2).

b) Change the central differences to advancing differences.

c) Use the identity in Section 7.2.4 to rearrange your expression in part (b) into (7.17).

d) Match your coefficients of the various powers of Δ to those of the Gauss forward formula. This establishes the table of conditions.

7–15 Verify that if $B(s) = \frac{1}{6}s(s^2 - 1)$, then $B(s) + B(1 - s) = \frac{1}{2}s(s - 1)$.

7–16 What is the additional condition for 5 degrees of exactness?

7.3 Derivation of Four-Point Formulas

7–17 Show that, in the four-point case, $v'_{x-1+s}|_{s=1} = v'_{x+s}|_{s=0}$ will be satisfied for all u_x if $B'(0) = 0$ and $B'(1) = \frac{1}{2}$, given that $A(s) = s$.

7–18 Derive (7.19) from the conditions listed in (7.18).

7–19 Show that the Karup–King formula, given by (7.20), satisfies the condition for two degrees of exactness.

7–20 Verify that the formula given by (7.22) is osculatory.

7–21 Formula (7.22) is osculatory, but not reproducing. Formula (7.20) is reproducing, but not osculatory. Derive the $B(s)$ for a four-point formula that is osculatory *and* reproducing, with one degree of exactness.

7.4 Derivation of Six-Point Formulas

7–22 Derive the result that, for a six-point formula, $v'_{x-1+s}|_{s=1} = v'_{x+s}|_{s=0}$ implies $C'(0) = 0$ and $C'(1) = -\frac{1}{12}$, given that $A(s) = s$ and $B(s) = \frac{1}{6}s(s^2 - 1)$.

7–23 Derive (7.24) from the conditions listed in (7.23).

7–24 Does the reproducing member of the six-point family, given by (7.25), have four degrees of exactness? (c.f., Exercise 7–19) Does *any* member of the family have four degrees of exactness?

7–25 Let us derive a six-point *tangential* formula with four degrees of exactness. (This is called Shovelton's formula.)

a) Since we must have $C(0) = 0$, then $C(1)$ is implied by the degree-of-exactness requirement. What is $C(1)$?

b) What must be $C(\frac{1}{2})$?

c) What conditions are implied by the tangential requirement?

d) Use the above five conditions to derive $C(s)$.

e) Verify that your result satisfies all the desired properties, especially the four degrees-of-exactness requirement.

7–26 Now let us derive a six-point formula with the properties of Shovelton's formula *plus* the osculatory property. (This is called Sprague's formula; it dates from 1880, and was the first published smooth-junction interpolation formula.)

a) What condition, in addition to those of Exercise 7–25, must $C(s)$ satisfy?

b) Derive $C(s)$, and verify that it satisfies all the desired properties.

7–27 Henderson's formula is

$$v_{x+s} = su_{x+1} + \tfrac{1}{6}s(s^2 - 1)(\delta^2 u_{x+1} - \tfrac{1}{6}\delta^4 u_{x+1})$$
$$+ tu_x + \tfrac{1}{6}t(t^2 - 1)(\delta^2 u_x - \tfrac{1}{6}\delta^4 u_x).$$

a) How many degrees of exactness does it have?

b) Is it reproducing or smoothing?

c) Is it tangential or osculatory?

7.5 Determination of the Pivotal Points

7–28 An observed population produces the following data:

Age Group	Exposure	Deaths
23–27	100,000	75
28–32	120,000	100
33–37	200,000	225

Use King's pivotal-point formula, correct to third differences, to determine the pivotal rate of mortality at age 30.

7–29 King's formula, given by (7.30), is a special case of the M-W-A formula, defined by (3.1). When viewed as an M-W-A formula,

a) What is its range?

b) What is its weight?

c) What is its smoothing coefficient?

d) What degree polynomial will it reproduce?

TWO-DIMENSIONAL GRADUATION

8

8.1
INTRODUCTION

Thus far in this text we have been considering the graduation of a one-dimensional sequence of values, defined over an index, such as age for mortality data.

In this chapter we consider the problem of graduating data which is a function of two variables. Thus, in place of a sequence, or vector, of data, we have an array, or matrix. The most common example, at least for actuaries, is the familiar select and ultimate mortality model.

The variables we consider in this model are age at selection, denoted by $[x]$, and duration since selection, denoted by r. Thus $q_{[x]+r}$ is the mortality rate (which we wish to estimate) prevailing at attained age $x + r$ for a person selected at age x. We prefer to retain the notation used throughout this text, so we will use $t_{[x]+r}$ for the true rate, $U_{[x]+r}$ for the estimator random variable of this true rate, $u_{[x]+r}$ as a realization (or observed value) of $U_{[x]+r}$, and $v_{[x]+r}$ as our graduated rate, our revised estimate of $t_{[x]+r}$. Likewise, we will use $n_{[x]+r}$ for exposures.

The basic graduation theory developed and applied in earlier chapters holds equally well in our two-dimensional problem. Thus our revision of initial estimates is guided by our prior opinion about the array of $t_{[x]+r}$, including a concept of smoothness, while simultaneously trying to retain some degree of fit to observed data.

Experience shows that the effect of selection upon prevailing mortality tends to lessen with increasing duration since selection. Thus, whereas we might expect to find, for example,

$$t_{[35]} < t_{[33]+2},$$

we would probably expect to find, for example,

$$t_{[35]+15} \doteq t_{[33]+17}.$$

TABLE 8.1

Age at Selection [x]	Rate at Dur'n 0	Rate at Dur'n 1	Rate at Dur'n 2	Rate at Dur'n 3	Rate at Dur'n 4	Ultimate Rate	Attained Age
30	$t_{[30]}$	$t_{[30]+1}$	$t_{[30]+2}$	$t_{[30]+3}$	$t_{[30]+4}$	t_{35}	35
31	$t_{[31]}$	$t_{[31]+1}$	$t_{[31]+2}$	$t_{[31]+3}$	$t_{[31]+4}$	t_{36}	36
32	$t_{[32]}$	$t_{[32+1]}$	$t_{[32]+2}$	$t_{[32]+3}$	$t_{[32]+4}$	t_{37}	37
⋮	⋮	⋮	⋮	⋮	⋮	⋮	⋮

As a result, mortality models will generally show *select* rates only for about 5 to 10 years since selection, referred to as the *select period;* thereafter rates are shown as a function of attained age only, and are called *ultimate* rates. For these rates, the select notation is dropped. Thus, if the select period is k, then $t_{[x]+r}$ becomes just t_{x+r} for all $r \geq k$.

For convenience of reference, the standard format of the select and ultimate table is illustrated in Table 8.1, in terms of the true rates we wish to estimate. We have arbitrarily chosen a five-year select period.

8.2
PRIOR OPINION

We have already mentioned that smoothness, both across each row and down each column, will be an element of our prior opinion. In addition, we may have a prior concept concerning an increasing or decreasing pattern of the rates. This would likely depend on the meaning of the term "selection".

For insured data, we would expect that rates would increase down each column, since successive rates relate to persons at increasing ages, but a constant duration since selection. The same would hold across each row, as both age and duration since selection increase. Furthermore, the rates on a diagonal, reading from lower left to upper right, relate to persons at a constant attained age, but increasing duration since selection. Thus we might believe that, for example,

$$t_{[35]} < t_{[34]+1} < t_{[33]+2} < t_{[32]+3} < t_{[31]+4} < t_{35}.$$

These elements of prior opinion, smoothness and the three directions of increasing rates, along with considerations of fit, give us a good sense of direction in graduating such data.

In the above example, with mortality increasing by duration since selection, we have a case of *positive* selection. By that we mean that persons have been selected (for issuance of insurance) because of good health and other characteristics indicative of low mortality.

By contrast, clinical survival models generally are based on *negative* selection, whereby the selected persons are unhealthy. Examples would be selection because of treatment for a particular disease or due to a certain surgery. Then mortality may be expected to be high for a few years after selection, but then reducing as only the successful treatment cases continue to survive. In such cases, our prior opinion would suggest that rates should decrease across rows, and likewise up the Southwest to Northeast diagonal. Rates of termination from disability would likewise be expected to decrease by duration since disablement, which is the concept of "selection" in this case.

8.3
METHODS OF GRADUATION

Select and ultimate models can be graduated using the one-dimensional methods of prior chapters. When this is done, each column is graduated separately, with final adjustments made across rows and along diagonals to assure compliance with any strongly held prior opinion. The ultimate column, normally based on larger sample sizes, may be accorded greater importance than the others. Of course rows may be graduated by a formal method as well, but the small number of data in each row restricts this to some extent. Certainly the M-W-A method, with its end-value problem, would not be appropriate.

Alternatively, we can adapt our one-dimensional methods to handle two-dimensional models directly. In the next two sections, we will adapt Whittaker's method (Chapter 4), and comment briefly on the use of the mathematical formula, or parametric, approach (Chapter 6) to such models.

8.4
TWO-DIMENSIONAL WHITTAKER GRADUATION

The adaptation of formula (4.1) to select models is fairly straightforward. We define measures of smoothness both vertically and horizontally, as well as a measure of fit, combine the three measures linearly, and find the array of revised estimates which minimizes this combined measure. The matrix-vector formulation of Section 4.4 is used.

The method of this section is due to Wilkin and McKay [61]. For an expansion to higher dimensions, and other variations, see Knorr [39].

8.4.1 THE FUNCTION TO BE MINIMIZED

Assume that we have initial estimates at m ages at selection, and a select period of $n - 1$ years. Then there are n values in each row ($n - 1$ select rates plus the ultimate rate), and the array of initial estimates is expressed in an $m \times n$ matrix, with general term u_{ij}. Given also an $m \times n$ matrix of weights, we define our fit measure to be

$$F = \sum_{i=1}^{m} \sum_{j=1}^{n} w_{ij}(v_{ij} - u_{ij})^2. \qquad (8.1)$$

Smoothness is to be obtained both vertically (i.e., in each column), and horizontally (i.e., in each row). Let $\underset{v}{\Delta^z}$ be the differencing operator for the vertical smoothness measure, and $\underset{h}{\Delta^y}$ for the horizontal smoothness measure. Note that z and y need not be the same. Then a measure of vertical smoothness in the jth column is

$$\sum_{i=1}^{m-z} (\underset{v}{\Delta^z} v_{ij})^2,$$

and the over-all measure of vertical smoothness is

$$^{v}S = \sum_{j=1}^{n} \sum_{i=1}^{m-z} (\underset{v}{\Delta^z} v_{ij})^2. \qquad (8.2)$$

Similarly, a measure of horizontal smoothness in the ith row is

$$\sum_{j=1}^{n-y} (\underset{h}{\Delta^y} v_{ij})^2,$$

and the over-all measure of horizontal smoothness is

$$^{h}S = \sum_{i=1}^{m} \sum_{j=1}^{n-y} (\underset{h}{\Delta^y} v_{ij})^2. \qquad (8.3)$$

Then the function to be minimized is

$$M = F + \alpha\,{}^{v}S + \beta\,{}^{h}S, \qquad (8.4)$$

allowing for emphasis to be varried among fit, vertical smoothness, and horizontal smoothness.

8.4.2 THE MINIMIZATION OF M

To accomplish this, we again put M in a matrix-vector format.

First we transform the $m \times n$ matrix containing the u_{ij} into an $mn \times 1$ column vector, by arranging the successive rows of this matrix down the column. Thus the first row of the matrix becomes the first n elements in the column vector, the second row becomes elements $(n + 1)$ through $2n$ in the vector, and so on. In general,

$$u_{ij} \quad \text{becomes} \quad u_{n(i-1)+j}.$$

As before, we call this column vector **u**. The vector of graduated values **v** is similarly defined.

The $m \times n$ matrix of weights is transformed into an $mn \times mn$ diagonal matrix, by placing the rows successively down the principal diagonal. In general,

$$w_{ij} \quad \text{becomes} \quad w_{n(i-1)+j,\, n(i-1)+j},$$

and the new diagonal matrix of weights is called **w**. Then, just as for the one-dimensional case, F can be written as

$$F = (\mathbf{v} - \mathbf{u})'\mathbf{w}(\mathbf{v} - \mathbf{u}). \tag{8.1a}$$

Next we define an $n(m - z) \times mn$ matrix, which we call $^{\mathbf{v}}\mathbf{k}_z$, such that $^{\mathbf{v}}\mathbf{k}_z \mathbf{v}$ contains the values of $\underset{v}{\Delta^z} v_{ij}$ in the order suggested by (8.2). Then

$$^{v}S = (^{\mathbf{v}}\mathbf{k}_z\mathbf{v})'(^{\mathbf{v}}\mathbf{k}_z\mathbf{v}). \tag{8.2a}$$

Similarly, we define an $m(n - y) \times mn$ matrix, which we call $^{\mathbf{h}}\mathbf{k}_y$, such that $^{\mathbf{h}}\mathbf{k}_y\mathbf{v}$ contains the values of $\underset{h}{\Delta^y} v_{ij}$ in the order suggested by (8.3). Then

$$^{h}S = (^{\mathbf{h}}\mathbf{k}_y\mathbf{v})'(^{\mathbf{h}}\mathbf{k}_y\mathbf{v}). \tag{8.3a}$$

Therefore,

$$M = (\mathbf{v} - \mathbf{u})'\mathbf{w}(\mathbf{v} - \mathbf{u}) + \alpha(^{\mathbf{v}}\mathbf{k}_z\mathbf{v})'(^{\mathbf{v}}\mathbf{k}_z\mathbf{v}) + \beta(^{\mathbf{h}}\mathbf{k}_y\mathbf{v})'(^{\mathbf{h}}\mathbf{k}_y\mathbf{v}). \tag{8.4a}$$

By methods totally parallel to those used for the one-dimensional case (see Section 4.4), it can be shown that the $mn \times 1$ vector **v** of graduated values which will minimize (8.4a) is the vector which satisfies the matrix equation

$$(\mathbf{w} + \alpha\,^{\mathbf{v}}\mathbf{k}_z'\,^{\mathbf{v}}\mathbf{k}_z + \beta\,^{\mathbf{h}}\mathbf{k}_y'\,^{\mathbf{h}}\mathbf{k}_y)\mathbf{v} = \mathbf{w}\mathbf{u}. \tag{8.5}$$

8.4.3 THE MATRICES $^{\mathbf{v}}\mathbf{k}_z$ AND $^{\mathbf{h}}\mathbf{k}_y$

The proper construction of these two matrices is really the only aspect of this graduation problem which distinguishes it from its one-dimensional counterpart in Chapter 4, and we should explore this aspect a bit further.

First we note that $^{\mathbf{v}}\mathbf{k}_z$ can be defined in different ways. Since we sum the squares of the elements in $^{\mathbf{v}}\mathbf{k}_z\mathbf{v}$ to produce ^{v}S, we see that the same ^{v}S will result regardless of the order of the elements in $^{\mathbf{v}}\mathbf{k}_z\mathbf{v}$. In turn, the order of such elements will be implied by the particular form of $^{\mathbf{v}}\mathbf{k}_z$. In order to have a unique $^{\mathbf{v}}\mathbf{k}_z$, we have arbitrarily chosen to define it such that the order of the $\underset{v}{\Delta^z} v_{ij}$ elements will be that suggested by (8.2). That is, $^{\mathbf{v}}\mathbf{k}_z\mathbf{v}$ is to contain, from top to bottom, the $\underset{v}{\Delta^z} v_{ij}$ from the first column of the original matrix, then those from the second column, and so forth.

A numerical example (see Exercise 8–4) will make this clear. The reader should understand that this is simply our preferred definition of $^{\mathbf{v}}\mathbf{k}_z$.

The same remarks apply to $^{\mathbf{h}}\mathbf{k}_y$ as well. There we chose to define $^{\mathbf{h}}\mathbf{k}_y$ such that the order of the $\underset{h}{\Delta^y} v_{ij}$ in $^{\mathbf{h}}\mathbf{k}_y\mathbf{v}$ is those from the first row (left to right), then those from the second row, and so forth. This, too, is illustrated in Exercise 8–4.

8.5
MATHEMATICAL FORMULAS

The curve-fitting techniques of Section 6.3, particularly the regression approach, can be extended to the two-dimensional model. The basic problem, of course, is the selection of the functional form to be fit to the initial estimates. Such a form is a function of the two variables x and r, as well as the parameters to be determined.

No particular functional forms have attained broad acceptance for the select and ultimate model. The search for such forms is a fascinating subject in its own right, and there is a growing amount of literature on this subject. The interested reader is referred to the paper by Tenenbein and Vanderhoof [56], where several select models, all of a Gompertz type, are suggested and analyzed, and the weighted least-squares approach to determining their parameters is explored. This paper, and the discussions to it, list a considerable number of additional references.

We will explore an example from this paper in the exercises.

As an alternative to fitting initial estimates by regression (or otherwise), the parameters of an assumed select and ultimate form can be estimated directly from sample data by the method of maximum likelihood, analogous to the approach in Section 6.4 for the one-dimensional case. This approach can also be extended beyond two variables. For example, consider a parametric model which gives the force of mortality as a function of the three variables (1) age at selection, (2) duration since selection, and (3) an indicator variable denoting sex. Such problems are considered in Chapter 13 of Elandt-Johnson and Johnson [11].

8.6
SUMMARY

The extension of graduation theory to two-dimensional models is quite straightforward. One-dimensional methods can be used on various sections of the model, with care taken to assure an acceptable blending of the results.

Alternatively, direct two-dimensional methods can be developed. We have explored in detail only the application of Whittaker's method to this model, and have suggested references for the parametric approach. In addition, a formal Bayesian approach to the two-dimensional model is suggested by Hickman and Miller [28].

EXERCISES

8.1   Introduction; 8.2 Prior Opinion

8–1   Suppose the first-year select column and the ultimate column have been satisfactorily graduated, resulting in values of $v_{[x]}$ and v_x. Observed number of deaths $\theta_{[x]+r}$ and exposures $n_{[x]+r}$ are available. Each revised select rate is to be determined by the relationship

$$v_{[x]+r} = a_r \cdot v_{[x+r]} + (1 - a_r) \cdot v_{x+r}, \quad 0 < a_r < 1,$$

for $r = 1, 2, \ldots, k - 1$, and where a_r depends on r but not on x. That is, each graduated select rate is a linear interpolation "up the diagonal" between the first-year and ultimate rates of the same attained age.

For each r, a_r is to be determined so that the total observed deaths at duration r (for all select ages combined) is equal to the total graduated deaths.

a) What is the length of our select period?

b) What would you expect the pattern of the a_r to be, as r increases, in a model based on positive selection? How about a model based on negative selection?

c) Derive a formula for determining a_r.

8.3 Methods of Graduation

8–2 A mortality study with a 16-year select period has produced initial estimates for the first-year select rate $u_{[x]}$, and the ultimate rate u_{x+16}. In addition, for each age at selection, the deaths and exposures in the quinquennial duration groups (1 to 5), (6 to 10), (11 to 15) are available. Suggest methods that would be appropriate to graduate each row of this select and ultimate mortality model.

8.4 Two-Dimensional Whittaker Graduation

8–3 Suppose a select and ultimate model has 50 ages at selection and a five-year select period.

a) How many elements of data do we have?

b) If vertical smoothness is measured by $\Delta^3 v_{ij}$, how many elements are in ^vS, given by (8.2)?

c) If horizontal smoothness is measured by $\Delta^2 v_{ij}$, how many elements are in ^hS, given by (8.3)?

d) What element does $u_{42,4}$, in the original array, become in the column vector $\mathbf{u}$?

e) What will be the dimension of the matrix $^v\mathbf{k_z}$?

f) What will be the dimension of the matrix $^h\mathbf{k_y}$?

g) What is the size of the equation set represented by (8.5)?

8–4 Let $m = 4$, $n = 3$, $z = 2$, and $y = 1$.

a) Write the original *array* of graduated values to be determined.

b) Write the vector $\mathbf{v}$, showing the position of each element from the array in part (a).

c) Write the vector $^v\mathbf{k_z}\mathbf{v}$, with elements in the order suggested by (8.2).

d) Now that we have the result $^v\mathbf{k_z}\mathbf{v}$, and the vector $\mathbf{v}$, write the matrix $^v\mathbf{k_z}$.

e) Similarly, write the vector $^{h}\mathbf{k_y v}$, with elements in the order suggested by (8.3).

f) Finally, write the matrix $^{h}\mathbf{k_y}$ which will produce this result.

8.5   Mathematical Formulas

8-5 Suppose we adopt the model $\mu_{[x]+r} = Bd^r c^{x+r}$ to fit to forces of mortality observed for each of ten time intervals since selection, for each of 20 ages at selection, $a, a + 1, \ldots, b$. An array of weights $w_{[x]+r}$ is selected. Let the array $u_{[x]+r}$ be the logs of the observed forces of mortality. Define

$$SS = \sum_{r=0}^{9} \sum_{x=a}^{b} w_{[x]+r}\{u_{[x]+r} - \lambda_1 - \lambda_2 r - \lambda_3(x + r)\}^2.$$

a) What are λ_1, λ_2, λ_3?

b) Write the normal equations to solve for the least-squares estimates of λ_1, λ_2, λ_3.

8-6 We can apply the matrix approach of Section 8.4 to Exercise 8–5.

a) Arrange the array of $u_{[x]+r}$ values into the column vector $\mathbf{u}$. What element in $\mathbf{u}$ does $u_{[a+3]+7}$ become?

b) Arrange the array of $w_{[x]+r}$ weights into the diagonal matrix $\mathbf{w}$. What element in $\mathbf{w}$ does $w_{[b-1]}$ become?

c) Define $\boldsymbol{\lambda} = \begin{bmatrix} \lambda_1 \\ \lambda_2 \\ \lambda_3 \end{bmatrix}$. Then the normal equations in part (b) of Exercise 8–5 can be represented by equation (6.34),

$$\mathbf{x'wx\boldsymbol{\lambda}} = \mathbf{x'wu}.$$

Here's the tough part. What is the matrix $\mathbf{x}$?

ANALYSIS AND CRITIQUE

9

INTRODUCTION

Throughout this text the description of graduation methods has been mainly confined to the theory and mathematics involved. Such issues as suitable uses for a method, quality of results, and parameter selection were not addressed. In this final chapter we will explore some of these concerns.

9.2
PARAMETER SELECTION

In this section we will discuss the issue of parameter selection, and the effect of parameters on graduated results. In some cases, the parameters are capable of an interpretation, which guides their selection. In other cases, only a general idea of the effect of a parameter can be seen *a priori,* so that graduated results are often obtained by using different parameters, and then compared. Thus the effect of the parameter is seen empirically. In these cases, the illustrations presented in Appendix C are particularly valuable. We will discuss parameter selection method-by-method.

9.2.1 MOVING-WEIGHTED-AVERAGE

In the case of the Minimum-R_0 formula, only the range of the formula (i.e., the parameter n) is to be selected. In the general averaging approach, the error elements in the initial estimates are being averaged out over the terms in the formula. It follows that fewer terms in the range will result in less redistribution of error, so that revised estimates will more closely fit the initial. This is born out in the illustrations in Appendix C.

As we have already mentioned, Minimum-R_0 formulas do not produce smooth results (which can also be seen in the illustrations). Since smoothness is generally measured in third differences of graduated values, $z = 3$ or 4 will produce the desired smoothness. M-W-A formulas that had achieved popularity usually used such values of z, along with n in the vicinity of 7 to 11. An attempt to select n analytically, rather than empirically, is explored by Gerritson [13].

9.2.2 WHITTAKER'S METHOD

Again smoothness is related to the measure of smoothness incorporated in the function to be minimized (the parameter z in the traditional form). Fit is influenced by the choice of weights. Together both are influenced by the important parameter h, as described in Section 4.2.

In the statistical view of Whittaker's method (see Section 4.5), the final parameter h was developed as $\frac{\lambda}{w}$. Now λ was a parameter of the prior distribution of the vector of true rates $\mathbf{t}$, and, as such, might be loosely interpreted as a measure of confidence in that prior opinion. Similarly, w represented the assumed equal reciprocal of variance in the conditional distribution of $\mathbf{u}$, given $\mathbf{t}$. It is easier to see that w can likewise be interpreted as a measure of confidence in the data. Recall that Whittaker's prior was based entirely on smoothness. Then a larger h, which emphasizes smoothness, implies a larger λ relative to w, which suggests greater confidence in prior opinion relative to observed data. A smaller value of h has the converse interpretation. Thus we see that emphasis on smoothness versus fit can be undertaken to achieve a desired graduation result, or to reflect the statistical theory underlying the method.

9.2.3 THE BAYESIAN METHOD

For this method we gave a considerable bit of attention to parameter selection in our basic description of the method in Chapter 5. We emphasized the idea that these parameters have interpretations, which *should* guide their selection, but that subjectivity eventually enters in. The idea of revising the parameters in light of a graduation outcome is hard to do, because it is difficult to see what effect such a revision of parameters would have. The idea of doing several Bayesian graduations of the same data, and comparing the results, is not as practical for this method as for others because of the large volume of calculations involved, even for a computer. Bayesians solve this dilemma by contending that parameter specification is a function of prior opinion, not of graduated results. Undoubtedly this problem of parameter specification causes the Bayesian method to be the most controversial of our several graduation methods. A thorough critique of the method is given by Ryder [50].

9.2.4 PARAMETRIC METHODS

Here parameter selection is not really the issue. They are not selected, but rather are determined from the data. The choices to be made (the analogy to parameter selection) are the functional form, and the technique of determining the parameters. Regression and maximum likelihood, techniques not much used historically in parametric actuarial graduations, are recommended.

Clearly there is no uncertainty as to the smoothness of graduated results produced by a parametric method, so such results need be tested for fit only. Nonparametric results, on the other hand, do not have guaranteed smoothness, so they must be tested for both attributes.

9.2.5 INTERPOLATION METHODS

In our smooth-junction interpolation approach of Chapter 7, there are several parameters whose values will influence the results. Smoothness within each interpolation interval is assured by the use of polynomial arcs. Smoothness over a broader range is obtained by requiring these arcs to join with equal first (or first and second) derivatives. The number of points upon which a formula is based can also have an influence.

The pattern of the pivotal points, to which the interpolation is hinged, will certainly influence the results. Some preliminary smoothing of the pivotal-point pattern itself may be desirable. Greater smoothness in final values can be achieved by deviation away from the pivotal points via use of a smoothing (versus reproducing) formula.

This method is certainly one for which *a priori* parameter selection is hard to do. The illustrations in Appendix C show results based on different combinations of parameters.

9.3
CHOICE OF METHOD

No one graduation method can be viewed as "best" or "correct" in a universal sense. In certain situations, however, one particular method might be preferred over another. Such choice might be guided, for example, by the intended purpose of the model. In particular, if smoothness is of paramount importance, then a Min-R_0 M-W-A or Bayesian approach is not recommended.

Another important factor influencing the choice of a method is the form and extent of the initial data. In particular, we have seen that only an interpolation or other parametric approach (or an informal graphic approach) are appropriate for use with grouped data. Because many actuarial mortality studies have reported the basic data in grouped form, the interpolation approach has been an historically popular one.

The range of the data is also important. For a short sequence of terms, methods which have an "end-value" problem (M-W-A and central-difference interpolation) are clearly not appropriate.

Certain methods require a greater amount of numerical computation than others, and in earlier times this factor could well have been influential in choosing a method. With today's computer facilities, however, this is no longer an important issue.

Although we do not wish to imply an official endorsement of any one method, the remarkable versatility of Whittaker's method should be noted. It has been satisfactorily used with various kinds of data, including some very significant mortality studies.

9.4
FUTURE DIRECTIONS

Research in the topic of graduation is an ongoing activity. In this final section of the text we will briefly survey some areas currently receiving attention. It is submitted that this text presents a considerably modernized view of the subject over that contained in prior texts. Perhaps the next one to be written will show as many new developments beyond this one.

9.4.1 BAYESIAN PARAMETERS

The work of Hickman and Miller [27], mentioned in Section 5.5.4, has made a good start on this thorny problem. If the degree of subjectivity in this parameter specification can be brought under reasonable control, this method should become one of the more frequently used graduation methods.

9.4.2 ROBUSTNESS

In all graduation methods, the revised estimates are partly influenced by the initial data being graduated. In some cases, observations may be particularly "out of line" because of unusually large statistical fluctuation. In mortality studies with exposure measured in amounts of insurance rather than number of lives, a few claims on exceptionally large policies could unrealistically distort an estimate of true prevailing mortality. Estimation procedures, including graduation methods, designed to resist the influences of such data are said to be robust.

In general, methods using least-squares fitting are not robust. Thus the variation of Whittaker's method suggested by Schuette in Section 4.6.4 is more robust. In a totally intuitive manner, we reflected a robust graduation procedure in our informal graphic graduation in Section 2.8. There we chose not to be influenced by obvious (to us) outliers. The problem, of course, lies in the situation where we can't see the outliers, as we could with our graphic approach. Robust procedures should be designed to deal properly with "hidden" outliers.

The Fourteenth Annual Actuarial Research Conference, in 1979, emphasized robust estimation procedures. A general overview of robust procedures was presented by Hogg [31]; particular application to mortality estimation was described by Klugman [38]. The entire Conference is reported in the 1979.3 issue of ARCH.

9.4.3 MORTALITY STUDIES BY AMOUNT OF INSURANCE

All of the statistical ideas presented in this text for the graduation of mortality data assumed that the data consisted of deaths and exposure (sample size) in numbers of persons. In fact, many mortality studies, in the insurance industry at least, are conducted in terms of amounts of insurance. Many people feel that such a basis for the study produces results which more accurately reflect the financial impact of mortality on the company.

Traditionally, statistical techniques which we have discussed were made applicable to amount studies by first converting amount data to persons data by dividing the amounts by an average policy size. Recent research has shown that this technique is an oversimplification (see Klugman [37]). In particular, the issue of robustness is significant here. More work in this area is going on.

9.4.4 FUNCTIONAL FORMS

It is interesting to note that the most frequently used mortality models in actuarial work were developed in the middle of the last century. The presence of computers now makes it easy to deal with much more complex forms, and research in this area is active. The work of Tenenbein and Vanderhoof [56], mentioned earlier, is one such example. Additional uses of the popular Gompertz form have been explored by Wetterstrand [58].

ANSWERS TO THE CHAPTER EXERCISES

A

CHAPTER 2

2–2 a) $L = \dfrac{n!}{h!(n-h)!} t^h (1-t)^{n-h}$

b) $\ell = \ln L = \ln \dfrac{n!}{h!(n-h)!} + h \ln t + (n-h) \ln (1-t)$

c) $t = \dfrac{h}{n}$ $\left(\text{To be notationally consistent with Section 2.2, we should write}\right.$

$\left. \hat{T} = \dfrac{H}{n}.\right)$

d) $\hat{\imath} = .4$

2–3 a) $50t$　　　　　　　　　　　b) $t = \dfrac{H}{50}$ $\left(\text{or, again, } \hat{T} = \dfrac{H}{50}\right)$

c) $\hat{\imath} = .4$

2–4 a) $.5; .0025$　　　　　　　　　b) About $.001$

2–5 $.2; .0016$

2–6 Prior opinion about the relationships among neighboring values in the sequence being estimated.

2–7 a) $v_d = 2v_n = 10v_p$

b) $.07, .35, .70$; the total absolute departure is $.09$

2–8 a) 3.145　　　　　b) $.27$　　　　　c) 23%

2–9 a) n　　　b) $\dfrac{\theta}{n}$　　　c) $n \cdot q_x$　　　d) q_x

e) Because it is a precise binomial proportion

2–10 a) $n + \tfrac{1}{2}m$　　　　　　　b) $\dfrac{\theta}{n + \tfrac{1}{2}m}$

c) $n \cdot q_x + m \cdot {}_{1/2}q_{x+1/2}$　　　d) $(n + \tfrac{1}{2}m)q_x$

f) q_x

2–11 a) Understate

b) It is greater than q_x. This estimator is positively biased in this case.

2–12 a) $n - \frac{1}{2}m$

b) $\dfrac{\theta_x}{n - \frac{1}{2}m}$

c) $n \cdot q_x - m \cdot {}_{1/2}q_{x+1/2}$

d) $(n - \frac{1}{2}m)q_x$

e) q_x

f) d) is greater than c)

g) It is less than q_x. This estimator is negatively biased in this case.

2–13 a) 0

b) $\dfrac{t_x(1 - t_x)}{n_x}$

c) Same as b)

2–14 Unit normal

2–18 a) 2.3736

b) 50%, using 3 degrees of freedom. However, the two relations imposed on v_p, v_n, v_d should reduce the degrees of freedom to 1, so that the better answer is about 13%.

2–19 a) 9.890

b) Less than 1%; note that here, as well, $v = .35$ was obtained, in part, from the datum $u = .20$, so that the assumption of 1 degree of freedom is questionable.

2–20 a) 8

b) .18329

2–21 a) 10

b) 10

2–22 a) 24.611   b) 15   c) About 5% [Note that the answers to (b) and (c) assume 15 degrees of freedom; a smaller number, reflecting the determination of v_x from the data, would be more appropriate.]

2–23 c) .163; 12.143

2–24 a) 17.529   b) About 30% [In this case, since v'_x is determined from v_x by imposing two conditions, the appropriate degrees of freedom is two less than for Exercise 2–22.]

2–25 a) $a = .90606812$; $b = .02029320$
   b) Because v'_x is not yet known, and using it would severely complicate the minimization.
   c) 17.565. Why is it not less than the 17.529 result from Exercise 2–24? Since we used $w_x = n_x$ in part (a), we have not minimized the ''real'' (2.10).

2–26 .31   .28

2–27 a) 8   b) 10   c) 21.167

CHAPTER 3

3–1 a) u_{38} b) a_3 c) 13   d) 15
   e) $x = 26, 27, \ldots, 53$

3–6 $E[V_x] = \delta^4 t_x$ Var $(V_x) = 70\sigma^2$

3–7 $36\sigma^2$

3–8 $\frac{1}{83}$; It increases the variance of V_x, thus making v_x a less reliable estimate of t_x than was u_x.

3–9 Chris. Ingrid needs to triple the sample size to achieve the same variance reduction.

3–10 a) $a_1 + a_2 + a_3 = 1$, because t is a polynomial of degree zero.

b) ^{I}Var $(V) = t(1 - t)\left[\dfrac{1}{n_1 + n_2 + n_3}\right]$ ^{C}Var $(V) = \dfrac{t(1 - t)}{9}\left[\dfrac{1}{n_1} + \dfrac{1}{n_2} + \dfrac{1}{n_3}\right]$

^{N}Var $(V) = t(1 - t)\left[a_1^2 \cdot \dfrac{1}{n_1} + a_2^2 \cdot \dfrac{1}{n_2} + a_3^2 \cdot \dfrac{1}{n_3}\right]$

c) ^{I}Var $(V) = {}^C$Var (V) if $n_1 = n_2 = n_3$

3–11 a)

		$a_{-2}U_x + a_{-1}U_{x+1} + a_0U_{x+2} + a_1U_{x+3} + a_2U_{x+4}$
$a_{-4}U_{x-2}$	$a_{-3}U_{x-1}$	
$a_{-3}U_{x-2}$	$a_{-2}U_{x-1}$ + $a_{-1}U_x + a_0U_{x+1}$ $+ a_1U_{x+2} + a_2U_{x+3}$	a_3U_{x+4}
$a_{-2}U_{x-2}$ + $a_{-1}U_{x-1} + a_0U_x$ $+ a_1U_{x+1}$ $+ a_2U_{x+2}$	a_3U_{x+3}	a_4U_{x+4}

b) The boxed-in values above, where $a_{-4} = a_{-3} = a_3 = a_4 = 0$

c) $\Delta^2 V_x = \displaystyle\sum_{-4}^{2} \Delta^2 a_r U_{x+2+r}$ d) Var $(\Delta^2 V_x) = \sigma^2 \displaystyle\sum_{-4}^{2} (\Delta^2 a_r)^2$

3–12 a) $\Delta^3 V_x = V_{x+3} - 3V_{x+2} + 3V_{x+1} - V_x$:

			$a_{-2}U_{x+1} + a_{-1}U_{x+2} + a_0U_{x+3} + a_1U_{x+4} + a_2U_{x+5}$
$a_{-5}U_{x-2}$	$a_{-4}U_{x-1}$	$a_{-3}U_x$	
$a_{-4}U_{x-2}$	$a_{-3}U_{x-1}$	$a_{-2}U_x + a_{-1}U_{x+1} + a_0U_{x+2}$ $+ a_1U_{x+3} + a_2U_{x+4}$	a_3U_{x+5}
$a_{-3}U_{x-2}$	$a_{-2}U_{x-1}$ + $a_{-1}U_x + a_0U_{x+1}$ $+ a_1U_{x+2}$ $+ a_2U_{x+3}$	a_3U_{x+4}	a_4U_{x+5}
$a_{-2}U_{x-2}$ + $a_{-1}U_{x-1} + a_0U_x$ $+ a_1U_{x+1}$ $+ a_2U_{x+2}$	a_3U_{x+3}	a_4U_{x+4}	a_5U_{x+5}

b) The boxed-in values above, where $a_{-5} = a_{-4} = a_{-3} = a_3 = a_4 = a_5 = 0$

c) We add the top, minus three times the second, plus three times the third, minus the fourth to obtain $\Delta^3 V_x = \displaystyle\sum_{-5}^{2} - \Delta^3 a_r U_{x+3+r}$. Note well that the coefficients are really *negatives* of $\Delta^3 a_r$'s.

d) Var $(\Delta^3 V_x) = \sigma^2 \displaystyle\sum_{-5}^{2} (\Delta^3 a_r)^2$. The minus sign in part c) is immaterial.

3–14 Var $(\Delta^3 U_x) = 20\sigma^2$ $R_3^2 = \dfrac{1}{20} \displaystyle\sum_{-n-3}^{n} (\Delta^3 a_r)^2$

3–16 a) 197.8

b) 14 .06

c) It produces a v_x sequence that is rougher than the u_x sequence (nearly 200 times so!) We saw in Exercise 3–8 that this formula was also unsuccessful under the reduction-of-variance criterion.

3–17 b) $^{I}R_0{}^2 = \dfrac{43}{81} = .53086$; $^{II}R_0{}^2 = \dfrac{595}{1225} = .48571$; formula II is "better"

c) $^{I}R_3{}^2 = \dfrac{43}{135} = .31852$; $^{II}R_3{}^2 = \dfrac{617}{6125} = .10073$; again II is "better"

3–18 a)

	Min-R_0	Min-R_3
$R_0{}^2$:	.25541	.28334
$R_3{}^2$:	.02010	.00337

3–19 $x = y = \frac{1}{2}$

3–21 a) $a_1 = -4a_2$; $a_0 = 1 + 6a_2$

b) $924a_2{}^2 + 140a_2 + 6$

c) $a_2 = -\dfrac{5}{66}$, $a_1 = \dfrac{20}{66}$, $a_0 = \dfrac{36}{66}$

3–22 a) $a_1 = -4a_2 - 9a_3$; $a_0 = 1 + 6a_2 + 16a_3$

b) $1416a_3{}^2 + 252a_2{}^2 + 1176a_2a_3 + 100a_3 + 40a_2 + 2$

c) $a_3 = -\dfrac{35}{462}$; $a_2 = \dfrac{45}{462}$; $a_1 = \dfrac{135}{462}$; $a_0 = \dfrac{172}{462}$

3–25 a) $a_r = \beta_0 + \beta_2r^2 + \beta_4r^4 + \beta_6r^6$

b)
$$a_3 = \beta_0 + 9\ \beta_2 + 81\ \beta_4 + 729\ \beta_6 = 0$$
$$a_4 = \beta_0 + 16\beta_2 + 256\beta_4 + 4096\beta_6 = 0$$
$$a_0 + 2a_1 + 2a_2 = 5\beta_0 + 10\beta_2 + 34\ \beta_4 + 130\ \beta_6 = 1$$
$$a_1 + 4a_2 = 5\beta_0 + 17\beta_2 + 65\ \beta_4 + 257\ \beta_6 = 0$$

3–26 a) $a_r = \beta_0 + \beta_2r^2 + \beta_4r^4$

b)
$$a_4 = \beta_0 + 16\beta_2 + 256\beta_4 = 0$$
$$a_0 + 2a_1 + 2a_2 + 2a_3 = 7\ \beta_0 + 28\beta_2 + 196\beta_4 = 1$$
$$a_1 + 4a_2 + 9a_3 = 14\beta_0 + 98\beta_2 + 794\beta_4 = 0$$

3–29 b) $\displaystyle\sum_{-n}^{n} a_r = h \sum_{-n}^{n} [(n + 1)^2 - r^2] + k \sum_{-n}^{n} [n^2 - r^2][(n + 1)^2 - r^2] = 1$

$$\sum_{-n}^{n} [(n + 2)^2 - r^2]a_r = h \sum_{-n}^{n} [(n + 1)^2 - r^2][(n + 2)^2 - r^2]$$

$$+ k \sum_{-n}^{n} [n^2 - r^2][(n + 1)^2 - r^2][(n + 2)^2 - r^2] = (n + 2)^2$$

c) $h \cdot S_{n,1} + k \cdot S_{n-1,2} = 1$

$h \cdot S_{n,2} + k \cdot S_{n-1,3} = (n + 2)^2$

d) $h = \dfrac{S_{n-1,3} - (n + 2)^2 S_{n-1,2}}{S_{n,1} \cdot S_{n-1,3} - S_{n,2} \cdot S_{n-1,2}}$; $k = \dfrac{(n + 2)^2 S_{n,1} - S_{n,2}}{S_{n,1} \cdot S_{n-1,3} - S_{n,2} \cdot S_{n-1,2}}$

3–30 a) $a_r = h[(n + 1)^2 - r^2][(n + 2)^2 - r^2]$
$+ k[n^2 - r^2][(n + 1)^2 - r^2][(n + 2)^2 - r^2]$

b) $h \cdot S_{n,2} + k \cdot S_{n-1,3} = 1$

$h \cdot S_{n,3} + k \cdot S_{n-1,4} = (n + 3)^2$

3-31 a) $h \cdot S_{n,z} + k \cdot S_{n-1,z+1} = 1$
$h \cdot S_{n,z+1} + k \cdot S_{n-1,z+2} = (n + z + 1)^2$

CHAPTER 4

4-1 a) They will be the same

b) They will be the same; the minimized value of M, call it M^*, in the second case will be $\dfrac{1}{w}$ times the value of M in the first case, but the same values of v_x will produce this minimum.

4-2 a) $v_x = u$ for all x, and $M = 0$.

b) Then $v_x = u_x$ for all x, and $M = 0$.

4-3

$$
\begin{array}{rl}
(w_1 + h)v_1 - 2h\, v_2 + h\, v_3 & = w_1 u_1 \\
-2h\, v_1 + (w_2 + 5h)v_2 - 4h\, v_3 + h\, v_4 & = w_2 u_2 \\
h\, v_1 - 4h\, v_2 + (w_3 + 6h)v_3 - 4h\, v_4 + h\, v_5 & = w_3 u_3 \\
h\, v_2 - 4h\, v_3 + (w_4 + 6h)v_4 - 4h\, v_5 + h\, v_6 & = w_4 u_4 \\
h\, v_3 - 4h\, v_4 + (w_5 + 5h)v_5 - 2h\, v_6 & = w_5 u_5 \\
h\, v_4 - 2h\, v_5 + (w_6 + h)v_6 & = w_6 u_6
\end{array}
$$

4-4

$$
\begin{array}{rl}
(w_1 + h)v_1 - 3h\, v_2 + 3h\, v_3 - h\, v_4 & = w_1 u_1 \\
-3h\, v_1 + (w_2 + 10h)v_2 - 12h\, v_3 + 6h\, v_4 - h\, v_5 & = w_2 u_2 \\
3h\, v_1 - 12h\, v_2 + (w_3 + 19h)v_3 - 15h\, v_4 + 6h\, v_5 - h\, v_6 & = w_3 u_3 \\
-h\, v_1 + 6h\, v_2 - 15h\, v_3 + (w_4 + 20h)v_4 - 15h\, v_5 + 6h\, v_6 - h\, v_7 & = w_4 u_4 \\
-h\, v_2 + 6h\, v_3 - 15h\, v_4 + (w_5 + 19h)v_5 - 12h\, v_6 + 3h\, v_7 & = w_5 u_5 \\
-h\, v_3 + 6h\, v_4 - 12h\, v_5 + (w_6 + 10h)v_6 - 3h\, v_7 & = w_6 u_6 \\
-h\, v_4 + 3h\, v_5 - 3h\, v_6 + (w_7 + h)v_7 & = w_7 u_7
\end{array}
$$

4-5 2 [Note that $z = 3$ and $h = 2$]

4-6 a) $\mathbf{k_2' k_2} = \begin{bmatrix} 1 & -2 & 1 & 0 & 0 & 0 \\ -2 & 5 & -4 & 1 & 0 & 0 \\ 1 & -4 & 6 & -4 & 1 & 0 \\ 0 & 1 & -4 & 6 & -4 & 1 \\ 0 & 0 & 1 & -4 & 5 & -2 \\ 0 & 0 & 0 & 1 & -2 & 1 \end{bmatrix}$

4-7 a) $\mathbf{k_3' k_3} = \begin{bmatrix} 1 & -3 & 3 & -1 & 0 & 0 & 0 \\ -3 & 10 & -12 & 6 & -1 & 0 & 0 \\ 3 & -12 & 19 & -15 & 6 & -1 & 0 \\ -1 & 6 & -15 & 20 & -15 & 6 & -1 \\ 0 & -1 & 6 & -15 & 19 & -12 & 3 \\ 0 & 0 & -1 & 6 & -12 & 10 & -3 \\ 0 & 0 & 0 & -1 & 3 & -3 & 1 \end{bmatrix}$

4–8 a) $\sum_{1}^{n} w_x v_x$ b) The vector **0**

c) That $\sum_{1}^{n} w_x v_x = \sum_{1}^{n} w_x u_x$, or that $F = \sum_{1}^{n} w_x(v_x - u_x) = 0$

4–9 a) $\sum_{1}^{n} x \cdot w_x v_x$ b) The vector **0**

c) That $\sum_{1}^{n} x \cdot w_x v_x = \sum_{1}^{n} x \cdot w_x u_x$, or that $F = \sum_{1}^{n} x \cdot w_x(v_x - u_x) = 0$

4–10 13

4–11 $\frac{1}{2}(-3v_1 + 9v_2 - 9v_3 + 5v_4)$

4–15 a) $(w_1 + h_2 + h_3)v_1 - (2h_2 + 3h_3)v_2 + (h_2 + 3h_3)v_3 - h_3v_4 = w_1u_1$

b) $w_r v_r + h_2 \delta^4 v_r - h_3 \delta^6 v_r = w_r u_r$

c) $(\mathbf{v} - \mathbf{u})'\mathbf{w}(\mathbf{v} - \mathbf{u}) + h_2(\mathbf{k_2 v})'\mathbf{k_2 v} + h_3(\mathbf{k_3 v})'\mathbf{k_3 v}$

d) $(\mathbf{w} + h_2\mathbf{k_2'k_2} + h_3\mathbf{k_3'k_3})\mathbf{v} = \mathbf{wu}$

4–16 a) $\mathbf{b} = \begin{bmatrix} 2 & -3 & 1 & 0 & 0 \\ -3 & 7 & -5 & 1 & 0 \\ 1 & -5 & 8 & -5 & 1 \\ 0 & 1 & -5 & 7 & -3 \\ 0 & 0 & 1 & -3 & 2 \end{bmatrix}$

b) $\mathbf{c} = \begin{bmatrix} 3 & -3 & 1 & 0 & 0 \\ -3 & 8 & -5 & 1 & 0 \\ 1 & -5 & 9 & -5 & 1 \\ 0 & 1 & -5 & 8 & -3 \\ 0 & 0 & 1 & -3 & 3 \end{bmatrix}$

4–19 b) $[w_1 + h(1 + r)^2]v_1 - [h(1 + r)(2 + r)]v_2 + [h(1 + r)]v_3 = w_1u_1$

c) $-[h(1 + r)(2 + r)]v_1 + \{w_2 + h[(1 + r)^2 + (2 + r)^2]\}v_2$
$- [h(2 + r)^2]v_3 + [h(1 + r)]v_4 = w_2u_2$

d) $[h(1 + r)]v_{n-2} - [h(2 + r)]v_{n-1} + [w_n + h]v_n = w_nu_n$

e) $[h(1 + r)]v_{n-3} - [h(2 + r)^2]v_{n-2} + \{w_{n-1} + h[1 + (2 + r)^2]\}v_{n-1}$
$- [h(2 + r)]v_n = w_{n-1}u_{n-1}$

f) $\begin{bmatrix} (1+r)^2 & -(1+r)(2+r) & (1+r) & 0 & 0 & 0 \\ -(1+r)(2+r) & (2+r)^2 + (1+r)^2 & -(2+r)^2 & (1+r) & 0 & 0 \\ (1+r) & -(2+r)^2 & 1 + (2+r)^2 + (1+r)^2 & -(2+r)^2 & (1+r) & 0 \\ 0 & (1+r) & -(2+r)^2 & 1 + (2+r)^2 + (1+r)^2 & -(2+r)^2 & (1+r) \\ 0 & 0 & (1+r) & -(2+r)^2 & 1 + (2+r)^2 & -(2+r) \\ 0 & 0 & 0 & (1+r) & -(2+r) & 1 \end{bmatrix}$

4–21 a) $\mathbf{g_3 v} = \begin{bmatrix} \Delta^3 v_1 & -r\,\Delta^2 v_1 \\ \Delta^3 v_2 & -r\,\Delta^2 v_2 \\ \Delta^3 v_3 & -r\,\Delta^2 v_3 \\ \vdots & \vdots \\ \Delta^3 v_{n-3} & -r\,\Delta^2 v_{n-3} \end{bmatrix}$

b) $\mathbf{g_3} = \begin{bmatrix} -(1+r) & (3+2r) & -(3+r) & 1 & 0 & \cdots & \cdots & 0 \\ 0 & -(1+r) & (3+2r) & -(3+r) & 1 & 0 & \cdots & 0 \\ & & \ddots & & \ddots & & & \\ 0 & 0 & \cdots & & \cdots & -(1+r) & (3+2r) & -(3+r) & 1 \end{bmatrix}$

c) $\mathbf{r_3} = \begin{bmatrix} -r & 2r & -r & 0 & 0 & 0 & \cdots & \cdots & & & 0 \\ 0 & -r & 2r & -r & 0 & 0 & 0 & \cdots & \cdots & & 0 \\ & \ddots & & & & \ddots & & & & \ddots & \\ 0 & 0 & 0 & \cdots & \cdots & \cdots & \cdots & -r & 2r & -r & 0 \end{bmatrix}$

d) $\mathbf{r_z}$ is $(n-z) \times n$, whereas $\mathbf{k_{z-1}}$ is $(n-z+1) \times n$. If we define $\mathbf{k_{z-1}^*}$ to be $\mathbf{k_{z-1}}$ without its last row, then $\mathbf{r_z} = -r\mathbf{k_{z-1}^*}$.

4–22 a) $(1-h_1)(\mathbf{v}-\mathbf{u})'\mathbf{w}(\mathbf{v}-\mathbf{u}) + h_1(\mathbf{v}-\mathbf{s})'\mathbf{w^s}(\mathbf{v}-\mathbf{s}) + h_2\mathbf{v}'(\mathbf{g_z'g_z})\mathbf{v}$

b) $[(1-h_1)\mathbf{w} + h_1\mathbf{w^s} + h_2\mathbf{g_z'g_z}]\mathbf{v} = [(1-h_1)\mathbf{wu} + h_1\mathbf{w^s s}]$

CHAPTER 5

5–1 a) $f_M(m) = \lambda e^{-\lambda m}$, $m > 0$, $\lambda > 0$

b) $p_{Y|M}(y|m) = \dfrac{m^y e^{-m}}{y!}$, $m > 0$, $y = 0, 1, \ldots$

c) $p_Y(y) = \dfrac{\lambda}{(1+\lambda)^{y+1}}$, $\lambda > 0$, $y = 0, 1, \ldots$ e) 10

f) $\dfrac{(1+\lambda)^{y+1} m^y e^{-m(1+\lambda)}}{y!}$, $\lambda > 0$, $m > 0$, $y = 0, 1, \ldots$ g) 15

5–4 $\dfrac{a-1}{a+b-2}$

5–5 .5667

5–6 .5700 $a = 113.5$ $b = 138.5$

5–7 a) $\mathbf{A} = \begin{bmatrix} \sigma_1^2 & \mathrm{cov}_{12} \\ \mathrm{cov}_{21} & \sigma_2^2 \end{bmatrix}$, where $\mathrm{cov}_{12} = \mathrm{cov}_{21}$

b) $|\mathbf{A}| = \sigma_1^2\sigma_2^2 - (\mathrm{cov}_{12})^2$

d) $\mathbf{A}^{-1} = \begin{bmatrix} \dfrac{1}{\sigma_1^2(1-\rho^2)} & -\dfrac{\rho}{\sigma_1\sigma_2(1-\rho^2)} \\ -\dfrac{\rho}{\sigma_1\sigma_2(1-\rho^2)} & \dfrac{1}{\sigma_2^2(1-\rho^2)} \end{bmatrix}$

5–8   a) $|\mathbf{B}| = \prod_1^n b_i$

b) $\mathbf{B}^{-1} = \begin{bmatrix} b_1^{-1} & & \bigcirc \\ & b_2^{-1} & \\ & & \ddots \\ \bigcirc & & b_n^{-1} \end{bmatrix}$

c) $\sum_1^n \dfrac{1}{b_i}(u_i - t_i)^2$

5–9   a) $-\frac{1}{2}[\mathbf{t}'\mathbf{A}^{-1}\mathbf{t} - \mathbf{m}'\mathbf{A}^{-1}\mathbf{t} - \mathbf{t}'\mathbf{A}^{-1}\mathbf{m} + \mathbf{m}'\mathbf{A}^{-1}\mathbf{m} + \mathbf{u}'\mathbf{B}^{-1}\mathbf{u} - \mathbf{t}'\mathbf{B}^{-1}\mathbf{u}$
         $- \mathbf{u}'\mathbf{B}^{-1}\mathbf{t} + \mathbf{t}'\mathbf{B}^{-1}\mathbf{t}]$

b) $k_5 = k_4 \cdot \exp\{-\frac{1}{2}[\mathbf{u}'\mathbf{B}^{-1}\mathbf{u} + \mathbf{m}'\mathbf{A}^{-1}\mathbf{m}]\}$

c) Because they are symmetric

5–10 $\mathbf{v}' = \left[\dfrac{13}{9}, \dfrac{34}{7}, \dfrac{120}{7}\right]$

5–14 .00000009

5–16 110

5–17 $\mathbf{A} = \begin{bmatrix} .0022 & .0024 & .0013 & .0004 & 0 & 0 \\ .0024 & .0032 & .0034 & .0020 & .0006 & 0 \\ .0013 & .0034 & .0045 & .0053 & .0029 & .0010 \\ .0004 & .0020 & .0053 & .0077 & .0085 & .0054 \\ 0 & .0006 & .0029 & .0085 & .0117 & .0150 \\ 0 & 0 & .0010 & .0054 & .0150 & .0238 \end{bmatrix}$

5–20 a) It is not a variable, since it is uniquely determined by t_1 and t_2

b) $t_3 = 1 - t_1 - t_2$

c) $[0, 1 - t_1]$ d) $[0, 1]$

f) $\displaystyle\int_0^1 \int_0^{1-t_1} \int_0^{1-t_1-t_2} \cdots \int_0^{1-t_1-\cdots-t_{n-1}} t_1^{a_1-1} \cdots t_{n-1}^{a_{n-1}-1}$
   $(1 - t_1 - \cdots - t_{n-1})^{a_n-1}\, dt_{n-1} \cdots dt_2\, dt_1$

5–22 a) $t_i = \dfrac{a_i - 1}{a - 3}$

b) Whenever $a_1 = a_2 = a_3$, which implies $t_1 = t_2 = t_3 = \frac{1}{3}$

5–23 a) $\dfrac{d!\,\Gamma(a_1 + a_2 + a_3)\Gamma(a_1 + d_1)\Gamma(a_2 + d_2)\Gamma(a_3 + d_3)}{d_1!\cdot d_2!\cdot d_3!\,\Gamma(a_1)\Gamma(a_2)\Gamma(a_3)\Gamma(a_1 + a_2 + a_3 + d_1 + d_2 + d_3)}$

b) $\dfrac{d!\cdot\Gamma(a)\cdot\prod\limits_{1}^{n}\Gamma(a_i + d_i)}{\prod\limits_{1}^{n}d_i!\cdot\prod\limits_{1}^{n}\Gamma(a_i)\cdot\Gamma(a + d)}$

CHAPTER 6

6–1 $c = 1.079$ $g = .997$

6–4 $n = 4.7681254$ $k = 5.8859 \times 10^{-11}$

6–5 $n = 2$ $k = .000003$

6–6 Makeham

6–7 a) $\ln \Delta^2 \mu_x$ b) $\dfrac{\Delta^2 \ln p_{x+1}}{\Delta^2 \ln p_x} = c$

6–8 -4

6–9 $.000003$

6–10 $c = 1.1020469$ $g = .99935293$ $s = .99921700$

6–11 $c = 1.133042$ $g = .999923$ $w = .999946$ $s = 1.001717$

6–12 a) $\hat{a} = -4.2093811$ $\hat{b} = .03641455$

b) $\hat{B} = .00006175$ $\hat{c} = 1.0874632$

6–13 a) $\hat{a} = -10.353891$ $\hat{b} = 4.682795$

b) $\hat{n} = 4.682795$ $\hat{k} = 4.427 \times 10^{-11}$

6–14 a) $\mathbf{x}*\mathbf{b} = \begin{bmatrix} a + b \\ a + 2b \\ \vdots \\ a + nb \end{bmatrix}$ b) $(\mathbf{u}* - \mathbf{x}*\mathbf{b})'\mathbf{w}(\mathbf{u}* - \mathbf{x}*\mathbf{b})$

6–15 c) $\mathbf{x}*'\mathbf{w}\mathbf{x}*\mathbf{b} = \mathbf{x}*'\mathbf{w}\mathbf{u}*$

6–16 *Only* that $\mathbf{x}*$ must be defined as $\mathbf{x}* = \begin{bmatrix} 1 & \log 1 \\ 1 & \log 2 \\ \vdots & \vdots \\ 1 & \log n \end{bmatrix}$

6–17 $\mathbf{x}* = \begin{bmatrix} 1 & 51.5 \\ 1 & 52.5 \\ \vdots & \vdots \\ 1 & 60.5 \end{bmatrix}$

6-18 $\mathbf{x}^* = \begin{bmatrix} 1 & 1.7118072 \\ 1 & 1.7201593 \\ \vdots & \vdots \\ 1 & 1.7817554 \end{bmatrix}$

6-20 a)

x	$c_0{}^x$	$c_0{}^{x-1}$	$c_0{}^{2x-1}$
51.5	52.64091	48.74159	2565.8015
52.5	56.85219	52.64091	2992.7509
53.5	61.40036	56.85219	3490.7447
54.5	66.31239	61.40036	4071.6046
55.6	71.61738	66.31239	4749.1196
56.5	77.34677	71.61738	5539.3731
57.5	83.53451	77.34677	6461.1247
58.5	90.21727	83.53451	7536.2559
59.5	97.43466	90.21727	8790.2889
60.5	105.22943	97.43466	10252.9929

6-20 b) $\begin{bmatrix} 10 & 762.58585 & 1.9992702 \\ 762.58585 & 60,966.062 & 161.50901 \\ 1.9992702 & 161.50901 & .42882386 \end{bmatrix}$ c) $\begin{bmatrix} .01144070 \\ 1.0129901 \\ .00273999 \end{bmatrix}$

d) $d_A = .00005249$; $d_B = -.00014270$; $d_c = .05989196$
$A_1 = .002052490$; $B_1 = -.000092704$; $c_1 = 1.139891963$

e) $A = .001373522$; $B = .000014398$; $c = 1.111402688$
(Convergence is obtained within 8 iterations.)

6-21 a) $\sum\limits_{i=1}^{n} [\ln b + \ln y_i - \tfrac{1}{2}b(y_i^2 - x^2)]$ b) $\hat{b} = \left[\dfrac{1}{2n} \sum\limits_{i=1}^{n} y_i^2 - \tfrac{1}{2}x^2 \right]^{-1}$

6-22 a) $\sum\limits_{i=1}^{n} \left[a_i(\ln B + w_i \ln c) - \dfrac{B}{\ln c}(c^{w_i} - c^{x_i}) \right]$

b) $\dfrac{1}{B} \sum\limits_{i=1}^{n} a_i - \dfrac{1}{\ln c} \sum\limits_{i=1}^{n} (c^{w_i} - c^{x_i}) = 0$

$\dfrac{1}{c} \sum\limits_{i=1}^{n} a_i w_i - B \sum\limits_{i=1}^{n} \left[\dfrac{1}{\ln c}(w_i c^{w_i - 1} - x_i c^{x_i - 1}) - \dfrac{1}{c(\ln c)^2}(c^{w_i} - c^{x_i}) \right] = 0$

6-23 a) $1 - \left(\dfrac{j}{j+1} \right)^b$

c) $\sum\limits_{j=a}^{h} \left\{ \theta_j \left[\dfrac{(j+1)^b \ln (j+1) - j^b \ln j}{(j+1)^b - j^b} \right] + (A_j - \theta_j) \ln j - A_j \ln (j+1) \right\}$

6–24 a) $c_1 \sum w_x + c_2 \sum x w_x + c_3 \sum x^2 w_x + c_4 \sum x^3 w_x = \sum w_x u_x$

b) $c_1 \sum x w_x + c_2 \sum x^2 w_x + c_3 \sum x^3 w_x + c_4 \sum x^4 w_x = \sum x w_x u_x$

c) $c_1 \sum x^2 w_x + c_2 \sum x^3 w_x + c_3 \sum x^4 w_x + c_4 \sum x^5 w_x = \sum x^2 w_x u_x$

d) $c_1 \sum x^3 w_x + c_2 \sum x^4 w_x + c_3 \sum x^5 w_x + c_4 \sum x^6 w_x = \sum x^3 w_x u_x$

$$\left[\text{Note: all } \sum \text{ represent } \sum_{x=a}^{b} \right]$$

6–28 $n + 4$

6–29 a) $p_1(x) = c_1 + c_2 x + c_3 x^2 + c_4 (x - 29.7)^2$

b) $p_3(x) = c_1 + c_2 x + c_3 x^2 + c_4 (x - 29.7)^2 + c_5 (x - 62.5)^2 + c_6 (x - 80.6)^2$

c) $\displaystyle\sum_{20}^{29} w_x [u_x - c_1 - c_2 x - c_3 x^2]^2$

$+ \displaystyle\sum_{30}^{62} w_x [u_x - c_1 - c_2 x - c_3 x^2 - c_4 (x - 29.7)^2]^2$

$+ \displaystyle\sum_{63}^{80} w_x [u_x - c_1 - c_2 x - c_3 x^2 - c_4 (x - 29.7)^2 - c_5 (x - 62.5)^2]^2$

$+ \displaystyle\sum_{81}^{89} w_x [u_x - c_1 - c_2 x - c_3 x^2 - c_4 (x - 29.7)^2 - c_5 (x - 62.5)^2$

$\qquad - c_6 (x - 80.6)^2]^2$

6–30 a) $c_1 \sum (x - k)^3 w_x + c_2 \sum x(x - k)^3 w_x + c_3 \sum x^2 (x - k)^3 w_x$

$+ c_4 \sum x^3 (x - k)^3 w_x + c_5 \sum (x - k)^6 w_x = \sum (x - k)^3 w_x u_x$

$$\left[\text{All } \sum \text{ represent } \sum_{h+1}^{b} \right]$$

6–31 a) $c_1 \sum (x - k_1)^3 w_x + c_2 \sum x(x - k_1)^3 w_x + c_3 \sum x^2 (x - k_1)^3 w_x$

$+ c_4 \sum x^3 (x - k_1)^3 w_x + c_5 \sum (x - k_1)^6 w_x + c_6 \displaystyle\sum_{h_2+1}^{b} (x - k_1)^3 (x - k_2)^3 w_x$

$= \sum (x - k_1)^3 w_x u_x$

$$\left[\text{All } \sum \text{ represent } \sum_{h_1+1}^{b} \right]$$

b) $c_1 \sum (x - k_2)^3 w_x + c_2 \sum x(x - k_2)^3 w_x + c_3 \sum x^2(x - k_2)^3 w_x$

$+ c_4 \sum x^3(x - k_2)^3 w_x + c_5 \sum (x - k_1)^3(x - k_2)^3 w_x + c_6 \sum (x - k_2)^6 w_x$

$= \sum (x - k_2)^3 w_x u_x$

$$\left[\text{All } \sum \text{ represent } \sum_{h_2+1}^{b} \right]$$

6–32 a)

$$
x = \begin{bmatrix}
1 & 20 & (20)^2 & 0 & 0 & 0 \\
\vdots & \vdots & \vdots & \vdots & \vdots & \vdots \\
1 & 29 & (29)^2 & 0 & 0 & 0 \\
1 & 30 & (30)^2 & (30 - 29.7)^2 & 0 & 0 \\
\vdots & \vdots & \vdots & \vdots & \vdots & \vdots \\
1 & 62 & (62)^2 & (62 - 29.7)^2 & 0 & 0 \\
1 & 63 & (63)^2 & (63 - 29.7)^2 & (63 - 62.5)^2 & 0 \\
\vdots & \vdots & \vdots & \vdots & \vdots & \vdots \\
1 & 80 & (80)^2 & (80 - 29.7)^2 & (80 - 62.5)^2 & 0 \\
1 & 81 & (81)^2 & (81 - 29.7)^2 & (81 - 62.5)^2 & (81 - 80.6)^2 \\
\vdots & \vdots & \vdots & \vdots & \vdots & \vdots \\
1 & 89 & (89)^2 & (89 - 29.7)^2 & (89 - 62.5)^2 & (89 - 80.6)^2
\end{bmatrix}
$$

CHAPTER 7

7–1 a) u_{x+5} b) $c_1 = s$; $c_2 = \frac{1}{2}s(s - 1)$;
$c_3 = \frac{1}{6}s(s - 1)(s + 1)$;
$c_4 = \frac{1}{24}s(s - 1)(s + 1)(s - 2)$

c) $A(s) = s$; $B(s) = \frac{1}{6}s(s^2 - 1)$; $C(s) = \frac{1}{120}s(s^2 - 1)(s^2 - 4)$

7–2 8

7–3 $7A(0) + 5B(0)$

7–5 4

7–6 $s = 0, .25, .50, .75, 1.00$

7–8 b) $\frac{1}{4}$ c) Because, coincidently, $\delta^2 u_{x-1} = \delta^2 u_{x+1}$. The requirement $B(0) = 0$ is to assure $v_{x-1+s}|_{s=1} = v_{x+s}|_{s=0}$ *regardless* of data.

7–9 No. To be osculatory, all three properties must be satisfied.

7–11 a) $A(0) = A'(0) = A'(1) = 0$
c) Any function of the form $A(s) = cs^2 + ds^3$, in which $c = -\frac{3}{2}d$.

7–12 a) Osculatory   b) Reproducing

7–13 Yes, if $\delta^2 u_x = 0$.

7–16 $C(s) = \frac{1}{120}s(s^2 - 1)(s^2 - 4)$

7–21 $B(s) = \frac{1}{2}(s^4 - s^3)$

7–24 No; no

7–25 a) $C(1) = 0$ b) $C(\frac{1}{2}) = \frac{3}{256}$

  c) $C'(0) = 0$; $C'(1) = -\frac{1}{12}$ d) $C(s) = \frac{1}{48}s^2(s - 1)(s - 5)$

7–26 a) $C''(0) = 0$ b) $C(s) = \frac{1}{24}s^3(s - 1)(5s - 7)$

7–27 a) 3 b) Reproducing c) Neither; second derivatives are matched, but first are not.

7–28 $\frac{1}{1225}$

7–29 a) 15 b) 4.275 c) .17362 d) Third

CHAPTER 8

8–1 a) k b) Decreasing, in both cases

  c) For each r, $a_r = \dfrac{\displaystyle\sum_x n_{[x]+r}v_{x+r} - \sum_x \theta_{[x]+r}}{\displaystyle\sum_x n_{[x]+r}(v_{x+r} - v_{[x+r]})}$

8–2 The presence of grouped data suggests that a parametric approach of some sort should be used. No doubt we would use King's pivotal value formula (Section 7.5) to obtain rates for the middle age in each of the three quinquennial groups. We might then interpolate among the five rates in each row, adapting our interpolation formulas to avoid the "end-value" problem created by central difference formulas. We might also try to fit a single curve to the entire durational range by least squares. In light of the limited data, a simple, informal graphic approach may be as well as any.

8–3 a) 300 b) 282 c) 200 d) u_{250}

  e) 282×300 f) 200×300 g) 300×300

8–4

  a) $\begin{bmatrix} v_{11} & v_{12} & v_{13} \\ v_{21} & v_{22} & v_{23} \\ v_{31} & v_{32} & v_{33} \\ v_{41} & v_{42} & v_{43} \end{bmatrix}$ b) $\mathbf{v} = \begin{bmatrix} v_{11} \\ v_{12} \\ v_{13} \\ v_{21} \\ v_{22} \\ v_{23} \\ v_{31} \\ v_{32} \\ v_{33} \\ v_{41} \\ v_{42} \\ v_{43} \end{bmatrix}$ c) $\begin{bmatrix} \Delta^2 v_{11} \\ \Delta^2 v_{21} \\ \Delta^2 v_{12} \\ \Delta^2 v_{22} \\ \Delta^2 v_{13} \\ \Delta^2 v_{23} \end{bmatrix}$

d)
$$\begin{bmatrix}
1 & 0 & 0 & -2 & 0 & 0 & 1 & 0 & 0 & 0 & 0 & 0 \\
0 & 0 & 0 & 1 & 0 & 0 & -2 & 0 & 0 & 1 & 0 & 0 \\
0 & 1 & 0 & 0 & -2 & 0 & 0 & 1 & 0 & 0 & 0 & 0 \\
0 & 0 & 0 & 0 & 1 & 0 & 0 & -2 & 0 & 0 & 1 & 0 \\
0 & 0 & 1 & 0 & 0 & -2 & 0 & 0 & 1 & 0 & 0 & 0 \\
0 & 0 & 0 & 0 & 0 & 1 & 0 & 0 & -2 & 0 & 0 & 1
\end{bmatrix}$$

e)
$$\begin{bmatrix}
\Delta v_{11} \\
\Delta v_{12} \\
\Delta v_{21} \\
\Delta v_{22} \\
\Delta v_{31} \\
\Delta v_{32} \\
\Delta v_{41} \\
\Delta v_{42}
\end{bmatrix}$$

f)
$$\begin{bmatrix}
-1 & 1 & 0 & 0 & 0 & 0 & 0 & 0 & 0 & 0 & 0 & 0 \\
0 & -1 & 1 & 0 & 0 & 0 & 0 & 0 & 0 & 0 & 0 & 0 \\
0 & 0 & 0 & -1 & 1 & 0 & 0 & 0 & 0 & 0 & 0 & 0 \\
0 & 0 & 0 & 0 & -1 & 1 & 0 & 0 & 0 & 0 & 0 & 0 \\
0 & 0 & 0 & 0 & 0 & 0 & -1 & 1 & 0 & 0 & 0 & 0 \\
0 & 0 & 0 & 0 & 0 & 0 & 0 & -1 & 1 & 0 & 0 & 0 \\
0 & 0 & 0 & 0 & 0 & 0 & 0 & 0 & 0 & -1 & 1 & 0 \\
0 & 0 & 0 & 0 & 0 & 0 & 0 & 0 & 0 & 0 & -1 & 1
\end{bmatrix}$$

8-5 a) $\lambda_1 = \log B$; $\lambda_2 = \log d$; $\lambda_3 = \log c$

b) $\lambda_1 \cdot \sum^2 w_{[x]+r} + \lambda_2 \cdot \sum^2 r w_{[x]+r} + \lambda_3 \cdot \sum^2 (x+r)w_{[x]+r} = \sum^2 w_{[x]+r} u_{[x]+r}$

$\lambda_1 \cdot \sum^2 r w_{[x]+r} + \lambda_2 \cdot \sum^2 r^2 w_{[x]+r} + \lambda_3 \cdot \sum^2 r(x+r)w_{[x]+r}$

$$= \sum^2 r w_{[x]+r} u_{[x]+r}$$

$\lambda_1 \cdot \sum^2 (x+r)w_{[x]+r} + \lambda_2 \cdot \sum^2 r(x+r)w_{[x]+r} + \lambda_3 \cdot \sum^2 (x+r)^2 w_{[x]+r}$

$$= \sum^2 (x+r)w_{[x]+r} u_{[x]+r}$$

$$\left[\text{Note: all } \sum^2 \text{ represent } \sum_{r=0}^{9} \sum_{x=a}^{b} \right]$$

8–6 a) u_{38} b) $w_{181,181}$

$$\mathbf{x} = \begin{bmatrix} 1 & 0 & a \\ 1 & 1 & a+1 \\ 1 & 2 & a+2 \\ \cdot & \cdot & \cdot \\ \cdot & \cdot & \cdot \\ \cdot & \cdot & \cdot \\ 1 & 9 & a+9 \\ 1 & 0 & a+1 \\ 1 & 1 & a+2 \\ \cdot & \cdot & \cdot \\ \cdot & \cdot & \cdot \\ \cdot & \cdot & \cdot \\ 1 & 9 & a+10 \\ 1 & 0 & a+2 \\ 1 & 1 & a+3 \\ \cdot & \cdot & \cdot \\ \cdot & \cdot & \cdot \\ \cdot & \cdot & \cdot \\ 1 & 9 & a+11 \\ \cdot & \cdot & \cdot \\ \cdot & \cdot & \cdot \\ 1 & 0 & b \\ 1 & 1 & b+1 \\ \cdot & \cdot & \cdot \\ \cdot & \cdot & \cdot \\ \cdot & \cdot & \cdot \\ 1 & 9 & b+9 \end{bmatrix}$$

c) $\mathbf{x} =$

Note: the matrix $\mathbf{x}$ is 200×3, with 20 partitions of 10 rows each

BIBLIOGRAPHY

B

1. Andrews, G.H. and Nesbitt, C.J. "Periodograms of Graduation Operators", TSA, XVII (1965), 1.

2. Batten, R.W. *Mortality Table Construction*. Englewood Cliffs: Prentice-Hall, Inc., 1978.

3. Beers, H.S. Discussion of "The General Theory of Osculatory Interpolation", by T.N.E. Greville, TASA, XLVI (1945), 83.

4. Benjamin, B. and Haycocks, H.W. *The Analysis of Mortality and Other Actuarial Statistics*. Cambridge: Cambridge University Press, 1970.

5. Borgan, Ø. "On the Theory of Moving Average Graduation", Scand. Actuar. J. (1979), 83.

6. Burden, R.L. and Faires, J.D. *Numerical Analysis* (Third Edition). Boston: Prindle, Weber & Schmidt, 1985.

7. Camp, K. "New Possibilities in Graduation", TSA, VII (1955), 6.

8. Chan, B. "A Revision of the Minimum-R_z Theorem", ARCH, 1982.2, 17.

9. Chan, L.K. and Panjer, H.H. "A Statistical Approach to Graduation by Mathematical Formula", ARCH, 1979.2, 27.

10. DeBoor, C. *A Practical Guide to Splines*. New York: Springer-Verlag, 1978.

11. Elandt-Johnson, R.C. and Johnson, N.L. *Survival Models and Data Analysis*. New York: John Wiley and Sons, 1980.

12. Elphinstone, M.D.W. "Summation and Some Other Methods of Graduation: The Foundations of Theory", TFA, XX (1951), 15.

13. Gerritson, P. "A New Class of M-W-A Formulas", ARCH, 1978.1,

14. Gompertz, B. "On the Nature of the Function Expressive of the Law of Human Mortality", Phil. Trans., Royal Society of London, 1825.

15. Greenlee, H.R. and Keh, A.D. "The 1971 Group Annuity Mortality Table", TSA, XXIII (1971), 569.

16. Greville, T.N.E., Boom, H.J., Jones, D.A., and Nesbitt, C.J. *Part 5 Study Notes: Graduation*. Chicago: Society of Actuaries, 1973.

17. Greville, T.N.E. (ed.) *Theory and Application of Spline Functions*. New York: Academic Press, 1969.

18. Greville, T.N.E. "Moving-Weighted-Average Smoothing Extended to the Extremities of the Data. I. Theory", Scand. Actuar. J. (1981), 38.

19. Greville, T.N.E. "Moving-Weighted-Average Smoothing Extended to the Extremities of the Data. II. Methods", Scand. Actuar. J. (1981), 65.

20. Greville, T.N.E. "Moving-Weighted-Average Smoothing Extended to the Extremities of the Data. III. Stability and Optimal Properties", J. Appx. Theory, 33 (1981), 43.

21. Henderson, R. *Mathematical Theory of Graduation*. New York: Actuarial Society of America, 1938.

22. Henderson, R. "Graduation by Adjusted Average", TASA, XVII (1916), 43.

23. Henderson, R. "A New Method of Graduation", TASA, XXV (1924), 29.

24. Henderson, R. "Further Remarks on Graduation", TASA, XXVI (1925), 52.

25. Hickman, J.C. Discussion of "Bayesian Graduation", by G.S. Kimeldorf and D.A. Jones, TSA, XIX, (1967), 114.

26. Hickman, J.C. and Miller, R.B. Discussion of "A Linear Programming Approach to Graduation", by D.R. Schuette, TSA, XXX (1978), 433.

27. Hickman, J.C. and Miller, R.B. "Notes on Bayesian Graduation", TSA, XXIX (1977), 7.

28. Hickman, J.C. and Miller, R.B. "Bayesian Bivariate Graduation and Forecasting", ARCH, 1979.3, 99.

29. Hoel, P.G. *Introduction to Mathematical Statistics,* 4th ed. New York: John Wiley and Sons, 1971.

30. Hoem, J.M. "A Contribution to the Statistical Theory of Linear Graduation", Ins.: Math. and Econ. 3 (1984), 1.

31. Hogg, R.V. "Statistical Robustness: One View of Its Use in Applications Today", ARCH, 1979.3, 9.

32. Jenkins, W.A. "Graduation Based on a Modification of Osculatory Interpolation", TASA, XXVIII (1927), 198.

33. Jones, D.A. "Bayesian Statistics", TSA, XVII (1965), 33.

34. Kellison, S.G. *Fundamentals of Numerical Analysis*. Homewood: Richard D. Irwin, Inc., 1975.

35. Kimeldorf, G.S. and Jones, D.A. "Bayesian Graduation", TSA, XIX (1967), 66.

36. King, G. Discussion of "The Graphic Method of Adjusting Mortality Tables", by T.B. Sprague, JIA, XXVI (1887), 114.

37. Klugman, S.A. "On the Variance and Mean Squared Error of Decrement Estimators", TSA, XXXIII (1981), 301.

38. Klugman, S.A. "Robust Mortality Estimation", ARCH, 1979.3, 61.

39. Knorr, F.E. "Multidimensional Whittaker-Henderson Graduation", TSA, XXXVI (1984), 213.

40. Leamer, E.E. *Specification Searches*. New York: John Wiley and Sons, 1978.

41. London, R.L. "In Defense of Minimum-R_0 Linear Compound Graduation, and a Simple Modification for its Improvement", ARCH, 1981.2, 75.

42. Lowrie, W.B. "An Extension of the Whittaker-Henderson Method of Graduation", TSA, XXXIV (1982), 329.

43. Makeham, W.M. "On the Law of Mortality, and the Construction of Annuity Tables", JIA, VIII (1860).

44. McCutcheon, J.J. "Recently Published U.K. Mortality Tables Methods of Construction and Possible Developments Therefrom", ARCH, 1980.2, 61.

45. McCutcheon, J.J. "Some Remarks on Splines", TFA, XXXVII (1981), 421.

46. Miller, M.D. *Elements of Graduation*. New York: Actuarial Society of America and American Institute of Actuaries, 1946.

47. Miller, R.B. and Wichern, D.W. *Intermediate Business Statistics*. New York: Holt, Rinehart and Winston, 1977.

48. Nesselle, D. "A Least-Squares Method for Determining the Makeham Constants", (unpublished Master's paper) Boston: Northeastern University, 1965.

49. Peterson, R.M. "Group Annuity Mortality", TSA, IV (1952), 246.

50. Ryder, J.M. "A Review of Graduation and Bayesian Methods", Trans. Inst. Act. of Australia and New Zealand, 1972, 1.

51. Schuette, D.R. "A Linear Programming Approach to Graduation", TSA, XXX (1978), 73.

52. Seal, H.L. "Tests of a Mortality Table Graduation", JIA, LXXI (1941), 5.

53. Spoerl, C.A. "The Whittaker-Henderson Graduation Formula A, the Mixed Difference Case", TASA, XLII (1941), 292.

54. Sheppard, W.F. "Graduation by Reduction of Mean Square Error", JIA, XLVIII (1914), 171.

55. Taylor, G.C. "The Chi-square Test of a Graduation by Linear Compound Formula", Bull. Assn. Roy. Actu. Belges, 71 (1976), 26.

56. Tenenbein, A. and Vanderhoof, I. "New Mathematical Laws of Select and Ultimate Mortality", TSA, XXXII (1980). 119.

57. Vaughan, H. "Notes on Graduation by Linear Compound", Trans. Act. Soc. of Australia and New Zealand, 12 (1960–61), 449.

58. Wetterstrand, W.H. "Parametric Models for Life Insurance Mortality Data: Gompertz' Law Over Time", TSA, XXXIII (1981), 159.

59. Whittaker, E.T. "On a New Method of Graduation", Proc. Edin. Math. Soc., XLI (1923), 63.

60. Whittaker, E.T. and Robinson, G. *The Calculus of Observations,* 4th ed. London and Glasgow: Blackie and Son, Ltd., 1944.

61. Wilkin, J.C. and McKay, S.F. Appendix to *Experience of Disabled-Worker Benefits under OASDI, 1965–74,* by F.R. Bayo and J.C. Wilkin. Baltimore: Social Security Administration, 1975.

62. Wilks, S.S. *Mathematical Statistics.* New York: John Wiley and Sons, 1962.

63. Wolfenden, H.H. "On the Development of Formulae for Graduation by Linear Compounding, with Special Reference to the Work of Erastus L. DeForest", TASA, XXVI (1925), 81.

C.1
INTRODUCTION

In this appendix we illustrate the results of graduating a sequence of initial estimates by the various methods discussed in the text.

The data, presented below in Table C-1, is an approximation to the data underlying the 1971 Group Annuity Mortality Table, Female Lives [15]. As stated throughout the text, we interpret the number of deaths (θ_x) as a binomial random variable, based on a sample size of n_x. Then $u_x = \dfrac{\theta_x}{n_x}$ is our initial estimate of the true mortality rate t_x. We have also calculated the natural log of each initial estimate plus .1 [i.e., $\ln(u_x + .1)$]. These transformed values will be used for all illustrations, along with the similar transformation of the revised estimates (graduated values) v_x. Figure C-1 illustrates these transformed initial estimates.

Each of the following major graduation approaches are illustrated in this appendix: moving-weighted-average, Whittaker, Bayesian, Makehamization, spline, and interpolation. In each case a description of approach is given, and results are presented in both tabular and graphic form, with comments. Fit measure (2.10) is calculated for each result, using $w_x = \dfrac{n_x}{v_x(1 - v_x)}$, as is the smoothness measure

$S = \sum_x (\Delta^3 v_x)^2$, and these two measures are given for each individual graduation.

Both fit and smoothness can also be observed on the graphs. Note that the transformed initial estimates are shown on each graph for this purpose.

For those methods with an "end-value" problem (moving-weighted-average and interpolation), only the truncated sequence is reported and illustrated. That is, no attempt is made to extend the revised estimates at each end.

TABLE C-1

x	θ_x	n_x	u_x	x	θ_x	n_x	u_x
55	1	84	.01190	80	374	6140	.06091
56	2	418	.00478	81	348	4718	.07376
57	10	1066	.00938	82	304	3791	.08019
58	21	2483	.00846	83	249	2806	.08874
59	35	3721	.00941	84	167	2240	.07455
60	62	5460	.01136	85	192	1715	.11195
61	50	6231	.00802	86	171	1388	.12320
62	55	8061	.00682	87	126	898	.14031
63	88	9487	.00928	88	86	578	.14879
64	132	10,770	.01226	89	97	510	.19020
65	267	24,267	.01100	90	93	430	.21628
66	300	26,791	.01120	91	75	362	.20718
67	432	29,174	.01481	92	84	291	.28866
68	491	28,476	.01724	93	31	232	.13362
69	422	25,840	.01633	94	75	196	.38265
70	475	23,916	.01986	95	29	147	.19728
71	413	21,412	.01929	96	25	100	.25000
72	480	20,116	.02386	97	20	161	.12422
73	537	18,876	.02845	98	5	11	.45455
74	566	17,461	.03242	99	3	10	.30000
75	581	15,012	.03870	100	2	8	.25000
76	464	11,871	.03909	101	0	5	.00000
77	461	10,002	.04609	102	2	4	.50000
78	433	8949	.04839	103	0	2	.00000
79	515	7751	.06644	104	1	2	.50000

It should be understood that the choices of graduation methods and parameters which we have made are for illustrative purposes only, and are not necessarily being advocated as "best" choices for the data under consideration.

C.2
MOVING-WEIGHTED-AVERAGE

Using $n = 8$, our initial estimates have been graduated with $z = 0, 2, 4$. To illustrate the effect of n, we have used $n = 11, 8, 3$, with the Min-R_3 formula. The results are presented below in Table C-2.

Caution must be exercised in interpreting the fit and smoothness measures given in Table C-2. Because different values of n will produce different numbers of final graduated values, the measures are based on different ranges. Thus the result with $n = 11$, which would *not* be expected to fit as well as the result with $n = 3$, gives a smaller value of fit measure (2.10) simply because it is calculated over 16

Fɪɢᴜʀᴇ **C-1**

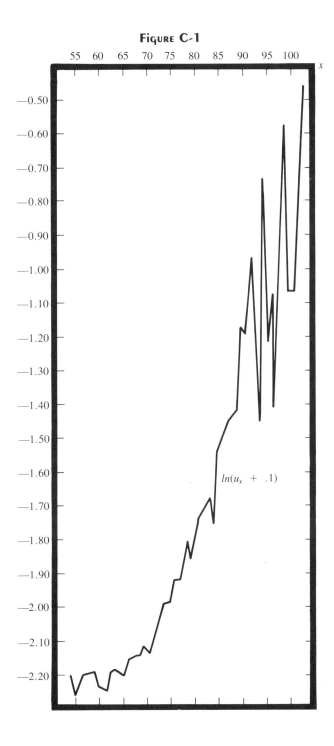

TABLE C-2

x	$n = 8$ $z = 0$	$n = 8$ $z = 2$	$n = 8$ $z = 4$	$n = 11$ $z = 3$	$n = 8$ $z = 3$	$n = 3$ $z = 3$
63	.00991	.00975	.00962		.00968	.00922
64	.01089	.01050	.01036		.01042	.01073
65	.01129	.01137	.01137		.01137	.01143
66	.01226	.01248	.01260	.01237	.01255	.01243
67	.01330	.01376	.01394	.01367	.01387	.01418
68	.01511	.01530	.01540	.01521	.01536	.01630
69	.01726	.01711	.01707	.01706	.01708	.01758
70	.01970	.01924	.01910	.01923	.01916	.01853
71	.02135	.02161	.02155	.02176	.02159	.02051
72	.02469	.02452	.02447	.02468	.02450	.02370
73	.02810	.02792	.02789	.02815	.02790	.02821
74	.03195	.03179	.03182	.03214	.03180	.03295
75	.03613	.03621	.03626	.03655	.03623	.03710
76	.04249	.04152	.04132	.04125	.04139	.04020
77	.04662	.04702	.04686	.04622	.04695	.04540
78	.05132	.05247	.05263	.05138	.05259	.05228
79	.05663	.05789	.05840	.05673	.05820	.05955
80	.06296	.06363	.06420	.06253	.06394	.06594
81	.06840	.06965	.07015	.06893	.06994	.07377
82	.07532	.07628	.07656	.07692	.07646	.07829
83	.08640	.08467	.08426	.08636	.08442	.08216
84	.09467	.09440	.09380	.09781	.09407	.08908
85	.11787	.10882	.10683	.11153	.10756	.10428
86	.12181	.12388	.12288	.12800	.12336	.12166
87	.14554	.14217	.14162	.14569	.14184	.13844
88	.16490	.16263	.16232	.16349	.16240	.15966
89	.19130	.18557	.18453	.18093	.18487	.18191
90	.18995	.20327	.20482	.19873	.20437	.21555
91	.20731	.21687	.22047	.21505	.21909	.22159
92	.22769	.22849	.23139	.23000	.23006	.23161
93	.25823	.24312	.24109	.24178	.24161	.24867
94	.24280	.25136	.24924		.25032	.26724
95	.26922	.25986	.25691		.25824	.23870
$F =$	115.19006	100.04398	97.20914	80.10746	98.27059	94.48030
$S =$	0.02634	0.00032	0.00004	0.00001	0.00008	0.04729

fewer values than used in the calculation of (2.10) for the $n = 3$ case. Similarly, the $n = 11$ case should be smoother than the $n = 3$ case, but the reported measures are a bit misleading in that they are based on different numbers of graduated values.

A different means of illustrating these results is presented in Figures C-2a and C-2b. An attempt to portray ln $(v_x + .1)$ for three different results on the same graph

Figure C-2a

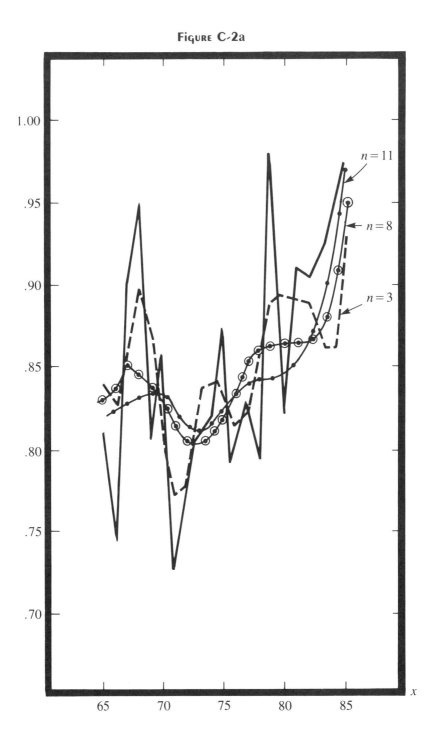

Figure C-2b

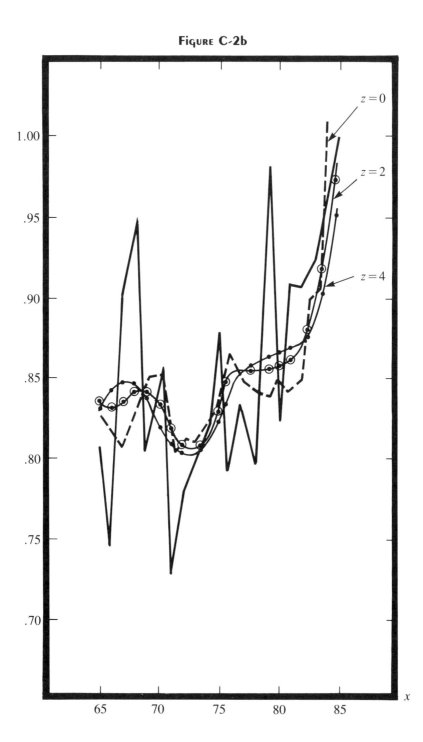

was unsuccessful, since the results were too similar to be illustrated on our graphing scale. As an alternative, we have utilized the idea of reference to a standard table, as described in Section 2.9. The chosen standard table is the 1951 Group Annuity Table, Female Lives [49].

Figure C-2a illustrates results for $z = 3$, and $n = 3, 8, 11$. First the ratios of our initial estimates to the '51-GA values are shown by the solid, jagged line. The ratios for each of the three graduation results are similarly presented. Note how the results for $n = 3$, which fit the initial estimates more closely, reflect the pattern of the ratios for the initial estimates as well. The two larger values of n produce smoother graduation results, reflected by the smoother progression of ratios (since the values in the standard table are quite smooth).

Figure C-2b illustrates the ratios for the three graduations using $n = 8$, and $z = 0, 2, 4$. As expected, the larger values of z produce the more acceptable graduations. Here also the ratios for the initial estimates are shown for comparative purposes. In both graphs the range of illustrated results has been reduced to [65, 85].

C.3
WHITTAKER

Two graduations have been performed using the basic Whittaker formula given by (4.1). The value of z is 4 in both cases, and the weights have been calculated as $w_x = \dfrac{n_x}{u_x(1 - u_x)}$, as discussed in Section 4.2.1. To illustrate the effect of the parameter h, two different values have been used. The results illustrated in Figure C-3a used $h = 1000$, and those of Figure C-3b used $h = 426,138$ (the average value of w_x). As expected, the larger value of h produces greater smoothness in the graduated results, deviating from the initial estimates in order to do so. The results are presented below in Table C-3.

In order to avoid division by zero in the calculation of the weights, the initial estimate values of $u_{101} = u_{103} = 0$ were arbitrarily replaced by $u_{101} = .25$ and $u_{103} = .50$.

C.4
BAYESIAN

Several Bayesian graduations of our data were performed, using the Kimeldorf-Jones method described in Section 5.4, with results produced by (5.12). The vector **m** of prior means was specified as the mortality rates of the 1951 Group Annuity Table [49], Female Lives. Elements of the diagonal matrix **B** were determined by (5.20). An index number of some interest is the average value of b_{ii}, $\bar{b} = .00875$.

As described in Section 5.2.2, specification of the matrix **A** is considerably

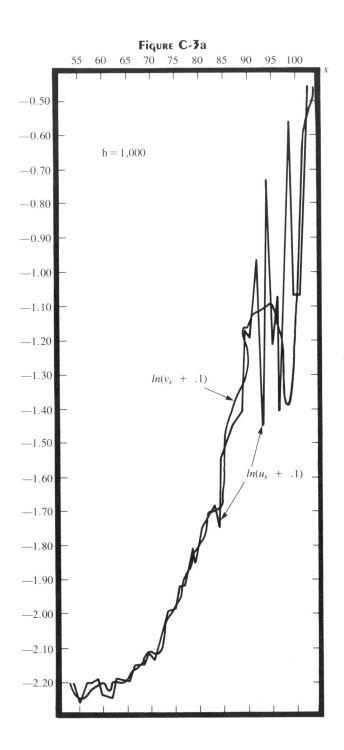

Figure C-3a

Figure C-3b

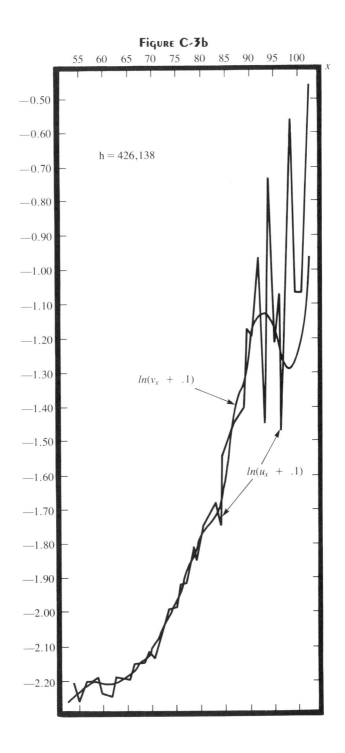

h = 426,138

$ln(v_x + .1)$

$ln(u_x + .1)$

TABLE C-3

x	Results using $h = 1,000$	Results using $h = 426,138$	x	Results using $h = 1,000$	Results using $h = 426,138$
55	.00990	.00387	80	.06387	.06540
56	.00548	.00620	81	.07225	.07140
57	.00854	.00815	82	.08109	.07698
58	.00862	.00939	83	.08313	.08317
59	.00954	.00971	84	.08352	.09157
60	.01115	.00916	85	.10236	.10362
61	.00810	.00830	86	.12349	.11976
62	.00681	.00813	87	.14048	.13935
63	.00931	.00902	88	.15951	.16085
64	.01218	.01016	89	.18469	.18209
65	.01102	.01102	90	.20726	.20069
66	.01121	.01226	91	.21917	.21453
67	.01481	.01430	92	.22253	.22212
68	.01718	.01624	93	.22449	.22290
69	.01645	.01746	94	.23026	.21739
70	.01969	.01862	95	.22027	.20708
71	.01943	.02047	96	.19142	.19453
72	.02378	.02372	97	.16012	.18312
73	.02840	.02803	98	.15134	.17683
74	.03263	.03257	99	.17660	.17992
75	.03828	.03683	100	.23486	.19680
76	.03972	.04102	101	.31745	.23194
77	.04493	.04593	102	.41135	.28982
78	.05036	.05197	103	.50127	.37493
79	.06290	.05877	104	.57134	.49176
				$F = 68.12450$	$F = 113.40598$
				$S = 0.00461$	$S = 0.00019$

subjective. For illustrative purposes, we have specified the matrix by formula (5.17), using $r = .8$, and arbitrarily limiting the number of non-zero entries in the matrix by setting $a_{ij} = 0$ for $j > i + 10$ and $j < i - 10$. The several graduations were produced by changing the constant variance denoted by p^2 in formula (5.17).

The largest value of p^2 used was $p^2 = \bar{b} = .00875$. The results are presented in Table C-4. These results fit our u_x data so closely (see values of F and S) that their graphs largely overlap, and are therefore not illustrated.

A logical value of p^2 would be the average approximate variance implied by the sample sizes which produced the m_x values initially. Since this data was not avail-

TABLE C-4

x	$p^2 = .00875$	$p^2 = .00100$	$p^2 = .00001$	x	$p^2 = .00875$	$p^2 = .00100$	$p^2 = .00001$
55	.01175	.01070	.00598	80	.06084	.06114	.06618
56	.00482	.00512	.00666	81	.07407	.07418	.07423
57	.00938	.00932	.00826	82	.07965	.07925	.08139
58	.00845	.00845	.00844	83	.08907	.08833	.08994
59	.00941	.00942	.00956	84	.07485	.07850	.09801
60	.01135	.01134	.01028	85	.11204	.11010	.10870
61	.00802	.00802	.00833	86	.12275	.12288	.11962
62	.00682	.00684	.00757	87	.14014	.13933	.13056
63	.00928	.00927	.00932	88	.15059	.15544	.14243
64	.01226	.01225	.01167	89	.18905	.18369	.15470
65	.01100	.01100	.01111	90	.21385	.20709	.16777
66	.01120	.01121	.01159	91	.21304	.21428	.18009
67	.01481	.01479	.01456	92	.26653	.23761	.19429
68	.01724	.01725	.01698	93	.18001	.22148	.20876
69	.01634	.01634	.01669	94	.32224	.25846	.22529
70	.01985	.01984	.01936	95	.22738	.23826	.24273
71	.01930	.01931	.02018	96	.22504	.24227	.26256
72	.02386	.02389	.02393	97	.16757	.23516	.28397
73	.02845	.02841	.02828	98	.23715	.27004	.30823
74	.03241	.03244	.03285	99	.26506	.30103	.33494
75	.03870	.03866	.03778	100	.29225	.33596	.36447
76	.03910	.03917	.04084	101	.31545	.36936	.39700
77	.04607	.04597	.04641	102	.36273	.40847	.43296
78	.04841	.04864	.05263	103	.41586	.45310	.47271
79	.06642	.06605	.06092	104	.44874	.49567	.51786
				$F =$	17.89293	50.99612	126.40842
				$S =$	.61525	.05195	.00032

able to us, we calculated such variances by using the hypothetical sample sizes given by the ℓ_x values in the 1952 table. The average of these approximate variances is .00100, and this was used as p^2 in (5.17) for our second graduation. The results are presented in Table C-4. By decreasing p^2 (with no change in $\bar{b}$), the elements of $\mathbf{A}^{-1}$ are *increased* relative to $\mathbf{B}^{-1}$, so the result, $\mathbf{v}$, reflects a heavier weighting of $\mathbf{m}$ than of $\mathbf{u}$. Thus, as expected, this graduation is smoother than the first one, but with poorer fit.

Finally we decreased p^2 arbitrarily to .00001, thereby weighting $\mathbf{m}$ considerably more heavily than $\mathbf{u}$, and producing the smoothest results (with poorest fit). These results are also presented in Table C-4, and illustrated in Figure C-4.

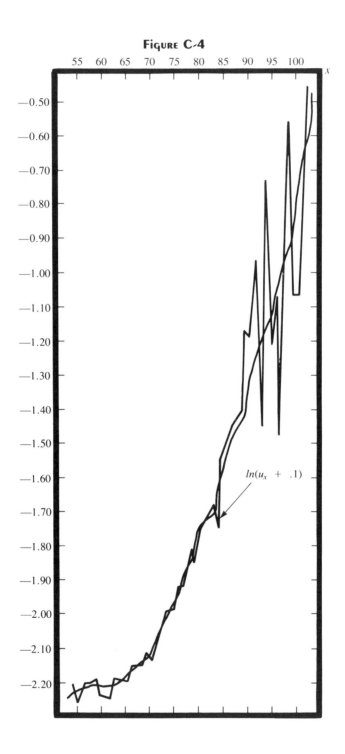

Figure C-4

C.5
PARAMETRIC GRADUATIONS

Three graduations of our data were performed using various curve-fitting approaches. Since parametric graduations are inherently smooth, no smoothness measure is calculated in these cases.

The first graduation fits the Makeham form, using the non-linear regression technique of Section 6.3.4, with $A_0 = .002$, $B_0 = .00005$, $c_0 = 1.08$. Fifteen iterations were required for convergence of A, B, c to nine decimal places, the final values being $A = -.008380064$, $B = .000044299$, $c = 1.097365940$. Although a negative value of A is mathematically permissible, positive values are generally used in the Makeham form. (Our fitted curve also produces a negative value for v_{55}!) Thus this Makeham result might well be considered unsatisfactory.

TABLE C-5A

x	Makeham	Spline	x	Makeham	Spline
55	−.00069	.00715	80	.06771	.06489
56	.00006	.00747	81	.07481	.07251
57	.00088	.00773	82	.08254	.08079
58	.00178	.00796	83	.09094	.08977
59	.00277	.00819	84	.10008	.09948
60	.00385	.00846	85	.11000	.10994
61	.00504	.00878	86	.12076	.12119
62	.00634	.00920	87	.13241	.13325
63	.00777	.00973	88	.14503	.14615
64	.00933	.01041	89	.15866	.15959
65	.01104	.01126	90	.17337	.17298
66	.01291	.01232	91	.18921	.18572
67	.01496	.01361	92	.20625	.19722
68	.01721	.01516	93	.22454	.20686
69	.01967	.01701	94	.24412	.21405
70	.02236	.01918	95	.26504	.21819
71	.02531	.02170	96	.28733	.21867
72	.02853	.02459	97	.31101	.21488
73	.03206	.02790	98	.33610	.20624
74	.03591	.03164	99	.36257	.19213
75	.04012	.03585	100	.39042	.17196
76	.04472	.04055	101	.41957	.14511
77	.04974	.04578	102	.44996	.11100
78	.05522	.05156	103	.48149	.06901
79	.06120	.05792	104	.51400	.01855
				$F = 672.183$	$F = 153.787$

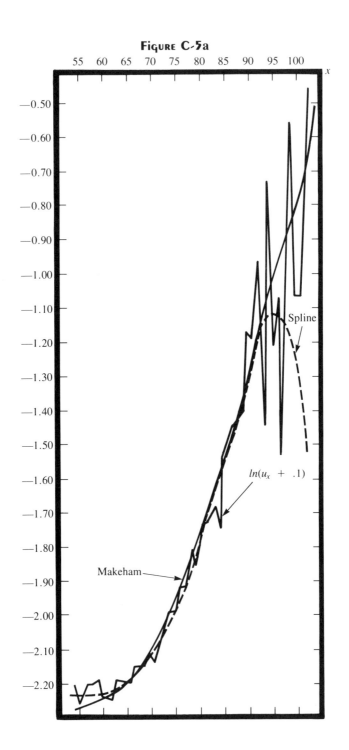

Figure C-5a

The second graduation fits a two-arc cubic spline, using the technique of Section 6.5, with the internal knot at $x = 87.5$. Both graduation results are presented in Table C-5a, and illustrated in Figure C-5a. Note the considerably better fit which can be obtained by using the spline, even with only one internal knot. On the other hand, if monotonicity is important, then the Makeham result may be preferred to the spline result.

The final illustration shows an excerpt from a smooth-junction interpolation graduation, using Jenkins' formula given by (7.26). The excerpted results are presented in Table C-5b and illustrated in Figure C-5b. In particular, interpolation results might logically be compared with those produced by a spline fit, since the two approaches are somewhat similar.

TABLE C-5b _____

x	v_x
72	.02472
73	.02439
74	.02672
75	.03135
76	.03791
77	.04602
78	.04356
79	.04382
80	.04833
81	.05863
82	.07624
83	.06953
84	.07248
85	.08588
86	.11055

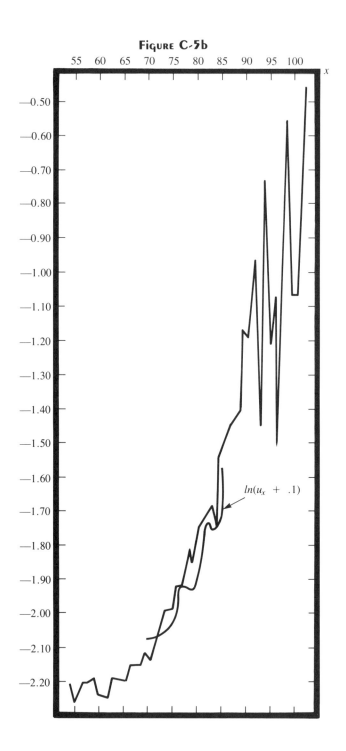

Fiɢuʀᴇ C-5b

FINITE DIFFERENCES

D

D.1
INTRODUCTION

In this appendix we briefly summarize the definitions and properties of the finite difference operators, to the extent needed for understanding their uses in the graduation theory contained in this text.

For a more thorough treatment of the subject, see Kellison [34], Sections 2.1–2.2 and 4.1–4.2. For the derivation of interpolation formulas using finite differences, see Kellison's Sections 3.1, 3.2, 4.3, and 4.7.

D.2
THE FORWARD DIFFERENCE OPERATOR

The *forward difference operator* over interval h, denoted by Δ_h, is defined by

$$\Delta_h f(x) = f(x + h) - f(x). \tag{D.1}$$

In words, the difference (or differencing) operator, when applied to a function at argument x, in general, produces the difference $f(x + h) - f(x)$. In particular, at $h = 1$, we have

$$\Delta f(x) = f(x + 1) - f(x). \tag{D.2}$$

Note that when $h = 1$, we use merely Δ, not Δ_1. The remainder of this appendix will assume $h = 1$ for simplicity.

The second order differencing operator, Δ^2, is defined by

$$
\begin{aligned}
\Delta^2 f(x) &= \Delta[\Delta f(x)] \\
&= \Delta[f(x + 1) - f(x)] \\
&= \Delta f(x + 1) \quad \Delta f(x) \\
&= [f(x + 2) - f(x + 1)] - [f(x + 1) - f(x)] \\
&= f(x + 2) - 2f(x + 1) + f(x).
\end{aligned}
\tag{D.3}
$$

Note that Δ^2 means a repetition of the differencing operation, and *not* Δ times Δ. Since Δ is an operator, not an algebraic quantity, "multiplication" is not a meaningful concept.

Higher order differences follow analogously.

$$\Delta^3 f(x) = \Delta[\Delta^2 f(x)]$$

$$= \Delta[f(x + 2) - 2f(x + 1) + f(x)]$$

$$= [f(x + 3) - f(x + 2)] - 2[f(x + 2) - f(x + 1)] + [f(x + 1) - f(x)]$$

$$= f(x + 3) - 3f(x + 2) + 3f(x + 1) - f(x). \tag{D.4}$$

By now the pattern should be clear. In general, $\Delta^n f(x)$ will involve $n + 1$ terms, from $f(x + n)$ back through $f(x)$. We prefer to say it this way (rather than to say $f(x)$ up through $f(x + n)$), to aid in determining the signs of the coefficients. $f(x + n)$ is always positive, $f(x + n - 1)$ will be negative, with signs alternating, so that $f(x)$ will be positive or negative depending on whether n is even or odd. Note the sign patterns in $\Delta^2 f(x)$ and $\Delta^3 f(x)$ above. The coefficients of the $n + 1$ terms in $\Delta^n f(x)$ are the binomial coefficients of order n.

An important property of finite differences is that the application of the Δ operator to a polynomial function reduces the degree of that polynomial by one. Thus, if $f(x)$ is a polynomial of degree n, $\Delta f(x)$ is a polynomial of degree $n - 1$. In this respect, differencing is analogous to differentiation. It follows that if $f(x)$ is a polynomial of degree n, then $\Delta^n f(x)$ is a polynomial of degree 0, which is a constant. That is

$$\Delta^n f(x) = c, \tag{D.5}$$

if $f(x)$ is a polynomial of degree n, and, furthermore,

$$\Delta^{n+1} f(x) = 0. \tag{D.6}$$

It is for this reason that we say, for example, that requiring $\Delta^4 v_x$ to approach zero is to require the v_x sequence to approach a third degree polynomial (see Section 1.6).

For an exponential function of the form $f(x) = c^x$, the differencing operation produces

$$\Delta c^x = c^{x+1} - c^x = c^x(c - 1). \tag{D.7}$$

The recurrence of the exponential function itself is again an analogy between differencing and differentiation.

The forward differencing operator is distributive. That is

$$\Delta[f(x) + g(x)] = \Delta f(x) + \Delta g(x). \tag{D.8}$$

It is also commutative with respect to a constant. Thus

$$\Delta[c \cdot f(x)] = c \cdot \Delta f(x). \tag{D.9}$$

It is frequently required to determine the finite differences of a table of data. To do this, we construct a difference table by tabulating the data in a column, and finding the differences between successive pairs of numbers in the table. Then second differences are found by differencing the first difference column, third differences by differencing the second differences, and so on. The reader should verify the entries in each column of differences in the following table.

TABLE D. 1

x	$f(x)$	$\Delta f(x)$	$\Delta^2 f(x)$	$\Delta^3 f(x)$	$\Delta^4 f(x)$
0	6				
1	2	−4			
2	−2	−4	0	66	
3	60	62	66	138	72
4	326	266	204	210	72
5	1006	680	414	282	72
6	2382	1376	696		

The constant value obtained for $\Delta^4 f(x)$ is no coincidence, since the function which generated the data was $f(x) = 3x^4 - 7x^3 + 6$, a fourth degree polynomial. As we saw above, the fourth differences of such a function must be constant. Furthermore,

$$\Delta^4[3x^4 - 7x^3 + 6] = 3 \cdot \Delta^4 x^4 - 7 \cdot \Delta^4 x^3 + \Delta^4 6$$

$$= 3(4!) - 7(0) + 0 = 72.$$

D.3
THE CENTRAL DIFFERENCE OPERATOR

The *central difference operator* over interval h, denoted by δ_h, is defined by

$$\delta_h f(x) = f(x + \tfrac{1}{2}h) - f(x - \tfrac{1}{2}h). \tag{D.10}$$

Here we find that the argument of the differenced function is *central* to the arguments of the functions used to define it, from which it gets its name. With $h = 1$ we have

$$\delta f(x) = f(x + \tfrac{1}{2}) - f(x - \tfrac{1}{2}). \tag{D.11}$$

Note that the interval of differencing is one, so, in order that $f(x)$ be central in the interval, half-values of the argument must be used. Specifically, for example, $\delta f(3) = f(3\tfrac{1}{2}) - f(2\tfrac{1}{2})$. Now if we were presented with data such as that in Table D.1, we see that $\delta f(3)$ simply cannot be determined.

The second order central difference is defined by

$$\begin{aligned}
\delta^2 f(x) &= \delta[\delta f(x)] \\
&= \delta[f(x + \tfrac{1}{2}) - f(x - \tfrac{1}{2})] \\
&= \delta f(x + \tfrac{1}{2}) - \delta f(x - \tfrac{1}{2}) \\
&= [f(x + 1) - f(x)] - [f(x) - f(x - 1)] \\
&= f(x + 1) - 2f(x) + f(x - 1).
\end{aligned} \tag{D.12}$$

Then, for example, $\delta^2 f(3) = f(4) - 2f(3) + f(2)$ can be determined from Table D.1. This situation arises frequently in actuarial applications of finite differences. The data will frequently be tabulated at intergal values of the argument x, so that odd powers of δ cannot be determined, but even powers can. We note that our uses of central differences in graduation *always* call for even powers (e.g., δ^{2z} in Section 3.6, and δ^2 and δ^4 in Chapter 7).

We obtain the fourth order central difference, $\delta^4 f(x)$ by

$$\begin{aligned}
\delta^4 f(x) &= \delta^2[\delta^2 f(x)] \\
&= \delta^2[f(x + 1) - 2f(x) + f(x - 1)] \\
&= [f(x + 2) - 2f(x + 1) + f(x)] - 2[f(x + 1) - 2f(x) + f(x - 1)] \\
&\quad + [f(x) - 2f(x - 1) + f(x - 2)] \\
&= f(x + 2) - 4f(x + 1) + 6f(x) - 4f(x - 1) + f(x - 2).
\end{aligned} \tag{D.13}$$

By now the pattern should be clear. If n is even, then $\delta^n f(x)$ will involve $n + 1$ terms, which is an odd number, with $f(x)$ in the middle. The extreme upper and lower terms will be positive, with the other coefficients alternating in sign. Note that $f(x)$ can be positive (as it is in δ^4) or negative (as it is in δ^2). As was true for Δ^n, the coefficients are the binomial coefficients of order n.

Just as was true for forward differences, if $f(x)$ is a polynomial of degree n, then $\delta f(x)$ is a polynomial of degree $n - 1$, $\delta^n f(x)$ is a polynomial of degree 0 (i.e., a constant), and $\delta^{n+1} f(x) = 0$.

INDEX